Understanding the Department of State

The Cabinet Series

Understanding the Department of State

Don Philpott

The Cabinet Series

Lanham • Boulder • New York • London

Published by Bernan Press
An imprint of The Rowman & Littlefield Publishing Group, Inc.
4501 Forbes Boulevard, Suite 200, Lanham, Maryland 20706
www.rowman.com
800-865-3457; info@bernan.com

Unit A, Whitacre Mews, 26-34 Stannary Street, London SE11 4AB

Library of Congress Control Number: 2015949516

ISBN: 978-1-59888-745-7
E-ISBN: 978-1-59888-746-4

♾™ The paper used in this publication meets the minimum requirements of
American National Standard for Information Sciences—Permanence of Paper
for Printed Library Materials, ANSI/NISO Z39.48-1992.

Printed in the United States of America

Contents

PART III: APPENDICES

Acknowledgement

This book has relied heavily on the vast wealth of information that is in the public domain. Almost all the material comes from federal, state and local websites as well as national and international agencies and organizations. These include the State Department, White House, Library of Congress, Department of Homeland Security, Central Intelligence Agency, Federal Bureau of Investigations, and many more.

It is an attempt to gather together information from as many sources as possible so that you don't have to.

Part I: Structure and Role

1

Introduction

Department Mission Statement

Shape and sustain a peaceful, prosperous, just, and democratic world and foster conditions for stability and progress for the benefit of the American people and people everywhere.

—From the FY 2013 Agency Financial Report

Under the Constitution, the President of the United States determines U.S. foreign policy. The Secretary of State, appointed by the President with the consent of the Senate, is the President's chief foreign affairs adviser. The Secretary carries out the President's foreign-policies through the State Department and the Foreign Service of the United States.

Created in 1789 by the Congress as the successor to the Department of Foreign Affairs, the Department of State is the senior executive Department of the U.S. Government. The Secretary of State's duties relating to foreign affairs have not changed significantly since then, but they have become far more complex as international commitments multiplied. These duties—the activities and responsibilities of the State Department—include the following:

- Serves as the President's principal adviser on U.S. foreign policy;

- Conducts negotiations relating to U.S. foreign affairs;
- Grants and issues passports to American citizens and exequaturs to foreign consuls in the United States;
- Advises the President on the appointment of U.S. ambassadors, ministers, consuls, and other diplomatic representatives;
- Advises the President regarding the acceptance, recall, and dismissal of the representatives of foreign governments;
- Personally participates in or directs U.S. representatives to international conferences, organizations, and agencies;
- Negotiates, interprets, and terminates treaties and agreements;
- Ensures the protection of the U.S. Government to American citizens, property, and interests in foreign countries;
- Supervises the administration of U.S. immigration laws abroad;
- Provides information to American citizens regarding the political, economic, social, cultural, and humanitarian conditions in foreign countries;
- Informs the Congress and American citizens on the conduct of U.S. foreign relations;
- Promotes beneficial economic intercourse between the United States and other countries;
- Administers the Department of State;
- Supervises the Foreign Service of the United States.

In addition, the Secretary of State retains domestic responsibilities that Congress entrusted to the State Department in 1789. These include the custody of the Great Seal of the United States, the preparation of certain presidential proclamations, the publication of treaties and international acts as well as the official record of the foreign relations of the United States, and the custody of certain original treaties and international agreements. The Secretary also serves as the channel of communication between the Federal Government and the States on the extradition of fugitives to or from foreign countries.

The Department of State has grown significantly over the years. In 1789, the first Secretary of State, Thomas Jefferson, oversaw a small staff of one chief clerk, three other clerks, a translator, and a messenger and only maintained two diplomatic posts, in London and Paris, as well as 10 consular posts.

To address ever changing global circumstances, the number of domestic and overseas employees grew to 1,228 in 1900, 1,968 in 1940, 13,294 in 1960 and 15,751 in 2000. The number of diplomatic posts increased from 41 in 1900 to 168 in 2004 and continues to grow.

World War I (1914-1918) and World War II (1939-1945) brought vastly increased global responsibilities to the United States as it emerged as a preeminent power. New challenges after the end of the Cold War and the fall of the Soviet Union, included: the newly independent states, the global economy, terrorism, and the security of the American overseas presence.

John Kerry, the current Secretary of State, travels to all corners of the world to do his job. His duties as Secretary include acting as the President's representative at all international forums, negotiating treaties and other international agreements, and conducting every day, face-to-face diplomacy. The challenges are daunting as are the travel requirements.

Last year between January 1 and October 10, Secretary Kerry traveled 566,218 mile and visited 55 countries. He was out of the country for 249 days and of that he spent the equivalent of 50.8 days in the air.

2

An Overview of the State Department

Diplomacy is one of the best ways to protect the United States and the American people. The State Department uses diplomacy with other nations to successfully deal with many challenges that cross national boundaries and affect us here in the United States, including:

- Terrorism;
- The threat of weapons of mass destruction;
- HIV/AIDS and other infectious diseases;
- Illegal drug trafficking and crime;
- Humanitarian needs of migrants and refugees; and
- Environmental degradation.

Americans at home and abroad face threats to their physical and economic well-being. The State Department protects our nation, its people, and our prosperity by helping to:

- Prevent terrorist attacks and strengthen international alliances to defeat global terrorism;
- Ensure America's homeland security by promoting policies and practices to keep travel, trade, and important infrastructure safe;

- Serve on the front line of America's borders, facilitating the entry of legitimate visitors to the United States while denying visas to those who do not qualify or would do us harm;
- Promote stability in all regions of the world;
- Prevent enemies from threatening the United States or our allies with weapons of mass destruction;
- Reduce the impact of international crime and illegal drugs on Americans;
- Protect and assist American citizens who travel, conduct business, and live abroad; and
- Nurture common interests and values between the people of the United States and the people of other countries.

Following are a few of the many ways the State Department uses diplomacy to protect America:

Fighting Terrorism

International terrorism threatens the United States, its allies and interests, and the world community. Defeating international terrorism requires sound policies, concerted U.S. Government effort, and international cooperation.

This reflects the goals of the National Strategy for Combating Terrorism:

- Defeat terrorists and their organizations;
- Deny sponsorship, support, and sanctuary to terrorists;
- Diminish the underlying conditions that terrorists seek to exploit; and
- Defend U.S. citizens and interests at home and abroad.

In the fight against terrorism, the State Department provides foreign policy oversight and guidance to all U.S. Government international counterterrorism activities. These include:

- Designating Foreign Terrorist Organizations to freeze their assets and isolate them internationally;
- Providing deterrence and rapid response to international terrorist incidents;
- Delivering creative and flexible anti-terrorism and counterterrorism finance training;
- Enhancing border security and global terrorism watch listing
- Providing expert counterterrorism assistance in support of embassies and partner nations;
- Integrating homeland security initiatives with foreign policy; and
- Leading technology development to effectively combat terrorism.

The State Department's annual Country Reports on Terrorism is a congressionally mandated assessment of trends in international terrorism and the nature of the terrorist threat. The narrative is focused on policy-related assessments, a country-by-country breakdown of foreign government cooperation, and chapters on State Sponsors of Terrorism, Foreign Terrorist Organizations, WMD terrorism, and Terrorist Safe Havens.

Homeland Security

Security for Americans begins at home but extends beyond our borders. In pursuit of homeland security, the State Department conducts visa operations and leads U.S. diplomatic efforts to gain international cooperation on measures to deter threats to travel, communications, and other critical infrastructure networks—information systems, transportation, and energy—and to secure our borders.

Visas: Welcoming Foreign Citizens

Immigrants and visitors have contributed greatly to our country, and make important contributions. Immigrants and many visitors who want to enter the United States must apply for a visa from the State Department. The State Department carefully reviews more than 8 million visa applications per year. The visa regulations help ensure that no visas are approved for foreign citizens who might harm our country, thereby keeping us safe while continuing to welcome citizens from around the globe.

Regional Stability

The State Department uses diplomacy in all regions of the world to keep local conflicts from becoming wider wars that may harm U.S. interests. The State Department joins with other countries in international organizations to promote stability and economic prosperity.

Following are some of the regional issues the State Department manages:

Middle East

Promote and support the development of democracy in Iraq. Continue to work with Israel, Egypt, other Middle Eastern countries, and the Palestinians to find a way for them to live peacefully together.

Western Hemisphere

Join with other countries to confront terrorism and illegal drug trafficking, while promoting institutions that support democracy and freedom.

Africa

Support democratization, rule of law, and economic development by reducing poverty, fighting disease, and encouraging regional leadership for conflict resolution.

East Asia and the Pacific

Work within organizations such as the Asia-Pacific Economic Cooperation forum to build prosperity and peace in the region by creating economic opportunities, building societies, and preventing threats to sustainable growth.

South and Central Asia

Support developing democracy in Afghanistan. Work with India and Pakistan and the international community to deal with problems between these countries, including the status of Kashmir and nuclear arms.

Europe and Eurasia

Work with European and Eurasian partners, and with key institutions such as NATO, on a range of global issues to promote stability and international cooperation.

Weapons of Mass Destruction

Weapons of mass destruction—such as nuclear, chemical, or biological weapons—pose a serious danger to the United States and the world. We must be concerned about the possibility that terrorists may acquire these weapons for use against innocent people. The State Department works to ensure that more countries do not obtain these weapons and to verify that international agreements restricting such weapons are being honored.

Criminal Justice

The State Department plays an important role in formulating and implementing international narcotics and crime control strategies. Strong law enforcement institutions, rooted in democratic principles and protective of human rights, are vital to preventing transnational threats, from drugs to organized criminal activity to terrorism. The State Department helps countries combat international narcotics production and trafficking, reduce international crime and terrorism, and strengthen international criminal justice institutions through bilateral, regional, and global assistance programs. The State Department's annual report on international narcotics control (see www.state.gov/p/inl) outlines the strategies dealing with these issues.

The State Department plays a critical role in developing civilian police and supporting justice reform in post- conflict societies. This assistance helps countries recovering from post-conflict or authoritarian regimes to reform their police, corrections, and judicial systems to create the stability necessary for economic prosperity and strong, democratic institutions.

Trafficking in persons is a modern- day form of slavery involving victims who are forced, defrauded, or coerced into labor or sexual exploitation. Annually, about 800,000 people, mostly women and children, are trafficked across national borders, which does not account for the millions trafficked within their own countries. The State Department's annual report on trafficking in persons (see www.state.gov/g/tip) assesses governments' efforts to combat trafficking and is an important diplomatic tool for ending modern day slavery.

Helping Americans

The State Department helps U.S. citizens travel, conduct business, and live abroad safely by:

- Providing information, including travel warnings and alerts, and country-specific information for those traveling and living abroad;
- Issuing passports to U.S. citizens;
- Helping U.S. citizens obtain emergency funds;
- Checking on the welfare and whereabouts of U.S. citizens abroad;
- Helping families with arrangements if a U.S. citizen dies overseas;
- Assisting U.S. travelers who become ill or are arrested while overseas;
- Assisting in international child custody disputes and adoptions; and
- Protecting and assisting U.S. citizens living or traveling abroad during crises.

Economic Prosperity and Security

The State Department supports U.S. businesses at home and abroad. Officers at U.S. embassies around the world are experts on the business practices of foreign countries and what products and markets are important in those countries. They identify opportunities for American firms and help support them in exporting or working within the country. The State Department:

- Helps ensure that American workers, businesspeople, and farmers can fairly compete for foreign investment and trade;
- Negotiates trade agreements to open foreign markets to increase opportunities to sell American products and services abroad;
- Supports U.S. business interests overseas by pointing out potential problems and helping make sure that American companies can sell products or services within a foreign country;

- Works with international and U.S. organizations to represent business interests;
- Promotes and licenses exports that contribute tens of billions of dollars to the U.S. economy;
- Protects American intellectual property rights, such as copyrights and patents; and
- Helps other countries develop strong, freemarket economies that provide investment and export opportunities.

Democracy and Human Rights

Promoting freedom and democracy and protecting human rights around the world are central to U.S. foreign policy. The values captured in the Universal Declaration of Human Rights and in other global and regional commitments are consistent with the values upon which the United States was founded centuries ago. The United States supports those persons who long to live in freedom and under democratic governments that protect universally accepted human rights.

Tools to advance a freedom agenda:

- Bilateral diplomacy;
- Multilateral diplomacy;
- Support for defenders of freedom;
- Foreign assistance;
- Reporting on human rights practices;
- Public outreach; and
- Economic sanctions.

State Department efforts to promote democracy seek to:

- Promote democracy as a means to achieve security, stability, and prosperity for the entire world;
- Assist newly formed democracies in implementing democratic principles;
- Assist democracy advocates around the world to establish vibrant democracies in their own countries; and
- Identify and denounce regimes that deny their citizens the right to choose their leaders in elections that are free, fair, and transparent.

State Department efforts to promote human rights seek to:

- Hold governments accountable to their obligations under universal human rights norms and international human rights instruments;
- Promote greater respect for human rights, based on those internationally accepted standards;
- Promote the rule of law, seek accountability, and change cultures of impunity; and
- Assist efforts to reform and strengthen the institutional capacity of the UN Commission on Human Rights.

Other Transnational Issues

The State Department also deals with many issues that are transnational, extending beyond any single country's borders. Examples include:

Health

HIV/AIDS, tuberculosis, and other infectious diseases pose health challenges for countries around the world. As disease spreads and more people become sick, the political and economic stability of countries is put at risk. Working with other agencies within the U.S. Government as well as other countries, the State Department prepares for and responds to world health problems and monitors the spread of potentially dangerous diseases.

Environment, Science, and Technology

The Department promotes transformational diplomacy through advancing environmental stewardship, encouraging economic growth, and promoting social development around the globe to foster a safer, more secure, and hopeful world. It also advances critical and diverse United States interests in the oceans. Science and technology cooperation led by the State Department helps make tangible improvements in the lives of people everywhere. Climate change and energy security pose serious interlinked challenges, the scale and scope of which will require a global response as well as national actions. The State Department is working with international partners on measures to slow, stop, and reverse greenhouse gas emissions in a way that promotes sustainable economic growth, increases energy security, and helps nations deliver greater prosperity for their people.

Refugees, Migration, and Population

The State Department helps millions of refugees and victims of conflict or natural disasters around the world. Each year, the United States also allows tens of thousands of refugees to live in America permanently. Population growth affects the environment and the ability of governments to provide services to the growing number of people who live in less space, use more fuel, and require more food.

Promoting Mutual Understanding

Mutual understanding between Americans and people in other countries advances U.S. national interests by fostering a sense of common interests and common values. To that end, the State Department engages international audiences on issues of foreign policy, society, and values to help create an environment receptive to U.S. national interests.

We communicate with foreign opinion makers and other publics through a variety of public diplomacy programs, using cutting edge technologies, including websites in English and six foreign languages, as well as traditional text publications. Additionally, experts in many fields travel to other countries to engage foreign audiences. The Department also provides information outreach support to U.S. embassies and consulates in more than 140 countries worldwide.

One of the most effective means of increasing mutual understanding is through people-to-people exchange programs. The State Department annually sponsors more than 40,000 educational and cultural exchanges—including visitors to the United States and Americans traveling abroad. These exchanges offer firsthand experiences of American society and culture to foreign visitors and provide opportunities for Americans to learn about other countries, cultures and peoples. Such intercultural experiences personify the universal values of human rights, freedom, equality, and opportunity that all civilized nations share.

Supporting Foreign and Civil Services

U.S. diplomacy requires a group of highly motivated people to accomplish the foreign policy goals of the United States. The Foreign Service and Civil Service work together both in the United States and at U.S. missions abroad to make U.S. foreign policy happen. In the wake of the terrorist attacks of September 11, 2001, our diplomatic presence and programs are more important than ever before.

The Foreign Service is a group of more than 11,000 employees who represent the United States in other countries. A Foreign Service career is a way of life that requires uncommon commitment, but through which one can achieve unique rewards. Members of the Foreign Service can be sent to any embassy, consulate, or other diplomatic mission anywhere in the world, at any time, to serve the diplomatic needs of the United States.

The Civil Service is made up of over 9,000 employees mostly in Washington, DC, who provide expertise, support, and continuity in accomplishing the mission of the Department. Some Civil Service employees are the domestic counterparts to consular officers abroad, issuing passports and assisting U.S. citizens at home and abroad.

In addition, more than 37,000 Foreign Service National employees, who are citizens of the country in which an embassy or other post is located, are a very valuable part of the State Department team overseas. These employees provide continuity by remaining in their jobs, while the Foreign Service officers move in and out of the country.

3

Organization

The following are the domestic organizational components of the State Department.

Secretary of State and Deputy Secretaries

The Secretary of State, appointed by the President with the advice and consent of the Senate, is the President's chief foreign affairs adviser. The Secretary carries out the President's foreign policies through the State Department, which includes the Foreign Service, Civil Service, and U.S. Agency for International Development. On February 1, 2013, John Kerry was sworn in as the 68th Secretary of State of the United States.

Deputy Secretary

The Deputy Secretary serves as the principal deputy, adviser, and alter ego to the Secretary of State; serves as Acting Secretary of State in the Secretary's absence; and assists the Secretary in the formulation and conduct of U.S. foreign policy and in giving general supervision and direction to all elements of the Department. Specific duties and supervisory responsibilities have varied over time.

Deputy Secretary of State for Management and Resources

The Deputy Secretary of State for Management and Resources as Chief Operating Officer of the Department. The Deputy Secretary also serves as principal adviser to the Secretary on overall supervision and direction of resource allocation and management activities of the Department. The Deputy Secretary for Management and Resources assists in carrying out the Secretary's authority and responsibility for the overall direction, coordination and supervision of operational programs of the State Department, including foreign aid and civilian response programs.

In addition, the Deputy Secretary for Management and Resources advises the Secretary on the Department's participation in the National Economic Council (NEC) and interagency economic policy matters. The Deputy Secretary also assists the Secretary in representing the United States at international meetings, in performing other representational assignments, and in presenting the Department's position before Congress.

The Deputy Secretary for Management and Resources also provides final recommendations to the Secretary on senior personnel appointments. The Director of the **Office of Small and Disadvantaged Business Utilization (OSDBU)** reports directly to the Deputy Secretary on small business policies and activities.

Under Secretaries

Arms Control and International Security

The Under Secretary of State for Arms Control and International Security leads the interagency policy process on nonproliferation and manages global U.S. security policy, principally in the areas of nonproliferation, arms control, regional security and defense relations, and arms transfers and security assistance. This entails overseeing the negotiation, implementation, and verification of international agreements in arms control and international security.

Other specific responsibilities include directing and coordinating export control policies and policies to prevent missile, nuclear, chemical, biological, and conventional weapons proliferation. All of these contribute to the State Department's strategic goal of countering threats to the United States and the international order. The Under Secretary for Arms Control and International Security serves as a Senior Adviser to the President and the Secretary of State.

Civilian Security, Democracy, and Human Rights

The Office of the Under Secretary for Civilian Security, Democracy, and Human Rights leads State Department efforts to prevent and counter threats to civilian security and effective governance, such as terrorism, violent extremism, mass atrocities and transnational crime. The bureaus and offices reporting to the Under Secretary contribute to the security of the American people and nations around the world by assisting countries to build more democratic, secure, stable, and just societies.

To achieve its mission, the Office works together, along with other U.S. Government agencies and foreign partners, to prevent and respond to conflict, promote peace and genuine stability, strengthen and develop the rule of law, achieve accountability for atrocities, counter terrorism and violent extremism, build democratic institutions, deepen respect for universal human rights, strengthen civilian protection and security, and advance the United States' humanitarian policies, practices, and programs around the world.

Economic Growth, Energy, and the Environment

The Under Secretary for Economic Growth, Energy, and the Environment leads the State Department's efforts to develop and implement economic growth, energy, agricultural, oceans, environmental, and science and technology policies to promote economic prosperity and address global challenges in a transparent, rules-based, and sustainable system. The bureaus and offices under her leadership work to:

- Advance the Department's economic statecraft agenda, using America's global leadership to strengthen our domestic economy;
- Elevate and intensify our efforts on energy security and environmental sustainability; and
- Foster innovation through robust science, entrepreneurship, and technology policies.

Management

The Under Secretary for Management is the State Department's representative on the President's Management Council, and is the Department official responsible for implementing the President's Management Agenda (PMA). The PMA is a set of management initiatives designed to make government more citizen-centered, effective, and efficient. There are five government-wide PMA initiatives: Human Capital (lead: Bureau of Human Resources); E-Government (Bureau of Information Resource Management); Competitive Sourcing (Bureau of Administration); Financial Management, and Budget and Performance Integration. The Department is also working with the White House Office of Management and Budget on the PMA initiative focused on "rightsizing" the U.S. Government's overseas presence.

Political Affairs

The Under Secretary for Political Affairs is the Department's fourth-ranking official. The Under Secretary serves as the day-to-day manager of overall regional and bilateral policy issues, and oversees the bureaus for Africa, East Asia and the Pacific, Europe and Eurasia, the Near East, South and Central Asia, the Western Hemisphere, and International Organizations.

The Assistant Secretaries of the geographic bureaus and offices advise the Under Secretary and guide the operation of the U.S. diplomatic missions within their regional jurisdiction. They are assisted by Deputy Assistant Secretaries, office directors, post management officers, and country desk officers. These officials work closely with U.S. embassies and consulates overseas and with foreign embassies in Washington, DC.

The Bureau of International Organization Affairs (IO) develops and implements the policies of the U.S. Government within the United Nations and its affiliated agencies, as well as within certain other international organizations. The IO Bureau engages in what is known as multilateral diplomacy to promote and defend the many overlapping interests of the American people. The IO Bureau also promotes effective and efficient management within international organizations.

Public Diplomacy and Public Affairs

The mission of American public diplomacy is to support the achievement of U.S. foreign policy goals and objectives, advance national interests, and enhance national security by informing and influencing foreign publics and by expanding and strengthening the relationship between the people and Government of the United States and citizens of the rest of the world.

The Under Secretary for Public Diplomacy and Public Affairs leads America's public diplomacy outreach, which includes communications with international audiences, cultural programming, academic grants, educational exchanges, international visitor programs, and U.S. Government efforts to confront ideological support for terrorism. The Under Secretary oversees the bureaus of Educational and Cultural Affairs, Public Affairs, and International Information Programs, as well as the Center for Strategic Counterterrorism Communications, and participates in foreign policy development.

Special Advisors, Envoys, and Representatives

These include:

Afghanistan and Pakistan

The Office of the Special Representative for Afghanistan and Pakistan co-ordinates across the government to meet U.S. strategic goals in the region while engaging NATO and other key friends, allies, and those around the world who are interested in supporting these efforts.

Arctic

The State Department's Special Representative for the Arctic was appointed in July of 2014, to lead the effort to advance U.S. interests in the Arctic Region, with a focus on Arctic Ocean governance, climate change, economic, environmental, and security issues in the Arctic region as the United States prepares to assume the chairmanship of the Arctic Council in 2015.

Climate Change

As the Administration's chief climate negotiator, the Special Envoy plays a central role in developing the United States' international policy on climate, representing the United States internationally at the Ministerial level in all bilateral and multilateral negotiations regarding climate change. The Envoy also participates in the development of domestic climate and clean energy policy.

The Obama administration is committed to combating climate change and meeting one of the greatest challenges of the 21st century. To meet this global challenge, the Office of the Special Envoy for Climate Change is actively engaging partners and allies around the world through international fora, such as the United Nations Framework Convention on Climate Change negotiating process, the Major Economies Forum on Energy and Climate, and key bilateral relationships. Special Envoy Stern believes that to achieve a strong international agreement and meet the climate challenge all countries must be fully engaged, and that, ultimately, such an agreement must complement and promote sustainable economic development by moving the world toward a low-carbon economy.

> The science is clear, and the threat is real. The facts on the ground are out-stripping the worst case scenarios. The costs of inaction—or inadequate actions—are unacceptable. But along with this challenge comes a great opportunity. By transforming to a low-carbon economy, we can stimulate global economic growth and put ourselves on a path of sustainable development for the 21st century.
>
> —*Special Envoy for Climate Change, Todd Stern, March 29, 2009*

Cyber Issues

In partnership with other countries, the State Department is leading the U.S. Government's efforts to promote an open, interoperable, secure, and reliable information and communications infrastructure that supports international trade and commerce, strengthens international security, and fosters free expression and innovation.

To more effectively advance the full range of U.S. interests in cyberspace, as outlined in the **U.S. International Strategy for Cyberspace**, the Office of the Coordinator for Cyber Issues (S/CCI) was established in February 2011. Its responsibilities include:

- Coordinating the Department's global diplomatic engagement on cyber issues
- Serving as the Department's liaison to the White House and federal departments and agencies on these issues
- Advising the Secretary and Deputy Secretaries on cyber issues and engagements
- Acting as liaison to public and private sector entities on cyber issues

- Coordinating the work of regional and functional bureaus within the Department engaged in these areas

S/CCI's coordination function spans the full spectrum of cyber-related issues to include security, economic issues, freedom of expression, and free flow of information on the Internet.

Global Food Security

The Special Representative for Global Food Security is responsible for coordinating all aspects of U.S. diplomacy related to food security and nutrition, including in support of Feed the Future, the U.S. government's global hunger and food security initiative. The Special Representative is part of the interagency leadership of the government-wide Presidential Initiative, serving concurrently as Deputy Coordinator for Diplomacy for Feed the Future. The Representative leads diplomatic efforts to advance the U.S. global hunger and food security initiative, with a particular focus on major donor and strategic partner countries as well as multilateral institutions such as the G8 and G20.

Global Health Diplomacy

The Office of Global Health Diplomacy (S/GHD) guides diplomatic efforts to advance the United States' global health mission to improve and save lives and foster sustainability through a shared global responsibility. In doing so, S/GHD focuses on providing diplomatic support in implementing the Global Health Initiative's principles and goals.

The U.S. Government is the leading contributor to global health efforts, with direct foreign assistance investments in over 80 countries, and support to other nations through our contributions to mechanisms like the Global Fund to Fight AIDS, Tuberculosis and Malaria. The United States invests in global health as an expression of American compassion, to strengthen fragile states by promoting social and economic progress, to protect America's security, and as a tool of public diplomacy.

S/GHD brings the full strength and voice of diplomacy into play to advance U.S. efforts to improve and save lives. These efforts are advanced through:

- **Strengthening Sustainable Health Programs:** S/GHD encourages sustainability of health programs by supporting partner countries as they strive to meet the health care needs of their citizens through effective leadership of their health care systems.
- **Promoting Shared Responsibility:** S/GHD uses diplomatic outreach across the family of nations to build shared global responsibility for sustained, ongoing improvements to health systems and health care delivery.
- **Supporting Our Embassies:** S/GHD supports our ambassadors and embassies on the ground, where our investments in health are translated into lives saved. Within the State Department, we champion global health training for diplomats, equipping them to elevate health in diplomatic discourse with partner countries.

Global Partnerships (S/GP)

The Secretary's Office of Global Partnerships is the entry point for collaboration between the U.S. Department of State, the public and private sectors, and civil society. Launched in 2009, S/GP aims to strengthen and deepen U.S. diplomacy and development around the world through partnerships that leverage the creativity, innovation, and core business resources of partners for greater impact. S/GP is working with partners across sectors, industries, and borders to promote economic growth and opportunity; to invest in the well-being of people from all walks of life; and to make democracy serve every citizen more effectively and justly.

S/GP's mission is to build public-private partnerships that strengthen diplomacy and development outcomes by serving as:

- **Convener**, bringing together people from across regions and sectors to work together on issues of common interest.
- **Catalyst**, launching new projects, actively seeking new solutions, and providing vital training and technical assistance to facilitate additional projects.
- **Collaborator**, working closely with our partners to plan and implement projects while avoiding duplication, learning from each other, and maximizing our impact by looking for best practices.
- **Cultivator**, nurturing innovative new partnerships by providing the space, access to networks and capital, and mentoring assistance to turn a good idea into reality.

Global Youth Issues

The Global Youth Issues portfolio is housed in the Policy, Planning, and Resources Office of the Under Secretary for Public Diplomacy and Public Affairs. The portfolio is focused on helping the U.S. Government better engage young people internationally to help solve the pressing challenges of today while also building greater global connectivity and networks to shape the world of tomorrow.

Its focus on global youth helps coordinate, amplify, and oversee efforts in three primary areas:

- Engaging youth in honest two-way dialogue -- including through our network of over 90 youth councils and regional networks;
- Empowering youth as drivers of their own destinies through programs on expanded economic opportunity and skills building;
- Elevating youth voices and causes by raising the profile of young people and the issues that they care about.

Haiti Special Coordinator

The Haiti Special Coordinator and his office oversee U.S. Government engagement with Haiti, including diplomatic relations and the implementation of a reconstruction strategy in partnership with the Government of Haiti. Promoting a stable and prosperous Haiti is a top U.S. policy objective. Following the 2010 earthquake, the United States committed $3.6 billion over five years to immediate humanitarian relief as well as longer-term reconstruction and development assistance. The plan, consistent with the Haitian Government's Action Plan, seeks to catalyze sustainable economic growth and promote stable democratic institutions. Much of the U.S. assistance is provided by the U.S. Agency for International Development (USAID). The U.S Government strategy focuses on four key pillars: (*a*) Infrastructure and energy, (*b*) Food and economic security, (*c*) Health and other basic services, and (*d*) Governance and rule of law.

Holocaust Issues

The Office of the Special Envoy for Holocaust Issues develops and implements U.S. policy with respect to the return of Holocaust-era assets to their rightful owners, compensation for wrongs committed during the Holocaust, and Holocaust remembrance. The Office does this in a manner that complements and supports broader U.S. interests and initiatives in a Europe committed to democracy, pluralism, human rights, and tolerance. The Office seeks to bring a measure of justice and assistance to Holocaust victims and their families and to create an infrastructure to assure that the Holocaust is remembered properly and accurately. This is an important issue in our bilateral relations with countries of central and eastern Europe and with the state of Israel.

Much of the Office's work relates to bringing closure to issues left outstanding during the Cold War. Before 1989, the governments of Russia and its satellites refused to permit research into Holocaust questions or the payment of compensation to Holocaust victims and their heirs. The end of communist governments in eastern Europe made it possible to extend Holocaust programs to those countries.

In addition, the Office has been involved in facilitating negotiations to reach, and in implementing, various agreements on the subject of Holocaust-era claims. Class action suits in the United States in the 1990's set the stage for the negotiation of a settlement agreement with Swiss Banks and executive agreements with Germany, France, and Austria that dealt with claims arising from unpaid Holocaust-era insurance policies, as the use of forced and slave labor, the illegal seizure of private and communal property, and other personal injuries. The Special Envoy is a member of the boards of directors overseeing the French and German payments programs. He maintains close relations with Austrian officials administering the programs negotiated with the Austrian Government. He also serves as an ex-officio member of the Holocaust Memorial Council (the board of directors of the U.S. Holocaust Memorial Museum).

In addition, the Office of the Special Envoy:

- Represents the United States on the Task Force for International Cooperation on Holocaust Education, Remembrance and Research. The U.S. chaired this organization from March 2003 to March 2004.
- Urges countries of eastern and central Europe to restitute illegally-confiscated communal and private property to rightful owners.
- Encourages the restitution of artworks to rightful owners.
- Supports the Special Envoy to Combat and Monitor Anti-Semitism, in coordinating U.S. efforts to combat anti-Semitism in the OSCE countries.
- Serves as the U.S. Government observer to the International Commission on Holocaust-Era Insurance Claims.

International Disability Rights

The Special Advisor for International Disability Rights (SADR) leads the U.S. comprehensive strategy to promote and protect the rights of persons with disabilities internationally. The United States, as part of its foreign policy, works to remove barriers and create a world in which disabled people enjoy dignity and full inclusion. Discrimination against people with disabilities is not simply unjust; it hinders economic development, limits democracy, and erodes societies.

The position of Special Advisor for International Disability Rights was created following U.S. signature of the Convention on the Rights of Persons with Disabilities (Disabilities Treaty) and resides in the Bureau of Democracy, Human Rights and Labor (DRL). As the senior-level disability human rights position at the State Department, the Special Advisor leads on disability human rights issues across the Department.

The Special Advisor for International Disability Rights also coordinates the interagency process for the ratification of the Disabilities Treaty; ensures that foreign assistance incorporates persons with disabilities; leads on disability human rights issues; ensures that the needs of persons with disabilities are addressed in international emergency situations; and conducts public diplomacy, including with civil society, on disability issues.

International Energy Affairs

The Special Envoy and Coordinator for International Energy Affairs advises the Secretary on energy issues, ensuring that energy security is advanced at all levels of U.S. foreign policy. The Office of the Coordinator for International Energy Affairs' (S/CIEA) primary goal is to integrate energy into our foreign policy agenda to advance U.S. national security interests. For the United States, energy resources remain strategic commodities and our economy relies on well-functioning energy markets, strategic stocks and diversity of supply. Providing an optimal mix of fuel types in adequate volumes is necessary to meet the various needs for industry, power generation, residential heating, transportation and many other activities. To that end, the Department of State and S/CIEA have taken a whole-of-government approach to expanding supplies of oil, natural gas and alternative energy sources to ensure adequate supplies for both the United States and the global market.

Since S/CIEA's creation, the office has worked to fulfill its mandate by engaging both energy producers and consumers. S/CIEA works with established and newly emerging energy producers to promote efficient production, management and distribution of energy products to ensure global markets function efficiently and fairly. S/CIEA also dialogues with emerging energy consumer countries to allay concerns about continued market access and cooperate on exploring development of alternative energy sources to diversify global supplies.

S/CIEA has also worked toward achieving energy security goals by implementing two whole-of-government programs in addition to ongoing bilateral discussions: the Energy Governance and Capacity Initiative (EGCI) and the Global Shale Gas Initiative (GSGI). Both programs facilitate development and expansion of available resources to maximize energy access.

Producing and consuming countries both share an interest in promoting energy security because of the major implications to global economic prosperity, peoples' wellbeing and national and international stability. S/CIEA will continue to engage with willing partners to promote energy security for the United States and the global market.

Israel and the Palestinian Authority (USSC)

The Secretary of State established the Office of the United States Security Coordinator for Israel and the Palestinian Authority (USSC) in 2005 to meet U.S. commitments under the Middle East Roadmap for Peace. The USSC is a joint, international, and interagency team with the core of the organization made up of Department of Defense service members who are assigned to the State Department.

The USSC directs all facets of U.S. security sector assistance to the Palestinian Authority and synchronizes international supporting efforts. The USSC headquarters is in Jerusalem with all members living in the local area. This persistent presence provides a positive and visible sign of the U.S. commitment to an enduring partnership with both Israel and the Palestinian people. The USSC assists the Palestinian Authority to transform and professionalize its security sector; engages with the Israelis and Palestinians on security initiatives that build trust and confidence in order to meet Roadmap obligations and supports U.S. and international whole-of-government efforts that set the conditions for a negotiated two-state solution.

The Palestinian Authority possesses professional and self-sustaining security institutions, accountable to and under legitimate civilian authority, that effectively combat terrorism and criminal threats to law and order, perpetuate an environment of security and stability for the Palestinian people, are able to provide for the national security of a future Palestinian State, and serve as a stable and peaceful neighbor to the State of Israel.

The USSC employs a phased campaign plan that directs U.S. efforts to achieve mutually beneficial objectives for the United States and our partners. The plan guides the common and collective actions toward the shared goal of building confidence between Israel and the Palestinian Authority in order to set the conditions for a negotiated, two-state solution. The USSC is currently transitioning its main effort from assisting the Palestinian Authority Security Forces (PASF) in building the force structure, infrastructure, equipment, and training required for a basic professional security capability to supporting institution-building in the Palestinian security sector. In this phase, it will help the PASF develop indigenous readiness, training, and logistics programs and the capability to maintain and sustain their operational readiness and support infrastructure. Additionally, the USSC will continue to advocate for enhanced security initiatives between Israel and the Palestinian Authority and will support other U.S. rule of law programs that assist the Palestinians improve the performance of the Justice and Corrections Sectors.

To achieve mission success, the USSC relies on a coalition effort that consists of security experts from the U.S., Canada, United Kingdom, Turkey, and the Netherlands. The team also includes other international partners from Germany, Finland, Denmark, and Greece who provide technical training experts and advisors. The USSC works very closely with its State Department counterparts especially the Bureau of International Narcotics and Law Enforcement Affairs to provide focused security assistance to the PASF and to support other interagency efforts to achieve broader U.S. national security objectives in the region.

USSC Vision Statement:
- Demonstrating **Excellence:** As a trusted, reliable partner and a responsible steward of assigned national resources
- Building Palestinian Authority Security Force **Competence:** So that they are accountable to civil leadership, able to provide security to its citizens, and enforce the rule of law
- Fostering Israeli-Palestinian Authority **Confidence:** To help set the conditions for a negotiated two-state solution

Kimberley Process

The Kimberley Process (KP) is an international, multi-stakeholder initiative created to increase transparency and oversight in the diamond industry in order to eliminate trade in conflict diamonds, or rough diamonds sold by rebel groups or their allies to fund conflict against legitimate governments. The KP, which became operational in 2003, controls trade in rough diamonds between participating countries through domestic implementation of a certification scheme that makes the trade more transparent and secure; and prohibits trade with non-participants. Fifty-four participants representing 81 countries participate in the KP, with industry and civil society participating as observers. Rough diamonds must be shipped in sealed containers and exported with a Kimberley Process Certificate that certifies that the rough diamonds have not benefited rebel movements. The State Department's Office of Threat Finance Countermeasures in the Bureau of Economic and Business Affairs coordinates

U.S. Government interagency implementation of the Kimberley Process pursuant to the Clean Diamond Trade Act of 2003.

Monitoring and Combating Anti-Semitism

The Special Envoy to Monitor and Combat Anti-Semitism advances U.S. Foreign Policy on anti-Semitism. Anti-Semitism is discrimination against or hatred toward Jews. The Special Envoy develops and implements policies and projects to support efforts to combat anti-Semitism. The Special Envoy was established by the Global Anti-Semitism Review Act of 2004, and is a part of the Bureau of Democracy, Human Rights and Labor (DRL). DRL produces the State Department's annual reports on Human Rights Practices and International Religious Freedom, and the Special Envoy provides input on anti-Semitism for these reports. The Special Envoy to Monitor and Combat Anti-Semitism welcomes information on anti-Semitic incidents, including personal and property attacks; government policies, including judicial/prosecutorial decisions and educational programs on the issue; and press and mass media reports. The office can be contacted at: SEASinfo@state.gov.

Muslim Communities

The Special Representative to Muslim Communities is responsible for executing Secretary Kerry's vision for engagement with Muslims around the world on a people-to-people and organizational level. He reports directly to the Secretary of State.

North Korea Human Rights

The Special Envoy for North Korean Human Rights Issues was created by the North Korea Human Rights Act of 2004, which called for a Special Envoy to "coordinate and promote efforts to improve respect for the fundamental human rights of the people of North Korea."

Nuclear Nonproliferation

The Special Representative of the President, with the rank of Ambassador, is responsible for working with other States to strengthen the Nuclear Non-Proliferation Treaty (NPT) and the international nonproliferation regime. The Ambassador plays a lead role in preparing for the NPT Review Conference, and through international diplomacy promoting the United States' goal of renewing and reinvigorating the NPT and the global regime.

Organization of Islamic Cooperation (OIC)

The Special Envoy is the President's representative to the Organization of Islamic Cooperation (OIC). The OIC is comprised of 56 nations and is the second largest international body after the UN.

Sudan and South Sudan

The Special Envoy is tasked with:

- Pressing the Government of Sudan to stop waging war on its own people, including by ending indiscriminate bombing, denial of unfettered humanitarian access and disregard of human rights and fundamental freedoms, as well as address the legitimate political concerns of all of the country's diverse population.
- Working to end the crisis in South Sudan by supporting the Intergovernmental Authority on Development (IGAD)-led talks, engaging the government, opposition and representatives of South Sudanese society, and supporting efforts to ensure justice, reconciliation, and accountability;
- Supporting the work of the African Union High-Level Implementation Panel to resolve outstanding issues related to the Comprehensive Peace Agreement between Sudan and South Sudan.

- Helping both governments meet the needs of their people and address humanitarian crises

Threat Reduction Programs

The Coordinator for Threat Reduction Programs for the Department of State and oversees Department of State (DOS) participation in interagency efforts to coordinate between DOS' threat reduction programs and those of other agencies.

In 2012, the United States Chaired the Global Partnership (GP) Against the Spread of Weapons and Materials of Mass Destruction. As Chair, the United States provided a road map to guide the GP towards becoming more of a coordinating mechanism for activities and programs under the extended mandate to continue the GP beyond 2012. The United States focused on the areas enunciated at the 2011 G8 Summit in Deauville --specifically nuclear and radiological security, biosecurity, scientist engagement, and facilitation of implementation of UN Security Council Resolution 1540. Officials collaborated on responses to assistance needs and coordinated possible projects in these areas as well as expansion of membership to start better reflecting global security threats. This expansion included the recent membership of Kazakhstan and also Mexico -- the first Latin American country to join the GP.

In an effort to provide a more integrated mechanism for funding and implementing programs under this extended mandate, relevant international organizations (IOs) were invited to attend the working group meetings for the first time. Furthermore, the U.S. focused on three sub- working groups in Biosecurity, Membership Expansion, and Centers of Excellence to facilitate and materialize the discussions of the full member GP working group. Two additional sub-working groups were approved late in 2012, focusing on Nuclear and Radiological Security, and Chemical Security.

Nuclear Security Summits

In his Prague speech in April 2009, President Obama highlighted the need for effective measures to secure nuclear material and prevent nuclear smuggling and terrorism. The Nuclear Security Summit in Washington, DC in April 2010 provided significant momentum toward this goal by bringing high-level attention and prominence to the issue of nuclear security and helping to develop a common understanding of the threat posed by nuclear terrorism. In Washington, 50 world leaders produced a Joint Communique and detailed Work Plan to articulate a common commitment to focus collectively on improving security while adapting to changing conditions, minimizing the use and locations of sensitive nuclear materials, and continually exchanging information on best practices and practical solutions. Significant progress toward improving nuclear security has already been made since April 2010.

Recognizing that the Summit's goals require a long-term commitment, the Republic of Korea hosted the second Nuclear Security Summit in Seoul in March 2012. In Seoul, President Obama and 57 other world leaders joined together to reduce the threat of nuclear terrorism. Summit participants agreed to a detailed Communiqué that advances important nuclear security goals. Many countries agreed to a number of multilateral joint commitments, including work on: implementing national legislation to implement nuclear security treaties; measures to prevent nuclear terrorism; and promoting the security of nuclear materials while in transit, among others. The international community has made great strides through the Summit process to prevent terrorists from acquiring nuclear weapons and material. Taken individually, these Summit initiatives may seem like small steps, but they add up to a significant shift.

The United States recognizes that work still needs to be done. Nuclear material continues to be stored without adequate protection, at risk of exploitation by terrorists and criminal gangs that have expressed an interest. The United States looks forward to working with its international partners to further secure vulnerable nuclear material and make progress toward the President's nonproliferation agenda.

Global Effort to Secure All Vulnerable Nuclear Material

In Prague, President Obama called for a new international effort to secure all vulnerable nuclear material around the world within four years. This effort will draw together international and domestic programs, including many supported directly by the United States, aimed at protecting such materials from theft or sabotage, raising international standards, converting civil applications that current use highly enriched uranium to the use of low enriched uranium, and reducing unnecessary stocks of such weapon-usable materials wherever feasible. The Coordinator oversees the coordination of DOS efforts in, and lead international diplomacy for the effort to improve nuclear security.

Non-Governmental Organizations (NGOs) Outreach

The Office has an active program for outreach to various U.S. and international NGOs, think tanks and research institutes as a means to determine ways in which they can work on promoting the overall goals of the global threat reduction programs.

Bureaus and Offices

Bureau of Administration

The Bureau of Administration (A) provides support programs to the Department of State and U.S. embassies and consulates. These programs include: real property and facilities management; procurement; supply and transportation; diplomatic pouch and mail services; official records, publishing, and library services; language services; setting allowance rates for U.S. Government personnel assigned abroad and providing support to the overseas schools educating their dependents; overseeing safety and occupational health matters; small and disadvantaged business utilization; and support for both White House travel abroad and special conferences called by the President or Secretary of State.

Direct services to the public and other government agencies include: authenticating documents used abroad for legal and business purposes; responding to requests under the Freedom of Information and Privacy Acts and providing the Electronic Reading Room for public reference to State Department records and information access programs; printing official publications; language support to the U.S. Government; and determining use of the Diplomatic Reception Rooms of the Harry S Truman headquarters building in Washington, DC.

The Office of Small and Disadvantaged Business Utilization (OSDBU), which reports to the Deputy Secretary for Management and Resources on small business policies and activities, is attached to the Bureau of Administration for administrative purposes and to facilitate collaboration with the Department's contracting function.

African Affairs

The division is focused on the development and management of U.S. policy concerning the continent. There are four pillars that serve as the foundation of U.S. policy toward Africa.

1) Strengthening Democratic Institutions;
2) Supporting African economic growth and development;
3) Advancing Peace and Security;
4) Promoting Opportunity and Development.

Allowances

The Office of Allowances in the Bureau of Administration develops and coordinates policies, regulations, standards, and procedures to administer the government-wide allowances and benefits program abroad under the Department of State Standardized Regulations (DSSR).

The office compiles statistics of living costs abroad, quarters allowances, hardship differentials, and danger pay allowances and computes the established allowances to compensate U.S. Government civilian employees for costs and hardships related to assignments abroad. The office is also responsible for establishing maximum per diem rates for foreign areas.

Arms Control, Verification and Compliance (AVC)

The AVC Bureau's core missions within the U.S. Department of State concern arms control, verification, and compliance with international arms control, nonproliferation, and disarmament agreements or commitments.

AVC advances national and international security through the negotiation and implementation of effectively verifiable and diligently enforced arms control and disarmament agreements involving weapons of mass destruction and their means of delivery as well as certain conventional weapons.

AVC also leads U.S. efforts to:

- Develop arms control policies for the implementation of existing agreements and negotiation of future agreements;
- Advance missile defense and space policy in support of U.S. national security policies and objectives; and
- Promote and implement bilateral and multilateral arms control, transparency and confidence-building measures.

Among the Bureau's core responsibilities are those ensuring that appropriate verification requirements and capabilities are fully considered and properly integrated throughout the development, negotiation, and implementation of arms control, nonproliferation and disarmament agreements and commitments.

AVC is also tasked with ensuring that other countries' compliance is carefully monitored, assessed, reported, and pursued, as well as that all treaties and agreements are fully implemented. The Bureau works with foreign governments and international organizations to acquire data and information for compliance assessments and to encourage Parties' compliance with their commitments.

AVC is the principal policy community representative to the Intelligence Community with regard to verification and compliance matters and ensures that verification requirements are met. As required by federal statute (22 U.S.C. § 2593a), AVC is responsible for ensuring that U.S. intelligence capabilities to collect, analyze, and disseminate precise and timely information bearing upon matters of verification and compliance (*e.g.,* on the nature and status of foreign governments' Weapons of Mass Destruction and delivery system programs) are effectively acquired, maintained, and enhanced.

The Bureau leads the State Department in all matters related to the implementation of certain international arms control, nonproliferation, and disarmament agreements and commitments; this includes staffing and managing treaty implementation commissions.

AVC also provides, through its **Nuclear Risk Reduction Center,** information technology support and secure, near-real-time government-to-government communications linkages with foreign government treaty partners.

Authentications

The U.S. Department of State issues both Authentication Certificates and Apostilles. The determination of which certificate is issued is based on the country in which the document will be used. Authentication Certificates are issued for documents which are destined for use in countries that are not parties to The Hague Apostille Convention. Apostille Certificates are issued for documents destined for use in countries that are parties to The Hague Apostille Convention.

In accordance with 22 CFR, Part 131, the Office of Authentications provides signed certificates of authenticity for a variety of documents to individuals, institutions, and government agencies. Examples of documents that may require authentication for use abroad may include, but are not limited to, company bylaws, powers of attorney, trademarks, diplomas, treaties, warrants, extraditions, agreements, certificates of good standing, and courier letters.

Budget and Planning

The Bureau of Budget and Planning (BP, formerly the Bureau of Resource Management) carries out the principal responsibilities of preparing and submitting the Department's budget requests, managing the Department's operational resource requirements, and ensuring that operational planning and performance management is synchronized with the Department's resource requirements. BP also coordinates with the Office of U.S. Foreign Assistance Resources in developing policies, plans, and programs to achieve foreign policy goals.

Civil Rights

At the Department of State, diversity is not just a worthy cause: it is a business necessity. Diversity of experience and background helps Department employees in the work of diplomacy. The Secretary believes that diversity is extremely important in making the State Department an employer of choice. The Secretary has delegated both tasks of advancing diversity within the Department and ensuring equal opportunity to all employees to the Director of the Office of Civil Rights (S/OCR), who also serves as the Chief Diversity Officer (CDO).

S/OCR advises and assists the Secretary and other principal officers in equal employment opportunity (EEO) policy and diversity management issues that relate to the Department of State. The office is symbiotically separated into three sections: Diversity Management and Outreach, Intake and Resolution, and Legal.

The Diversity Management and Outreach section helps the Department foster a work environment free of discrimination by maintaining an affirmative outreach program. It performs this task by preparing workforce diversity reports, managing special emphasis programs, delivering EEO and diversity briefings, conducting workforce analysis to eradicate barriers to equal employment opportunity for individuals and groups, organizing commemorative events to recognize the contributions of a diverse array of individuals and groups, and more.

The Intake and Resolution section handles all complaints surrounding employment discrimination in both the informal/counseling process and the formal complaint process. The Intake and Resolution section manages the Department's Alternative Dispute Resolution (ADR) program and the counseling program. Any employee or applicant who believes he/she has been discriminated against on the basis of race, color, national origin, sex, age, disability, religion, sexual orientation, or reprisal for protected EEO activity should contact S/OCR or an EEO counselor within 45 calendar days of the alleged discriminatory act.

S/OCR is one of the few EEO offices within the federal government to employ in-house counsel. The Legal section seeks to advance the mission of S/OCR by providing assistance with legal compliance as it relates to the administrative processing of EEO complaints and other EEO issues. The Legal section also investigates sexual and discriminatory harassment complaints within the Department reported pursuant to the requirements of 3 FAM 1525 and 1526.

S/OCR is in the forefront of establishing best practices for EEO and diversity management within a federal agency. The Department of State is the first cabinet-level agency to appoint a Chief Diversity Officer with oversight authority to integrate and transform diversity principles into practices in the Department's operations. Another best practice cited by the EEOC is a dialogue between S/OCR and each bureau within the Department to discuss the bureau's current diversity statistics and ways that each bureau can work to improve the diversity of staff, experiences, and thought.

Conflict and Stabilization Operations

The Bureau of Conflict and Stabilization Operations (CSO) advances U.S. national security by breaking cycles of violent conflict and mitigating crises in priority countries. It engages in conflict prevention, crisis response and stabilization, aiming to address the underlying causes of destabilizing violence.

Conflict prevention and crisis response is a vital diplomatic specialty--complementing traditional practices. Focusing on strategically significant countries, CSO believes in taking advantage of the astonishing advances in communications and data gathering and fully realizing the potential of women, young people, and other emerging local leaders. The vast energy generated by expressions of citizen power can move the world toward a brighter tomorrow, if fresh ideas and new alliances steer history toward that promise.

CSO breaks cycles of violence through locally grounded analysis that focuses on a top-priority opportunity to address conflict. When we began, we set three goals:

- Make an impact in three or four countries important to the United States.
- Build a respected team and trusted partnerships.
- Be innovative and agile.

By employing tools and expertise to fortify the Department in three areas related to conflict (analysis, strategy, and operations), CSO aims to connect policy and practice. Working with colleagues throughout the State Department and the interagency, CSO strives to forge a common U.S. government understanding of each conflict. The Bureau is now positioned to play a catalytic role as America's civilian power furthers global peace and prosperity.

CSO starts its engagements with joint, rapid, locally-grounded conflict analysis. Data-driven products draw on diverse sources, including diplomatic intelligence and media reports, "big data" platforms, polling, local interviews, and international expertise. Prioritized strategies then target the causes of instability and address high-risk periods such as political transitions and peace negotiations.

Rapid implementation requires host-country partners. CSO seeks to amplify local initiatives by managing nearly $100 million in programs (in FY2013). Working with an embassy, regional bureaus, and others, it uses these funds to ground theory in practice.

Real-time monitoring and evaluation enable us to adjust our plans. In Honduras, we saw an important new fiscal initiative get bogged down. In Kenya we should have mobilized already-active religious leaders, youth, civic activists, and police officers earlier. Better anticipation, greater speed, and improved partnership mechanisms are among recurring challenges. So is the need to provide "the right person, in the right place, at the right time," which is the goal of our new Civilian Response Network.

Finally, communications is central to diplomacy, and CSO is using both traditional media outlets and social media to break cycles of violence in Syria, Honduras, Nigeria, and elsewhere.

In every place CSO works, it counts on partners, starting with colleagues within the State Department and USAID and at the Department of Defense. In Syria, for example, U.S. partners include the Bureau of Near Eastern Affairs, the Office of Transition Initiatives, the U.S.-Middle East Partnership Initiative, and the Bureau of Democracy, Human Rights and Labor. It relies on allies such as the UK, Denmark, and Canada to support training and other efforts. CSO reaches out to civil society and host-country partners.

The support CSO teams has received from more than 20 U.S. ambassadors and their embassies is the best evidence that crisis response and conflict reduction are centerpieces of U.S. diplomacy. To build an enduring contributor to U.S. foreign policy, CSO understands that constant learning, close partnerships, and innovation are essential.

Counterterrorism

The primary mission of the Bureau of Counterterrorism (CT) is to forge partnerships with non-state actors, multilateral organizations, and foreign governments to advance the counterterrorism objectives and national security of the United States. Working with U.S. Government counterterrorism team, CT takes a leading role in developing coordinated strategies to defeat terrorists abroad and in securing the cooperation of international partners (see also Terrorism section).

Democracy, Human Rights, and Labor

Promoting freedom and democracy and protecting human rights around the world are central to U.S. foreign policy. The values captured in the Universal Declaration of Human Rights and in other global and regional commitments are consistent with the values upon which the United States was founded centuries ago. The United States supports those persons who long to live in freedom and under democratic governments that protect universally accepted human rights. The United States uses a wide range of tools to advance a freedom agenda, including bilateral diplomacy, multilateral engagement, foreign assistance, reporting and public outreach, and economic sanctions. The United States is committed to working with democratic partners, international and regional organizations, non-governmental organizations, and engaged citizens to support those seeking freedom.

The Bureau of Democracy, Human Rights and Labor leads the U.S. efforts to promote democracy, protect human rights and international religious freedom, and advance labor rights globally.

Diplomatic Security

The Bureau of Diplomatic Security (DS) is the security and law enforcement arm of the U.S. Department of State. DS is a world leader in international investigations, threat analysis, cyber security, counterterrorism, security technology, and protection of people, property, and information.

The Bureau is responsible for providing a safe and secure environment for the conduct of U.S. foreign policy. Every diplomatic mission in the world operates under a security program designed and maintained by Diplomatic Security. In the United States, Diplomatic Security personnel protect the Secretary of State and high-ranking foreign dignitaries and officials visiting the United States, investigates passport and visa fraud, and conducts personnel security investigations. Operating from a global platform in 31 U.S. cities and more than 160 foreign countries, DS ensures that America can conduct diplomacy safely and securely. DS plays a vital role in protecting 275 U.S. diplomatic missions and their personnel overseas, securing critical information systems, investigating passport and visa fraud, and fighting the war on terror.

Director General of the Foreign Service and Director of Human Resources

The Bureau handles recruitment, assignment evaluation, promotion, discipline, career development, and retirement policies and programs for the Department's Foreign and Civil Service employees.

East Asian and Pacific Affairs

The Bureau of East Asian and Pacific Affairs deals with U.S. foreign policy and U.S. relations with the countries in the Asia-Pacific region, particularly China and Korea.

Economic and Business Affairs

The Bureau of Economic and Business Affairs (EB) mission is to promote economic security and prosperity at home and abroad. The Bureau's work lies at the critical nexus of economic prosperity and national security. As the single point where international economic policy tools and threads converge, we help promote a coherent economic policy across the U.S. Government. On this site you will find links and resources for all of these tools and the ways the U.S. Department of State and EB are engaged to implement U.S. foreign economic policy.

The Bureau of Economic and Business Affairs is divided into seven areas:

- Commercial & Business Affairs (EB/CBA): Supports U.S. firms doing business overseas and foreign firms wishing to invest in the United States. Ensures that private sector business concerns are fully integrated into U.S. foreign and economic policy. Houses the Global Entrepreneurship Program to promote entrepreneurship worldwide.
- Trade Policy and Programs (EB/TPP): Furthers U.S. trade policy objectives and advances export opportunities for U.S. businesses through trade initiatives including free trade agreements and the World Trade Organization (WTO). Houses offices for trade, intellectual property, and agriculture.
- Counter Threat Finance and Sanctions (EB/TFS): Leads efforts to develop and implement economic sanctions, to deprive terrorist groups of funding, and to stem the trade in conflict gems and minerals.
- International Communications and Information Policy (EB/CIP): EB/CIP formulates, coordinates, and oversees the implementation of international telecommunications and information policy, leading U.S. delegations to bilateral and multilateral negotiations. EB/CIP works internationally to maintain a free, open and accessible global Internet, and also represents U.S. Government positions on telecommunications security, spectrum and other communications-related matters.
- International Finance and Development (EB/IFD): Uses financial channels to expand economic opportunities in the U.S. and abroad and support other U.S. foreign policy interests. Collaborates with other U.S. agencies, international financial institutions (e.g., IMF, World Bank), and private sector partners to promote sound economic policies and support U.S. exports and job creation. Houses offices focusing on investment, development and macroeconomic policies.

- Transportation Affairs (EB/TRA): Provides support to the U.S. global transportation industry. Leads negotiation of aviation agreements and coordinates international aviation and maritime policy, to support the highest level of safety, security, and environmental protection.
- Economic Policy Analysis & Public Diplomacy (EB/EPPD): Manages cross-cutting issues including strategic planning, economic analysis and public diplomacy. Promotes corporate social responsibility; leads the U.S. relationship with the Organization for Economic Cooperation and Development (OECD); and manages the Advisory Committee on International Economic Policy (ACIEP).

The Bureau of Educational and Cultural Affairs' (ECA)

The ECA's mission is to increase mutual understanding between the people of the United States and the people of other countries by means of educational and cultural exchange that assist in the development of peaceful relations.

As mandated by the Mutual Educational and Cultural Exchange Act of 1961, the U.S. Department of State's Bureau of Educational and Cultural Affairs (ECA) works to build friendly, peaceful relations between the people of the United States and the people of other countries through academic, cultural, sports, and professional exchanges, as well as public-private partnerships. Who We Engage In an effort to reflect the diversity of the United States and global society, ECA programs, funding, and other activities encourage the involvement of American and international participants from traditionally underrepresented groups, including women, racial and ethnic minorities, and people with disabilities. Opportunities are open to people regardless of their race, color, national origin, sex, age, religion, geographic location, socioeconomic status, disability, sexual orientation or gender identity. The Bureau is committed to fairness, equity and inclusion. Artists, educators, athletes, students, youth, and rising leaders in the United States and more than 160 countries around the globe participate in academic, cultural, sports, and professional exchanges.

Energy Resources

Energy is at the nexus of national security, economic prosperity, and the environment. The Department of State's work in national security, bilateral and multilateral diplomacy, commercial advocacy, environment and development are widely affected by energy concerns. The Bureau of Energy Resources (ENR) is working to ensure that all our diplomatic relationships advance our interests in having access to secure, reliable, and ever-cleaner sources of energy.

The Bureau of Energy Resources has three core objectives:

- **Energy Diplomacy:** To manage the geopolitics of today's energy economy through reinvigorated energy diplomacy with major producers and consumers of energy.
- **Energy Transformation:** To stimulate the market forces that will sustain transformational energy policies in terms of alternative and renewable energy sources, electricity, development, and reconstruction.
- **Energy Transparency and Access:** To expand good governance, increase transparency, and improve commercially viable and environmentally sustainable access to the 1.3 billion people without modern energy services.

European and Eurasian Affairs

The Bureau of European and Eurasian Affairs develops and implements U.S. foreign policy in Europe and Eurasia. The Bureau promotes U.S. interests in the region on issues such as international security, NATO, coordination with the European Union and other regional organizations, support for democracy, human rights, civil society, economic prosperity, counterterrorism, and nonproliferation.

Executive Secretariat

The Executive Secretariat (S/ES), comprised of the Executive Secretary and four Deputy Executive Secretaries, is responsible for coordination of the work of the Department internally, serving as the liaison between the Department's bureaus and the offices of the Secretary, Deputy Secretary, and Under Secretaries. It also handles the Department's relations with the White House, National Security Council, and other Cabinet agencies.

The Secretariat Staff (S/ES-S) works with the various offices of the Department in drafting and clearing written materials for the Secretary, Deputy Secretary, and Under Secretary for Political Affairs. This staff also is responsible for taking care of advance preparations for the Secretary's official trips -- domestic and international -- and staffing the "mobile office" and keeping the Secretary's schedule on track during the trip.

The Operations Center (S/ES-O) is the Secretary's and the Department's communications and crisis management center. Working 24 hours a day, the Operations Center monitors world events, prepares briefings for the Secretary and other Department principals, and facilitates communication between the Department and the rest of the world. The Operations Center also coordinates the Department's response to crises and supports task forces, monitoring groups, and other crisis-related activities.

Foreign Assistance Resources

The Office of U.S. Foreign Assistance Resources (F) ensures the strategic and effective allocation, management, and use of foreign assistance resources.

Foreign Missions

The Foreign Missions Act (22 U.S.C. 4301-4316) provides the legal foundation to facilitate secure and efficient operations of U.S. missions abroad, and of foreign missions and international organizations in the United States. Congress mandated the creation of the Office of Foreign Missions (OFM) in the Act to serve the interests of the American public, the American diplomatic community abroad, and the foreign diplomatic community residing in the United States ensuring that all diplomatic benefits, privileges, and immunities would be properly exercised in accordance with federal laws and international agreements.

The Office of Foreign Missions has four missions:

- Employment of reciprocity to ensure equitable treatment for United States diplomatic and consular missions abroad and their personnel through reciprocity;
- Regulation of the activities of foreign missions in the United States in a manner that will protect the foreign policy and national security interests of the United States;
- Protection of the United States public from abuses of privileges and immunities by members of the foreign missions; and
- Provision of service and assistance to the foreign mission community in the United States to assure appropriate privileges, benefits, and services on a reciprocal basis.

As an advocate for reciprocal agreements, OFM presses for fair treatment of U.S. personnel abroad while assuring foreign diplomats based in the United States receive the same treatment that each respective government provides in return. Additionally, OFM assists foreign missions in dealing with local government offices in the United States.

OFM also provides a range of services to the foreign diplomatic community, including issuance of vehicle titles, vehicle registrations, driver's licenses, and license plates; processing of tax exemption and duty-free customs requests; and facilitation of property acquisitions through local zoning law procedures. By assisting, advising, and regulating services for foreign diplomats, their dependents, and their staffs while residing in the United States.

Finally, OFM establishes and maintains relationships with U.S. law enforcement and security communities at the national, state, and local levels to

educate them about diplomatic privilege and immunity issues. OFM personnel conduct outreach and training seminars with these constituencies in con-
junction with other Department of State representatives, e.g., Diplomatic Security, Bureau of Consular Affairs, Office of the Chief of Protocol.

Foreign Service Institute

The Foreign Service Institute (FSI) is the Federal Government's primary
training institution for officers and support personnel of the U.S. foreign affairs community, preparing American diplomats and other professionals to
advance U.S. foreign affairs interests overseas and in Washington. At the
George P. Shultz National Foreign Affairs Training Center, the FSI provides
more than 600 courses—including some 70 foreign languages—to more than
100,000 enrollees a year from the State Department and more than 40 other
government agencies and the military service branches.

The Institute's programs include training for the professional development
of Foreign Service administrative, consular, economic/commercial, political,
and public diplomacy officers; for specialists in the fields of information management, office management, security, and medical practitioners and nurses;
for Foreign Service Nationals who work at U.S. posts around the world; and
for Civil Service employees of the State Department and other agencies. Ranging in length from one day to two years, courses are designed to promote successful performance in each professional assignment, to ease the adjustment
to other countries and cultures, and to enhance the leadership and management capabilities of the U.S. foreign affairs community.

Other courses and services help family members prepare for the demands
of a mobile lifestyle and living abroad, and provide employees and their families with important information about such critical and timely topics as emergency preparedness and cyber security awareness, among others. The Foreign
Service Institute is organized like a university and consists of five schools:

- The School of Language Studies
- The School of Applied Information Technology
- The School of Leadership and Management
- The School of Professional and Area Studies
- The Transition Center

Global AIDS Coordinator

The U. S. Global AIDS Coordinator's mission is to lead implementation of the U.S. President's Emergency Plan for AIDS Relief (PEPFAR).

PEPFAR is the U.S. Government initiative to help save the lives of those suffering from HIV/AIDS around the world. This historic commitment is the largest by any nation to combat a single disease internationally, and PEPFAR investments also help alleviate suffering from other diseases across the global health spectrum. PEPFAR is driven by a shared responsibility among donor and partner nations and others to make smart investments to save lives.

Global Criminal Justice

The Office of Global Criminal Justice advises the Secretary of State and the Under Secretary of State for Civilian Security, Democracy, and Human Rights on issues related to war crimes, crimes against humanity, and genocide. In particular, the office helps formulate U.S. policy on the prevention of, responses to, and accountability for mass atrocities. To this end, the office advises U.S. Government and foreign governments on the appropriate use of a wide range of transitional justice mechanisms, including truth and reconciliation commissions, lustrations, and reparations in addition to judicial processes.

The office also coordinates U.S. Government positions relating to the international and hybrid courts currently prosecuting persons responsible for genocide, war crimes, and crimes against humanity – not only for such crimes committed in the former Yugoslavia, Rwanda, Sierra Leone, and Cambodia – but also in Kenya, Libya, Côte d'Ivoire, Guatemala, and elsewhere in the world.

The office works closely with other governments, international institutions, and non-governmental organizations to establish and assist international and domestic commissions of inquiry, fact-finding missions, and tribunals to investigate, document, and prosecute atrocities in every region of the globe. The Ambassador-at-Large coordinates the deployment of a range of diplomatic, legal, economic, military, and intelligence tools to help expose the truth, judge those responsible, protect and assist victims, enable reconciliation, deter atrocities, and build the rule of law.

In the words of the President's May 2010 National Security Strategy:

> From Nuremberg to Yugoslavia to Liberia, the United States has seen that the end of impunity and the promotion of justice are not just moral imperatives; they are stabilizing forces in international affairs. The United States is thus working to strengthen national justice systems and is maintaining our support for ad hoc international tribunals and hybrid courts. Those who intentionally target innocent civilians must be held accountable, and we will continue to support institutions and prosecutions that advance this important interest. Although the United States is not at present a party to the Rome Statute of the International Criminal Court, and will always protect U.S. personnel, we are engaging with State Parties to the Rome Statute on issues of concern and are supporting the ICC's prosecution of those cases that advance U.S. interests and values, consistent with the requirements of U.S. law.

Global Food Security

The Office follows five Principles for Advancing Global Food Security

- Comprehensively address the underlying causes of hunger and under-nutrition
- Invest in country-led plans
- Strengthen strategic coordination
- Leverage the benefits of multilateral institutions
- Make sustained and accountable commitments

Global Women's Issues

The Secretary's Office of Global Women's Issues (S/GWI) seeks to ensure that women's issues are fully integrated in the formulation and conduct of U.S. foreign policy. The Office works to promote stability, peace, and development by empowering women politically, socially, and economically around the world.

> No country can get ahead if it leaves half of its people behind. This is why the United States believes gender equality is critical to our shared goals of prosperity, stability, and peace, and why investing in women and girls worldwide is critical to advancing U.S. foreign policy.
>
> —*"Why Women are Central to U.S. Foreign Policy," an Op-Ed by Secretary of State John Kerry*

Global Youth Issues

The Global Youth Issues portfolio is housed in the Policy, Planning, and Resources Office of the Under Secretary for Public Diplomacy and Public Affairs. The portfolio is focused on helping the U.S. Government better engage young people internationally to help solve the pressing challenges of today while also building greater global connectivity and networks to shape the world of tomorrow.

The focus on global youth helps coordinate, amplify, and oversee efforts in three primary areas:

- Engaging youth in honest two-way dialogue -- including through our network of over 90 youth councils and regional networks;
- Empowering youth as drivers of their own destinies through programs on expanded economic opportunity and skills building;

- Elevating youth voices and causes by raising the profile of young people and the issues that they care about.

Information Resource Management

The Bureau of Information Resource Management provides the information technology and services the Department needs to successfully carry out its foreign policy mission by applying modern IT tools, approaches, systems, and information products. It is expanding the use of collaborative information development and refinement to provide end users with the most accurate and useful information.

IRM constantly strives to improve its commitment for transparent, interconnected diplomacy, information systems and to incorporate new technologies for the advancement of U.S. foreign policy. Equally as important, the bureau is focused on enhancing security for the Department's computer and communications systems. IRM continues to aggressively confront these issues by strengthening IRM employee expertise and by enhancing the Department's information technology.

Inspector General

The Office of the Inspector General inspects each of the approximately 260 embassies, diplomatic posts, and international broadcasting installations throughout the world to determine whether policy goals are being achieved and whether the interests of the United States are being represented and advanced effectively. Additionally, OIG performs specialized security inspections and audits in support of the Department's mission to provide effective protection to our personnel, facilities, and sensitive information. OIG also audits Department and BBG operations and activities to ensure that they are as effective, efficient, and economical as possible. Finally, OIG investigates instances of fraud, waste, and mismanagement that may constitute either criminal wrongdoing or violation of Department and BBG regulations.

Bureau of Intelligence and Research

The Bureau of Intelligence and Research's (INR) primary mission is to harness intelligence to serve U.S. diplomacy. Drawing on all-source intelligence, INR provides value-added independent analysis of events to U.S. State Department policymakers; ensures that intelligence activities support foreign policy and national security purposes; and serves as the focal point in the State Department for ensuring policy review of sensitive counterintelligence and law enforcement activities around the world.

The bureau also analyzes geographical and international boundary issues. The Bureau of Intelligence and Research is a member of the U.S. intelligence community.

International Information Programs

The Bureau of International Information Programs (IIP) supports people-to-people conversations with foreign publics on U.S. policy priorities. To carry out this mission, IIP leverages digital communications technology to reach across platforms - from traditional forms of communications to new media channels. The bureau takes a strategic, data-driven approach to develop multimedia, digital communications products and to manage an overseas network of bricks-and-mortar American Spaces. Whether discussions take place in person or in virtual spaces, the bureau's top goal is to connect people with policy through dialogue that is relatable and understandable. In addition to IIP's ongoing programs, the bureau stands up timely special focus communications campaigns that respond to emerging issues.

International Narcotics and Law Enforcement Affairs (INL)

The Bureau of International Narcotics and Law Enforcement Affairs (INL) advises the President, Secretary of State, other bureaus in the Department of State, and other departments and agencies within the U.S. Government on the development of policies and programs to combat international narcotics and crime. INL programs support two of the Department's strategic goals

- To reduce the entry of illegal drugs into the United States; and
- To minimize the impact of international crime on the United States and its citizens

Focus areas are counternarcotics, combating crime and corruption, leveraging partnerships and rule of law. Its operating regions are Afghanistan and Pakistan, Africa and the Middle East, Europe and Asia and the Western Hemisphere.

International Organization Affairs

The Bureau of International Organization Affairs (IO) is the U.S. Government's primary interlocutor with the United Nations and a host of international agencies and organizations. As such, the Bureau is charged with advancing the President's vision of robust multilateral engagement as a crucial tool in advancing U.S. national interests. U.S. multilateral engagement spans the full range of important global issues, including peace and security, nuclear nonproliferation, human rights, economic development, climate change, global health, and much more.

International Security and Nonproliferation (ISN)

The Bureau of International Security and Nonproliferation (ISN) is responsible for managing a broad range of U.S. nonproliferation polices, programs, agreements, and initiatives. The proliferation of Weapons of Mass Destruction (WMD) and related materials, technologies, and expertise -- and the fact that terrorists are trying to acquire them -- is a preeminent challenge to American national security. Combating this threat through bilateral and multilateral diplomacy is one of the highest priorities of the Department of State. The ISN

Bureau leads the Department's efforts to prevent the spread of WMD --
whether nuclear, biological, chemical, or radiological -- and their delivery systems.

Legal Adviser

The Office of the Legal Adviser furnishes advice on all legal issues, domestic and international, arising in the course of the Department's work. This includes assisting Department principals and policy officers in formulating and
implementing the foreign policies of the United States, and promoting the
development of international law and its institutions as a fundamental element of those policies.

The Office is organized to provide direct legal support to the Department of
State's various bureaus, including both regional and geographic offices (those
which focus on specific areas of the world) and functional offices (those which
deal with specific subject matters such as economics and business, international environmental and scientific issues, or internal management).

Legislative Affairs

The Bureau of Legislative Affairs (H) coordinates legislative activity for the
Department of State and advises the Secretary, the Deputy, as well as the Under Secretaries and Assistant Secretaries on legislative strategy. H facilitates
effective communication between State Department officials and the Members
of Congress and their staffs. H works closely with authorizing, appropriations,
and oversight committees of the House and Senate, as well as with individual
Members that have an interest in State Department or foreign policy issues. H
manages Department testimony before House and Senate hearings, organizes
Member and staff briefings, and facilitates Congressional travel to overseas
posts for Members and staff throughout the year. H reviews proposed legislation and coordinates Statements of Administration Policy on legislation affecting the conduct of U.S. foreign policy. The H staff advises individual Bureaus

of the Department on legislative and outreach strategies and coordinates those strategies with the Secretary's priorities.

The Secretary of State is the principal Congressional Relations Officer of the Department. H supports the Secretary by ensuring that the administration's foreign policy priorities are reflected throughout the legislative process. H coordinates the annual testimony provided by the Secretary to Congressional committees with jurisdiction over State programs to explain Department priorities and budget requirements. The bureau succeeds in its overall mission by seeking passage of relevant foreign policy legislation and appropriations, obtaining advice and consent to treaties, as well as confirmation of the President's Departmental and Ambassadorial nominees by the Senate.

The Assistant Secretary, advises the Secretary of State on legislative matters, directs the Bureau of Legislative Affairs, and acts as the Department's principal liaison with the Congress.

Management Policy, Rightsizing, and Innovation

The Office of Management Policy, Rightsizing, and Innovation (M/PRI) is the Under Secretary for Management's central management analysis organization. M/PRI is comprised of three staffs that handle management policy, rightsizing, and innovation. M/PRI's Management Policy Staff provides analysis of cross-cutting issues for the Under Secretary for Management and other senior managers in the Department. Specifically, the Policy Staff:

- Manages and coordinates press and public outreach in addition to Congressional outreach for the entire M-family of bureaus;
- Coordinates and oversees the Department's initiatives within the President's Management Agenda;
- Manages the Accountability Review Board (ARB) function for the Secretary of State;

- Acts as liaison with the Office of Inspector General(OIG) and the Government Accountability Office (GAO) for M-family recommendations and findings;
- Provides advice and recommendations for cross-cutting issues when impasse is reached;
- Sets the policy for the Department's central system data warehouse; and,
- Serves as co-chair with the Office of Medical Services (MED) of the Avian Influenza Working Group to ensure that the Department is able to function in case of global pandemic.

M/PRI's Rightsizing Staff is responsible for managing the rightsizing of USG personnel serving abroad while under Chief of Mission authority and National Security Decision Directive 38 (NSDD 38). Through analyses and interaction with the field, the Rightsizing staff:

- Provides expertise to senior managers on policy matters related to chief of mission authority;
- Manages the NSDD-38 and country clearance processes;
- Conducts overseas staffing reviews of all missions on a rolling 5-year basis, as well as prior to planning any new capital construction projects abroad, in order to determine the minimum human resources required to meet foreign policy goals;
- Identifies potential efficiencies through outsourcing, empowerment of local staff, regionalization, consolidation and other rightsizing techniques;
- Works with the Office of Management and Budget (OMB) to provide advice and guidance regarding the President's Management Agenda for Rightsizing the entire U.S. Government presence overseas;
- Serves as the principal State Department interlocutor with other agency headquarters on management issues overseas to facilitate interagency cooperation, eliminate duplicative activity, and optimize productivity; and,

- With USAID counterparts, manages the day-to-day activities of the Joint Management Board to ensure ongoing consolidation of overseas management platforms.

M/PRI's Innovation Staff serves as the primary M representative to the Regional Initiatives Council (RIC) and leads standardization activities, especially those with an overseas focus. The Innovation Staff:

- Provides expertise in performance measurement and Department-wide management best practices to improve efficiency and customer satisfaction; and,
- Is the business case manager for Post Administrative Software Suite (PASS) and serves as co-chair of the PASS steering committee.

Medical Services

The Office of Medical Services (MED) has over 200 clinicians working in over 170 countries, supported by medical and administrative personnel in Washington, D.C. and abroad. MED provides healthcare to U.S. government employees and their families who are assigned to our embassies and consulates worldwide. We also advise our embassy and State Department management about health issues throughout the world. Although we cannot provide medical services to U.S. citizens abroad who are not affiliated with the U.S. government, we do collaborate with the State Department's Bureau of Consular Affairs to ensure the assistance they render is medically appropriate for the situation and available resources.

Near Eastern Affairs

The Bureau of Near Eastern Affairs (NEA), headed by Assistant Secretary Anne Patterson, deals with U.S. foreign policy and U.S. diplomatic relations with Algeria, Bahrain, Egypt, Iran, Iraq, Israel, Jordan, Kuwait, Lebanon, Libya,

Morocco, Oman, Palestinian Territories, Qatar, Saudi Arabia, Syria, Tunisia, United Arab Emirates, and Yemen. Regional policy issues that NEA handles include Iraq, Middle East peace, terrorism and weapons of mass destruction, and political and economic reform.

Oceans and International Environmental and Scientific Affairs

The Bureau of Oceans and International Environmental and Scientific Affairs, often referred to as "Oceans, Environment and Science" or "OES," was created in 1974 by Congress.

OES is currently headed by acting Assistant Secretary Ambassador Judith G. Garber and works to advance U.S. foreign policy goals in such critical areas as climate change, wildlife trafficking, water, polar issues, oceans policy, infectious diseases, science and technology, and space policy, to name a few.

Ombudsman

The Office of the Ombudsman assists employees of the Department of State manage workplace conflicts and help to identify mutually satisfactory solutions. The Department of State is a complex and far flung organization with over many employees spread over 200 countries, 178 embassies, 86 consulates and 9 missions. We state routinely that people are our most important asset; however there are times for nearly all of us when we need assistance or relief to solve difficulties in our work lives. When these problems defy easy categorization as potential HR grievances, EEO complaints, Union grievances, or IG investigations, that is precisely when you should call on the Ombudsman.

The Office provides a variety of services to Department employees, bureaus, and offices including coaching and mediation. Their services are independent, neutral, confidential, and informal whereby employees can consensually resolve workplace disputes and reach a fair and quick solution to workplace conflicts. We are committed to fostering a workplace culture that proactively manages conflict and benefits from innovative and creative resolutions.

The Ombudsman advises the Secretary and senior management on non-union, systemic issues affecting our workforce. The Ombuds experience and observation may result in policy recommendations, while feedback may uncover unintended, previously overlooked negative consequences as a result of procedures and practice. The Ombudsman may address a variety of issues—obtain information regarding agency policy, delete red tape, uncover evidence of prohibited personnel practices and workplace safety issues. Through all of this, the goal is to facilitate and support a fair, equitable, and nondiscriminatory workplace that ensures the essential well-being of the workforce especially in matters where problems are likely to be overlooked.

Overseas Buildings Operations

The Bureau of Overseas Buildings Operations (OBO) directs the worldwide overseas building program for the Department of State and the U.S. Government community serving abroad under the authority of the chiefs of mission. In concert with other State Department bureaus, foreign affairs agencies, and Congress, OBO sets worldwide priorities for the design, construction, acquisition, maintenance, use, and sale of real properties and the use of sales proceeds.

OBO's mission is to provide safe, secure and functional facilities that represent the U.S. government to the host nation and support our staff in the achievement of U.S. foreign policy objectives. These facilities should represent American values and the best in American architecture, design, engineering, technology, sustainability, art, culture and construction execution.

Policy Planning and Resources for Public Diplomacy and Public Affairs

The Office of Policy, Planning, and Resources for Public Diplomacy and Public Affairs (R/PPR) provides long-term strategic planning and performance measurement capability for public diplomacy and public affairs programs. It also enables the Under Secretary to better advise on the allocation of public diplomacy and public affairs resources, to focus those resources on the most urgent national security objectives, and provide realistic measurement of public diplomacy's and public affairs' effectiveness.

Policy Planning Staff

Created in 1947 by George Kennan at the request of Secretary of State George C. Marshall, the Policy Planning Staff (S/P) serves as a source of independent policy analysis and advice for the Secretary of State. The Policy Planning Staff"s mission is to take a longer term, strategic view of global trends and frame recommendations for the Secretary of State to advance U.S. interests and American values.

In his memoirs Present at the Creation, former Secretary of State Dean Acheson characterized the role of Policy Planning: "To anticipate the emerging form of things to come, to reappraise policies which had acquired their own momentum and went on after the reasons for them had ceased, and to stimulate and, when necessary, to devise basic policies crucial to the conduct of our foreign affairs."

For today's Policy Planning Staff, fulfilling this same, core mission for the Secretary requires striking a fine balance between engagement in the day-to-day requirements of diplomacy and development of long term, strategic plans. Broadly speaking, the daily work of the Policy Planning Staff may be divided into six areas:

- **Analysis**
  Policy Planning serves as an internal think tank for the Department of State - undertaking broad analytical studies of regional and functional issues, identifying gaps in policy, and initiating policy planning and formulation to fill these gaps. Policy Planning also serves as an institu-

tionalized "second opinion" on policy matters - providing recommendations and alternative courses of action to the Secretary of State.

- **Special Projects**
  Policy Planning assumes special projects or takes the lead on certain issues as tasked by the Secretary of State. Recent examples include Policy Planning's work on assembling the international coalition against terrorism, coordinating the reconstruction of Afghanistan through February 2002, and implementing the Good Friday agreement in Northern Ireland.

- **Policy Coordination**
  Policy Planning engages functional and regional bureaus within the State Department and relevant government agencies to ensure coordination and integration of policy with longer-term objectives.

- **Policy Articulation**
  The speechwriters for the Secretary of State are members of the Policy Planning Staff and work together with the whole Staff and all bureaus to draft the Secretary's speeches, public remarks, testimony before Congress, and contributions to print media.

- **Liaison**
  Policy Planning acts as a liaison with nongovernmental organizations, the academic community, think tanks, and others to exchange expert views on matters relevant to U.S. policy and to ensure that broad public opinion informs the policy formulation process.

- **Planning Talks**
  Policy Planning holds a series of dialogues -- known as planning talks -- with counterparts from other countries, including our key European allies, Japan, South Korea, Australia, China, and Russia. These talks

provide an opportunity to discuss broad strategic issues that go beyond crisis management or the day-to-day concerns of diplomacy.

The Director of the Policy Planning Staff manages the State Department's Dissent Channel. Consistent with its mandate to stimulate innovation and creativity in the Department, this unique process allows the Policy Planning Director to bring constructive, dissenting or alternative views on substantive foreign policy issues to the Secretary of State and Senior Department Officials. The Policy Planning Staff is typically a mix of career government officials and outside experts who bring differing perspectives and bases of experience to the conduct of U.S. diplomacy. Recently, the staff has included Foreign Service Officers, academics from universities and think tanks, intelligence analysts, former congressional staffers, an emergency room physician, a retired military officer, a business consultant, an arms control expert, and an economist. The staff is responsible for covering the full range of foreign policy issues facing the United States, although staff members exercise discretion and judgment in identifying the areas they focus on.

Political-Military Affairs (PM)

The Bureau of Political-Military Affairs (PM) is the Department of State's principal link to the Department of Defense. The PM Bureau provides policy direction in the areas of international security, security assistance, military operations, defense strategy and plans, and defense trade

Population, Refugees, and Migration

The Bureau of Population, Refugees, and Migration provides aid and sustainable solutions for refugees, victims of conflict and stateless people around the world, through repatriation, local integration, and resettlement in the United States. PRM also promotes the United States' population and migration policies.

Protocol

The Office of the Chief of Protocol seeks to advance the foreign policy goals of the United States by creating an environment for successful diplomacy. Its team extends the first hand that welcomes presidents, prime ministers, ruling monarchs, and other leaders to our country. By serving on the front lines of diplomatic engagement, it promote cross-cultural exchange and build new bridges of understanding between people and governments around the world.

Public Affairs

The Bureau of Public Affairs (PA) engages domestic and international media to communicate timely and accurate information with the goal of furthering U.S. foreign policy and national security interests as well as broadening understanding of American values. In carrying out its mission, PA employs a wide range of media platforms, provides historical perspective, and conducts public outreach.

The PA Bureau vigorously advances the State Department's mission to inform the American people and global audiences through a variety of ways, including:

- Strategic and tactical communications planning to advance America's foreign policy interests;
- Conducting press briefings for domestic and foreign press corps;
- Pursuing media outreach, enabling Americans everywhere to hear directly from key Department
- Managing the State Department's website at state.gov and developing web pages with up-to-date information about U.S. foreign policy;
- Using social media and other modern technologies to engage the public;
- Overseeing the State Department's six international Regional Media Hubs, which serve as overseas platforms for engagement of foreign audiences via the internet and broadcast and print media;

- Answering questions from the public about current foreign policy issues by phone, email, letter, or through social media;
- Arranging town meetings and scheduling speakers to visit universities, chambers of commerce, and communities to discuss U.S. foreign policy and why it is important to all Americans;
- Producing and coordinating audio-visual products and services in the U.S. and abroad for the public, the press, the Secretary of State, and Department bureaus and offices; and
- Preparing historical studies on U.S. diplomacy and foreign affairs matters.

Science & Technology Adviser

The Office of the Science and Technology Adviser to the Secretary (STAS) provides scientific and technical advice and resources to bureaus and offices at the U.S. Department of State, building upon the Secretary of State's emphasis on utilizing "smart power," "economic statecraft," and "whole-of-society" approaches.

Reporting to the Under Secretary for Economic Growth, Energy, and the Environment (E), E/STAS promotes science, technology, and engineering as integral components of U.S. diplomacy. The establishment of the E/STAS office in 2000 followed a National Research Council study that highlighted the attrition of scientists from the Department of State at a time when the importance of science and technology was increasing in many aspects of foreign policy. More recently, the 2010 Quadrennial Diplomacy and Development Review confirmed that in a world of increasingly fast-paced change, "science and technology must be enlisted in an unprecedented fashion."

South and Central Asian Affairs

The Bureau of South and Central Asian Affairs deals with U.S. foreign policy and U.S. relations with the countries of Afghanistan, Bangladesh, Bhutan,

India, Kazakhstan, Kyrgyzstan, Maldives, Nepal, Pakistan, Sri Lanka, Tajikistan, Turkmenistan, and Uzbekistan.

Trafficking in Persons

The U.S. Department of State leads the United States' global engagement to combat human trafficking and supports the coordination of anti-trafficking efforts across the U.S. government. Within the Department, and under the direction of the Ambassador-at-Large to Monitor and Combat Trafficking in Persons, the Office to Monitor and Combat Trafficking in Persons partners with foreign governments, international organizations, and civil society to develop and implement effective strategies for confronting modern slavery. The Office is responsible for bilateral and multilateral diplomacy, targeted foreign assistance, and public engagement on trafficking in persons.

The Office was established in accordance with the Trafficking Victims Protection Act (TVPA) of 2000. The TVPA updated the post-Civil War slavery statutes, furthering the guarantees of freedom from slavery and involuntary servitude set forth in the U.S. Constitution and articulated in the Universal Declaration of Human Rights.

The Office pursues policies, partnerships, and practices that uphold the "3P" paradigm of prosecuting traffickers, protecting victims, and preventing trafficking. The Office is organized into four sections: Reports and Political Affairs, International Programs, Public Engagement, and Resource Management and Planning.

Western Hemisphere Affairs

The Bureau of Western Hemisphere Affairs is responsible for managing and promoting U.S. interests in the region by supporting democracy, trade, and sustainable economic development, and fostering cooperation on issues such as citizen safety, strengthening democratic institutions and the rule of law, economic and social inclusion, energy, and climate change.

Part II: Major External Issues

Hopes that an end of the Cold War would mean a safer world have not materialized and in many respects the world is a more dangerous place than it was before. Putin's Russia has annexed Crimea and seems bent on acquiring more territory. China is flexing its economic and military muscle in the Far East. North Korea remains a threat to global security while the Middle East remains a powder keg. At the same time terrorism has taken on new dimensions with the emergence of ISIL, now the richest and most organized terrorist group in the world.

4

Terrorism

ISIL

ISIL—the Islamic State of Iraq and the Levant (also known as ISIS, or the Islamic State of Iraq and Syria)—poses the greatest terrorist threat the world has probably ever known. It is a Sunni ultra-extremist group that now controls areas in Iraq, Syria, Libya and Egypt. It believes in an extreme interpretation of Islam and all those who do not agree are infidels or apostates. It uses extreme violence to "purify" the community of unbelievers.

It has attracted tens of thousands of young fanatical jihadists from around the globe and it has billions of dollars to fund its cause. It has been officially branded as a terrorist organization by the United Nations and condemned by most countries because of its barbarity, especially the videotaping of beheadings. Many in the Muslim world have also denounced ISIS as being unrepresentative of Islam.

The group was founded in 1999 and became known as Al-Qa'ida in Iraq (AQI) in 2004 following the U.S. invasion. In 2006 it joined other Sunni insurgent groups to form the Mujahideen Shura Council which morphed into the Islamic State of Iraq (ISI). It enjoyed some popular support at first but its violence against civilians and execution of prisoners alienated many of the groups it was allied with. In April 2013, having entered the Syrian Civil War, it changed its name again to the Islamic State of Iraq and the Levant. In February 2014 Al-Qa'ida severed all ties with ISIL. Having occupied large tracts of land in Iraq and Syria, ISIL's leader Abu Bakr al-Baghdadi on June 29, 2014 declared himself Caliph of all Muslim nations demanding the allegiance of all devout Muslims worldwide. At the same time the organization changed its name again to the Islamic State (IS).

From 2006 until 2013 its primary goal, according to U.S. intelligence agencies, was to capture the central and western parts of Iraq and declare a Sunni Islamic State. By late 2007, however, because of indiscriminate attacks on civilians, many of the Sunni groups it was fighting alongside switched their allegiance and supported U.S. troops. Many senior AQI leaders were killed and the following year most AQI groups have been driven from their safe havens. In 2010 two top leaders, Abu Ayyub al-Masri and Abu Omar al-Baghadadi were killed in a joint U.S.-Iraqi raid. At a press conference in June 2010, General Odierno, commander of US forces in Iraq, reported that 80 percent of the ISI's top 42 leaders, including recruiters and financiers, had been killed or captured, with only eight remaining at large. He said that they had been cut off from al-Qaeda's leadership in Pakistan, and that improved intelligence had enabled the successful mission in April that led to the killing of al-Masri and al-Baghdadi; in addition, the number of attacks and casualty figures in Iraq for the first five months of 2010 were the lowest since 2003.

In May, 2012 Abu Bakr al-Baghdadi became leader of the Islamic State of Iraq. He appointed many of Saddam Hussein's former officers to senior positions, and in July 2012 he issued a statement announcing the start of a new offensive called "Breaking the Walls." In July 2013 in combined raids, ISIL broke down the walls of two prisons and released more than 500 fighters who then joined the cause.

The civil war in Syria started in 2011 and ISIL sent experienced fighters into the country to set up an organization and to support Syrians opposed to President Assad. Their trained fighters made rapid gains and ruthlessly introduced sharia law in the towns they controlled. In June 2014 the group announced that it was to be known as the Islamic State. In July, according to the Syrian Observatory for Human Rights, the group recruited more than 6,300 fighters many of them from western countries.

By August, ISIL advances were beginning to worry the international community. They captured several towns in northern Iraq and by October they were about 15 miles away from Baghdad airport. The UN accused ISIL of committing "mass atrocities" and war crimes On November 1, the U.S. and its allies began air strikes against ISIL in Syria and Iraq.

Amnesty International has found ISIL guilty of the ethnic cleansing of ethnic and religious minority groups in northern Iraq on a "historic scale". In a special report released on 2 September 2014, it describes how ISIL has "systematically targeted non-Arab and non-Sunni Muslim communities, killing or abducting hundreds, possibly thousands, and forcing more than 830,000 others to flee the areas it has captured since 10 June 2014." A United Nations report issued on 2 October 2014, based on 500 interviews with witnesses, said that ISIL took 450–500 women and girls to Iraq's Nineveh region in August where "150 unmarried girls and women, predominantly from the Yazidi and Christian communities, were reportedly transported to Syria, either to be given to ISIL fighters as a reward or to be sold as sex slaves."

In late August 2014, the Grand Mufti of Saudi Arabia, Abdul-Aziz ibn Abdullah Al ash-Sheikh, condemned the Islamic State and al-Qaeda saying, "Extremist and militant ideas and terrorism which spread decay on Earth, destroying human civilization, are not in any way part of Islam, but are enemy number one of Islam, and Muslims are their first victims."

ISIL imposes harsh Sharia law and teaching in the areas it controls but also uses sophisticated propaganda techniques, including social media, to get its message across. It is also reputed to have accumulated a war chest of more than $2 billion, much of it from looted banks in Mosul and the black market sale of oil from oilfields in areas that it now occupies. It controls about 300 oil wells in Iraq. Despite its teachings, it is not averse to raising money from kidnappings, extortion and bank robberies. Global efforts are underway to disrupt their cash flow.

The U.S. Response

In September 2014, in an address from the White House, President Obama outlines the threat that ISIL poses and how America and its allies planned to deal with it.

The President reiterated that as Commander-in-Chief, his "highest priority is the security of the American people," and noted that we have "consistently taken the fight to terrorists" that threaten the United States:

> We took out Osama bin Laden and much of al Qaeda's leadership in Afghanistan and Pakistan. We've targeted al Qaeda's affiliate in Yemen, and recently eliminated the top commander of its affiliate in Somalia. We've done so while bringing more than 140,000 American troops home from Iraq, and drawing down our forces in Afghanistan, where our combat mission will end later this year. Thanks to our military and counterterrorism professionals, America is safer."

"Still," he said, "we continue to face a terrorist threat."

> We can't erase every trace of evil from the world, and small groups of killers have the capacity to do great harm. That was the case before 9/11, and that remains true today. And that's why we must remain vigilant as threats emerge. At this moment, the greatest threats come from the Middle East and North Africa, where radical groups exploit grievances for their own gain. And one of those groups is ISIL—which calls itself the "Islamic State."

ISIL was formerly al Qaeda's affiliate in Iraq, and has since gained territory on both sides of the Iraq-Syrian border by taking advantage of sectarian strife and the Syrian civil war. Although ISIL calls itself the "Islamic State," the President emphasized that the terrorist group is neither Islamic nor a state.

"ISIL is not 'Islamic.' No religion condones the killing of innocents, and the vast majority of ISIL's victims have been Muslim," President Obama said. "And ISIL is certainly not a state.... It is recognized by no government, nor the people it subjugates."

Adding that ISIL's sole vision is the slaughter of anyone and everyone who stands in its way, the President detailed the threat that ISIL poses to Iraq, Syria, and the broader Middle East. And "if left unchecked," he said, "these terrorists could pose a growing threat beyond that region."

In a region that has known so much bloodshed, these terrorists are unique in their brutality. They execute captured prisoners. They kill children. They enslave, rape, and force women into marriage. They threatened a religious minority with genocide. And in acts of barbarism, they took the lives of two American journalists—Jim Foley and Steven Sotloff.

So ISIL poses a threat to the people of Iraq and Syria, and the broader Middle East -- including American citizens, personnel and facilities. If left unchecked, these terrorists could pose a growing threat beyond that region, including to the United States. While we have not yet detected specific plotting against our homeland, ISIL leaders have threatened America and our allies. Our Intelligence Community believes that thousands of foreigners—including Europeans and some Americans—have joined them in Syria and Iraq. Trained and battle-hardened, these fighters could try to return to their home countries and carry out deadly attacks.

Noting the concern that many Americans have about these threats, he made clear that the U.S. is "meeting them with strength and resolve."

In his address, the President outlined the four key parts of the United States' strategy to defeat ISIL:

1. **A systematic campaign of airstrikes against ISIL:** Working with the Iraqi government, we will expand our efforts beyond protecting our own people and humanitarian missions, so that we're hitting ISIL targets as Iraqi forces go on offense. Moreover, I have made it clear that we will hunt down terrorists who threaten our country, wherever they are. That means I will not hesitate to take action against ISIL in Syria, as well as Iraq. This is a core principle of my presidency: If you threaten America, you will find no safe haven.

2. **Increased support to forces fighting ISIL on the ground:** In June, I deployed several hundred American servicemembers to Iraq to assess how we can best support Iraqi security forces. Now that those teams have completed

their work -- and Iraq has formed a government -- we will send an additional 475 servicemembers to Iraq. As I have said before, these American forces will not have a combat mission -- we will not get dragged into another ground war in Iraq. But they are needed to support Iraqi and Kurdish forces with training, intelligence and equipment. We'll also support Iraq's efforts to stand up National Guard Units to help Sunni communities secure their own freedom from ISIL's control.

Across the border, in Syria, we have ramped up our military assistance to the Syrian opposition. Tonight, I call on Congress again to give us additional authorities and resources to train and equip these fighters. In the fight against ISIL, we cannot rely on an Assad regime that terrorizes its own people -- a regime that will never regain the legitimacy it has lost. Instead, we must strengthen the opposition as the best counterweight to extremists like ISIL, while pursuing the political solution necessary to solve Syria's crisis once and for all.

3. **Drawing on our substantial counterterrorism capabilities to prevent ISIL attacks:** Working with our partners, we will redouble our efforts to cut off its funding; improve our intelligence; strengthen our defenses; counter its warped ideology; and stem the flow of foreign fighters into and out of the Middle East. And in two weeks, I will chair a meeting of the U.N. Security Council to further mobilize the international community around this effort.

4. **Providing humanitarian assistance to innocent civilians displaced by ISIL:** This includes Sunni and Shia Muslims who are at grave risk, as well as tens of thousands of Christians and other religious minorities. We cannot allow these communities to be driven from their ancient homelands.

"This is our strategy," the President said, adding that the United States has a "broad coalition of partners" joining us in this effort:

Already, allies are flying planes with us over Iraq; sending arms and assistance to Iraqi security forces and the Syrian opposition; sharing intelligence; and providing billions of dollars in humanitarian aid. Secretary Kerry was in Iraq today meeting with the new government and supporting their efforts to promote unity. And in the coming days he will travel across the Middle East and Europe to enlist more partners in this fight, especially Arab nations who can help mobilize Sunni communities in Iraq and Syria, to drive these terrorists from their lands. This is American leadership at its best: We stand with people who fight for their own freedom, and we rally other nations on behalf of our common security and common humanity.

President Obama also noted the bipartisan support for this strategy here in the United States, and welcomed congressional support for the strategy "in order to show the world that Americans are united in confronting this danger."

The President made clear that eradicating ISIL won't happen overnight, but he also detailed how this effort isn't the same as our previous wars in Iraq and Afghanistan:

"Now, it will take time to eradicate a cancer like ISIL. And any time we take military action, there are risks involved -- especially to the servicemen and women who carry out these missions. But I want the American people to understand how this effort will be different from the wars in Iraq and Afghanistan. It will not involve American combat troops fighting on foreign soil. This counterterrorism campaign will be waged through a steady, relentless effort to take out ISIL wherever they exist, using our air power and our support for partner forces on the ground. This strategy of taking out terrorists who threaten us, while supporting partners on the front lines, is one that we have successfully pursued in Yemen and Somalia for years. And it is consistent with the approach I outlined earlier this year: to use force against anyone who threatens America's core interests, but to mobilize partners wherever possible to address broader challenges to international order.

President Obama called American leadership the "one constant in an uncertain world." From fighting terrorism, to rallying the world against Russian aggression, to helping to stop the outbreak of Ebola in West Africa, the U.S. continues to play a critical leading role across the globe:

"It is America that has the capacity and the will to mobilize the world against terrorists. It is America that has rallied the world against Russian aggression, and in support of the Ukrainian peoples' right to determine their own destiny. It is America -- our scientists, our doctors, our know-how -- that can help contain and cure the outbreak of Ebola. It is America that helped remove and destroy Syria's declared chemical weapons so that they can't pose a threat to the Syrian people or the world again. And it is America that is help-ing Muslim communities around the world not just in the fight against terror-ism, but in the fight for opportunity, and tolerance, and a more hopeful future.

"When we helped prevent the massacre of civilians trapped on a distant mountain, here's what one of them said: "We owe our American friends our lives. Our children will always remember that there was someone who felt our struggle and made a long journey to protect innocent people."

"That is the difference we make in the world. And our own safety, our own security, depends upon our willingness to do what it takes to defend this na-tion and uphold the values that we stand for—timeless ideals that will endure long after those who offer only hate and destruction have been vanquished from the Earth."

Other Terrorist Threats

Al-Qa'ida (AQ) and its affiliates and adherents worldwide continue to pre-sent a serious threat to the United States, its allies, and its interests. While the international community has severely degraded AQ's core leadership, the ter-rorist threat has evolved. Leadership losses in Pakistan, coupled with weak governance and instability in the Middle East and Northwest Africa, have ac-celerated the decentralization of the movement and led to the affiliates in the AQ network becoming more operationally autonomous from core AQ and increasingly focused on local and regional objectives. The past several years have seen the emergence of a more aggressive set of AQ affiliates and like-minded groups, most notably in Yemen, Syria, Iraq, Northwest Africa, and Somalia.

AQ leadership experienced difficulty in maintaining cohesion within the AQ network and in communicating guidance to its affiliated groups. AQ leader Ayman al-Zawahiri was rebuffed in his attempts to mediate a dispute among AQ affiliates operating in Syria – al-Nusrah Front and al-Qa'ida in Iraq (AQI), now calling itself the Islamic State of Iraq and the Levant (ISIL) – which resulted in the expulsion of ISIL from the AQ network in February 2014. In addition, guidance issued by Zawahiri in 2013 for AQ affiliates to avoid collateral damage was routinely disobeyed, notably in attacks by AQ affiliates against civilian religious pilgrims in Iraq, hospital staff and convalescing patients in Yemen, and families at a shopping mall in Kenya.

In many cases terrorist violence is being fueled by sectarian motivations, marking a worrisome trend, in particular in Syria, Lebanon, and Pakistan, where victims of violence were primarily among the civilian populations. Thousands of extremist fighters entered Syria during the year, among those a large percentage reportedly motivated by a sectarian view of the conflict and a desire to protect the Sunni Muslim community from the Alawite-dominant Assad regime. On the other side of the conflict, Iran, Hizballah, and other Shia militia continued to provide critical support to the Assad regime, dramatically bolstering its capabilities and exacerbating the situation. Many of these fighters are also motivated by a sectarian view of the conflict and a desire to protect the Shia Muslim community from Sunni extremists.

The relationship between the AQ core and its affiliates plays out in the financial arena as well. As was the case for the last few years, the affiliates have increased their financial independence through kidnapping for ransom operations and other criminal activities such as extortion and credit card fraud. Al-Qa'ida in the Arabian Peninsula (AQAP) and al-Qa'ida in the Islamic Maghreb (AQIM) are particularly effective with kidnapping for ransom and are using ransom money to fund the range of their activities. Kidnapping targets are usually Western citizens from governments or third parties that have established a pattern of paying ransom for the release of individuals in custody. Private donations from the Gulf also remained a major source of funding for Sunni terrorist groups, particularly for those operating in Syria.

While AQ core leadership in Pakistan is much diminished, Ayman al-Zawahiri remains the recognized ideological leader of a jihadist movement that includes AQ-affiliated and allied groups worldwide. Along with AQ, the Afghan Taliban, the Haqqani Network, Tehrik-e Taliban Pakistan (TTP), and other like-minded groups continue to conduct operations against U.S., Coalition, Afghan, and Pakistani interests from safe havens on both sides of the Afghanistan/Pakistan border, and in Pakistan, terrorist groups and AQ allies, such as TTP, have executed armed assaults not only on police stations, judicial centers, border posts, and military convoys, but also on polio vaccination teams and aid workers. Other South Asian terrorist organizations, including Lashkar e-Tayyiba (LeT), cite U.S. interests as legitimate targets for attacks. LeT, the group responsible for the 2008 Mumbai attacks, continues to pose a threat to regional stability.

Groups calling themselves Ansar al-Shari'a in Tunisia and the Libyan cities of Benghazi and Darnah also operated in the North Africa space. The three share some aspects of AQ ideology, but are not formal affiliates and generally maintain a local focus. In Libya, the terrorist threat to Western and Libyan government interests remains strong, especially in the eastern part of the country. Libya's porous borders, the weakness of Libya's nascent security institutions, and large amounts of loose small arms create opportunities for violent extremists. In Tunisia, Ansar al-Shari'a in Tunisia attempted suicide attacks against two tourist sites in late October 2013 and killed a political oppositionist in July that same year, suggesting the group remains intent on attacking Western and Tunisian interests.

In East Africa, al-Shabaab continued to pose a significant regional threat despite coming under continued pressure by African forces operating under the African Union's AMISOM command and steady progress in the establishment of Somali government capability. Perhaps because of these positive steps, al-Shabaab targeted its attacks on those participating in the effort to bring stability to Somalia. In September 2013, al-Shabaab struck outside of Somalia (its first external attack was in July 2010 in Kampala, Uganda), attacking the Westgate Mall in Nairobi, Kenya. The assault resulted in the death of at least 65 civilians, including foreign nationals from 13 countries outside of Kenya and six soldiers and police officers; hundreds more were injured. Al-Shabaab's attacks within Somalia continued in 2013, and resulted in the deaths of hundreds of people, including innocent women and children.

Boko Haram (BH) maintained a high operational tempo in 2013 and carried out kidnappings, killings, bombings, and attacks on civilian and military targets in northern Nigeria, resulting in numerous deaths, injuries, and destruction of property in 2013. The number and sophistication of BH's attacks are concerning, and while the group focuses principally on local Nigerian issues and actors, there continue to be reports that it has financial and training links with other violent extremists in the Sahel region. Boko Haram, along with a splinter group commonly known as Ansaru, has also increasingly crossed Nigerian borders to neighboring Cameroon, Chad, and Niger to evade pressure and conduct operations.

Africa

The Africa region has experienced significant levels of terrorist activity. In East Africa, the Somalia-based terrorist group al-Shabaab remained the primary terrorist threat. Somali security forces and the AU Mission in Somalia (AMISOM) continued to make gains against al-Shabaab but an inability to undertake consistent offensive operations against the group allowed al-Shabaab to develop and carry out asymmetric attacks, including outside of Somalia. Al-Shabaab issues persistent threats to other countries contributing troops to AMISOM. Driven out of major urban areas, al-Shabaab has returned to a strategy focused on asymmetric attacks intended to discredit and destabilize the nascent Federal Government of Somalia. The United States continues to support AMISOM and the establishment of a stable Somali government, and works to enhance counterterrorism capacity in Somalia and throughout the broader region.

Various East African countries continue to detect, deter, disrupt, investigate, and prosecute terrorist incidents; enhance domestic and regional efforts to bolster border security; and create integrated and dedicated counterterrorism strategies. In West Africa, conflict in Nigeria continue throughout the northern part of the country, with Boko Haram and related actors committing hundreds of attacks, reportedly resulting in over a thousand casualties in 2013 alone.

This violence reportedly spilled over into neighboring Cameroon, Chad, and Niger.

French and allied African forces successfully disrupted and pushed back efforts by al-Qa'ida in the Islamic Maghreb (AQIM) and other violent extremist groups to control northern Mali. France and other international partners continue to contribute forces to the region to assist the Malian government to rebuild and to deter terrorist threats. Western efforts to increase counterterrorism capacity in the region are focused on enhanced border security, regional information sharing and cooperation, and countering violent extremism.

East Asia and Pacific

Overall, countries in the East Asia and Pacific region continue to weaken the ability of terrorist groups to operate and constrain the activities of large terrorist organizations such as Jemaah Islamiya (JI), Jemaah Anshorut Tauhid (JAT), and the Abu Sayyaf Group (ASG). Ongoing concerns remain, however, notably in Indonesia, where terrorist attacks on police continue, and in the southern Philippines, where improvised explosive device (IED) attacks have occurred on several occasions in Mindanao and rogue elements of the Moro National Liberation Front (MNLF) conducted a violent three-week siege of Zamboanga City that killed dozens of Philippine Security Force members and displaced thousands. The tri-border region of the Sulu Sea remains an area of concern for cross-border weapons smuggling and kidnapping for ransom.

The trend of violent extremists focusing on domestic targets continues in Indonesia, with numerous attacks on police, including a series of separate high-profile attacks in which four Indonesia law enforcement officials were killed and seven were wounded. Indonesia also experienced its first suicide bombing in two years when a motorcycle-riding bomber targeted a police facility in Poso, Central Sulawesi. Challenges presented by overcrowded prisons and weaknesses in correctional facility management and security were highlighted when inmates, including convicted terrorists, escaped in a series of prison breaks.

Malaysia continues its legal reform efforts bringing charges under the new Security Offenses (Special Measures) Act of 2012 (SOSMA). Malaysia arrested former al-Qa'ida operative Yazid Sufaat, who was the first to be charged under SOSMA. In Thailand, two Iranians behind a failed 2012 plot, in which explosives were accidentally set off that allegedly were targeting Israeli diplomats in Bangkok, were convicted.

Australia maintains its position as a regional leader in the fight against terrorism and works to strengthen the Asia-Pacific region's counterterrorism capacity through a range of bilateral and regional initiatives in organizations such as ASEAN, the ASEAN Regional Forum, and the Pacific Island Forum. The Japanese government continus to participate in international counterterrorism efforts at multilateral, regional, and bilateral levels through the ASEAN-Japan Counterterrorism meeting and the Japan-China Counterterrorism Consultations.

Europe

Terrorist incidents, including deadly attacks, continue to plague Europe. Some attacks were apparently perpetrated by "lone offender" assailants while others were organized by groups claiming a range of extremist ideological motivations, from nationalism to right-wing and left-wing political theories to various religious beliefs, including violent Islamist extremism. In some cases the boundaries between ideologies were blurred.

A major challenge to Europe was the increasing travel of European citizens – mostly young men – to and from Syria seeking to join forces opposing the Assad regime. These "foreign fighters" sparked increasing concerns, and actions to address them, by European countries worried about the growing number of their citizens traveling to the battlefield and possibly returning radicalized. European governments, in particular the EU and several member states affected, took action to assess the problem and to devise an array of responses to discourage their citizens from going to Syria to take part in the conflict. These efforts ranged from new administrative procedures to prevent travel to Syria, to steps to counter recruitment and facilitation efforts, and programs to investigate and/or reintegrate persons returning from conflict zones. In the western Balkans, governments in EU candidate states and aspirants are also committed to responding effectively to the foreign fighter problem, and sought assistance to fill gaps in their capacity to do so from the United States, the EU, and others. European governments also work with the United States and other international partners in various fora, including the Global Counterterrorism Forum, to respond to the foreign fighter problem and strengthen general counterterrorism cooperation.

The Middle East and North Africa

The Near East region experiences significant levels of terrorist activity with instability and weak governance in North Africa, Syria, Iraq, and Yemen continuing to have ramifications for the broader region. Al-Qa'ida and its affiliates exploit opportunities to conduct operations amid this fragile political and security climate.

In Libya, lack of countrywide security coverage contributes to a high threat environment. Libya's weak security institutions, coupled with ready access to loose weapons and porous borders, provides violent extremists significant opportunities to act and plan operations.

Shia militants continue to threaten Iraqi security and were alleged to have been responsible for numerous attacks against Mujahadin-e Khalq members that continued to reside at Camp Hurriya near Baghdad. Hizballah provided a wide range of critical support to the Assad regime—including clearing regions of opposition forces, and providing training, advice, and logistical assistance to the Syrian Army —as the regime continues its brutal crackdown against the Syrian people.

Al-Qa'ida in the Islamic Maghreb (AQIM) has also taken advantage of the instability in the region, particularly in Libya and Mali. In Tunisia, the terrorist group Ansar al-Shari'a in Tunisia (AAS-T) precipitated a government crisis by assassinating, among others, two secular politicians.

The Government of Yemen continues its fight against al-Qa'ida in the Arabian Peninsula (AQAP), although struggling somewhat in this effort due to an ongoing political and security restructuring within the government itself. AQAP continues to exhibit its capability by targeting government installations and security and intelligence officials, but also strikes at soft targets, such as hospitals. President Hadi continues to support U.S. counterterrorism objectives in Yemen, and encourages greater cooperation between U.S. and Yemeni counterterrorism forces.

Despite these persistent threats, governments across the region continue to build and exhibit their counterterrorism capabilities, disrupting the activities of a number of terrorists. Although AQ affiliate presence and activity in the Sahel and parts of the Maghreb remains worrisome, the group's isolation in Algeria and smaller pockets of North Africa grew as partner efforts in Algeria, Morocco, and Tunisia increased.

In Egypt, significant political instability presents various security challenges for the government, leading to an increase in violent extremist activity in the Sinai and parts of lower Egypt, including Cairo. Government security forces aggressively target violent extremist activity in these areas.

Iran's state sponsorship of terrorism worldwide remains undiminished through the Islamic Revolutionary Guard Corps-Qods Force (IRGC-QF), its Ministry of Intelligence and Security, and Tehran's ally Hizballah, which remain a significant threat to the stability of Lebanon and the broader region. The U.S. government continues efforts to counter Iranian and proxy support for terrorist operations via sanctions and other legal tools.

South and Central Asia

South Asia remains a front line in the battle against terrorism. Although al-Qa'ida's (AQ) core in Afghanistan and Pakistan has been seriously degraded, AQ's global leadership continues to operate from its safe haven in the region and struggles to communicate effectively with affiliate groups outside of South Asia. AQ maintains ties with other terrorist organizations in the region, such as Tehrik-e Taliban Pakistan (TTP) and the Haqqani Network (HQN). These alliances continue to provide the group with additional resources and capabilities. In 2013, terrorists in South Asia carried out operations in heavily populated areas and continue to target regional governmental representatives and U.S. persons. On numerous occasions, civilians throughout South Asia were wounded or killed in terrorist events.

Afghanistan, in particular, continues to experience aggressive and coordinated attacks by the Afghan Taliban, HQN, and other insurgent and terrorist groups. A number of these attacks are planned and launched from safe havens in Pakistan.

Pakistan continues to experience significant terrorist violence, including sectarian attacks. The Pakistani military undertakes operations against groups that conduct attacks within Pakistan such as TTP, but does not take action against other groups such as Lashkar-e-Tayyiba (LeT), which continues to operate, train, rally, and fundraise in Pakistan. Afghan Taliban and HQN leadership and facilitation networks continue to find safe haven in Pakistan, and Pakistani authorities do not take significant military or law enforcement action against these groups.

India remains severely affected by and vulnerable to terrorism, including from Pakistan-based groups and their affiliates as well as left-wing violent extremists. The Government of India, in response, continues to undertake efforts to coordinate its counterterrorism capabilities more effectively and expand its cooperation and coordination with the international community and regional partners.

Bangladesh, an influential counterterrorism partner in the region, continues to make strides against international terrorism. The government's ongoing counterterrorism efforts have made it more difficult for transnational terrorists to operate in or use Bangladeshi territory. The United States and Bangladesh have signed a Counterterrorism Cooperation Initiative to enhance bilateral cooperation.

Western Hemisphere

Corruption, weak government institutions, insufficient interagency cooperation, weak or non-existent legislation, and a lack of resources remain the
primary causes for the lack of significant progress in some of the countries.
Transnational criminal organizations continue to pose a more significant
threat to the region than transnational terrorism, and most countries make
efforts to investigate possible connections with terrorist organizations. Iran's
influence in the Western Hemisphere remains a concern. However, due to
strong sanctions imposed on the country by both the United States and the
EU, Iran has been unable to expand its economic and political ties in Latin
America. The Revolutionary Armed Forces of Colombia commits the majority
of terrorist attacks in the Western Hemisphere.

The United States continues to work with partner nations to build capacity
to detect and address any potential terrorist threat. The Tri-Border area of Argentina, Brazil, and Paraguay continues to be an important regional nexus of
arms, narcotics, and human trafficking; counterfeiting; pirated goods; and
money laundering—all potential funding sources for terrorist organizations.

TERRORIST SAFE HAVENS	
Africa	Somalia, Trans-Sahara, and Mali.
Southeast Asia	The Sulu/Sulawesi Seas Littoral, the Southern Phil-ippines.
The Middle East	Iraq, Lebanon, Libya, and Yemen.
South Asia	Afghanistan and Pakistan.
Western Hemisphere	Colombia and Venezuela.

5

Russia

Vladimir Putin is proving a problem for the United States. However, the Russian leader is also an enigma to most world leaders. In the last year he has annexed Crimea, has and continues to ferment trouble in Ukraine, and has menacingly talked about his nuclear arsenal and his dream to reclaim all former Soviet Union territories. His refusal to end Russia's interference in Eastern Ukraine has led to punitive financial sanctions against many of his billionaire 'comrade capitalist' friends, banks and leading companies. In defiance he signed number of multi-billion dollar energy deals with China. A May 21 deal for a $77 billion pipeline to be jointly funded by Russia and China will be the world's largest construction project.

Vladimir Putin, a former Lieutenant Colonel in the KGB, has been President of Russia since May 2012 having previously served as President from 2000 to 2008. He had to step down in 2008 having served two four-year terms but effectively remained in control from 2008-2012 as Prime Minister. In November 2014 he issued a statement through the Tass news agency that he will step down no later than 2024.

Putin's friends control all Russia's infrastructure and for years the wealth from the country's vast oil and natural gas resources have funded the Russian military and defense industries and fueled the economy and his popularity at home. At the same time he has clamped down on critics, the opposition and the independent media. His frequent speeches to defend the rights of Russian-speaking peoples in the former Soviet Russia have propelled him to even greater popularity and stoked the country's growing nationalism.

Russia-U.S. relations have been cool for some time. The U.S. was furious that Russia granted asylum to NSA records-leaker Edward Snowden and also at Russia's continued support for Syria and vetoing UN motions against Iran. Russia is furious with the U.S. for its "monopolistic dominance in global relations" and its western allies for NATO encroachments into what he sees as Russia's sphere of influence.

On December 12, 2013 in his annual address to the Federal Assembly he warned," No one should entertain any illusions about achieving military superiority over Russia; we will never allow it. Russia will respond to all these challenges, both political and technological. We have all we need in order to do so."

Yet on August 1, 2014, on the 100th anniversary of Russia's entry into the Great War, he said," This tragedy reminds us what happens when aggression, selfishness and the unbridled ambitions of national leaders and political establishments push common sense aside, so that instead of preserving the world's most prosperous continent, Europe, they lead it towards danger. It is worth remembering this today.

"World history gives us so many examples of what a terrible price we pay for refusing to listen to each other, or for trampling on others' rights and freedoms and lawful interests in the name of our own interests and ambitions. It would be good if we could learn to open our eyes and to calculate at least a step ahead."

In March, 2014 German Chancellor Angela Merkel in a telephone call to President Obama said that she was not sure if Putin was in touch with reality."

Since then Putin has become more belligerent and has matched military action with the rhetoric. Russian military aircraft have made repeated probing sorties into NATO airspace, a Russian nuclear submarine is believed to have penetrated Sweden's territorial waters and Putin warned that long range bombers will be patrolling in the Gulf of Mexico.

In October, President Obama said sanctions against Russia could be lifted if Russia pursued peace and diplomacy. He was answered   by Russian Foreign Minister Lavrov, who said, "We are absolutely interested in bringing the ties to normal but it was not us who destroyed them."

On November 21, Vice President Joe Biden met with Ukrainian Prime Minister Arseniy Yatsenyuk to discuss Ukraine's process of government formation, its reform agenda, the situation in the east, and energy security. The Vice President congratulated the Prime Minister on initialing a coalition agreement, which will allow Ukraine to move ahead with delivering on reforms for the Ukrainian people. The Vice President underscored that the United States would work with its partners and the IMF to help secure the financial support Ukraine needs as it stabilizes its economy and pursues necessary reforms. The two leaders also discussed the situation in the east, and the Vice President noted that the United States would work with its European and G-7 partners to increase the costs to Russia if it continues on its current course of blatantly violating Ukraine's sovereignty and territorial integrity, and its obligations under the Minsk agreement.

On November 26, 2014 at a meeting of his military chiefs in Sochi, he said," We pose no threat to anyone and do not intend to get involved in any geopolitical games or intrigues, let alone conflicts, no matter who tries to draw us into them or how they do so. At the same time, it is indispensable to securely safeguard the sovereignty and integrity of Russia and the security of our allies."

It is these apparent contradictions that confuse those who have to deal with Putin.

Most Russians have no idea of what is happening in the Ukraine because of state-controlled media and the Russian Embassy in Washington does not even mention the crisis on its website. Their page on Russian-American Relations reads: "Russia consistently stands for cooperation with the United States based on the principles of equality, mutual consideration of interest and noninterference in each other's internal affairs.

The relations with the U.S. remain the most important factor in ensuring international security and stability. The key elements of Russia-U.S. cooperation are outlined in the Moscow Joint Declaration on New Strategic Relationship of 2002, Russia-U.S. Strategic Framework Declaration of 2008, as well as in the Joint Statement by President Putin and President Obama during their meeting in Los Cabos in June, 2012.

The current agenda of Russia-U.S. relations includes strengthening of strategic stability, supporting the resolution of regional conflicts, combating international terrorism and drug trafficking, counteracting other new global challenges and threats, building up trade and investment ties, expanding bilateral cultural exchanges and contacts between the people of both countries."

So what is the situation in Ukraine?

Ukraine

Ukraine had long been part of Tsarist and Soviet Russia but in July 1990 parliament adopted the Declaration of State Sovereignty of Ukraine and on August 21, 1991 adopted the Act of Independence. In 2010 Viktor Yanukovych was declared President and started developing closer ties with Russia even though the people had expressed their desire for closer ties with the west. This led to the formation of a protest movement with civil unrest and calls for the resignation of the President. At the same time, unrest broke out in largely Russian-speaking Eastern Ukraine which wanted to maintain ties with Russia and who opposed the pro-west protest movement.

On January 16, 2014 the government enacted anti-protest laws which led to an upsurge in violence. More than 98 people were killed and over 15,000 injured. On February 22, Parliament exercising constitutional powers, found the President "unable to fulfill his duties" and called a May 25 to elect a successor (Petro Poroshenko, who ran on a pro-European platform, won more than half the votes and was elected President). President Yanukovych fled to Russia and on March 1 asked Russia to use military forces "to establish legitimacy, peace, law and order, stability and defend the people of Ukraine". Putin described Yanukovych's ousting as a "coup perpetrated by nationalists, neo-Nazis, Russophobes and anti-Semites".

On March 3, 2014 Russia sent 16,000 troops into Crimea, a peninsular on the northeast coast of the Black Sea. Crimea had been part of Russia but was given to Ukraine by President Nikita Khrushchev in 1954.

The following day Putin defended his actions by claiming that the troops were to bolster Russia's military defenses of its Black Sea Fleet, headquartered in Crimea. He denied accusations by other nations, particularly the United States, that Russia intended to engage Ukraine in war. Putin also denied speculation that there would be further invasion into Ukrainian territory, saying, "Such a measure would certainly be the very last resort." The following day, it was announced that Putin had been nominated for the 2014 Nobel Peace Prize.

On March 17 The U.S. and European Union ordered a first round of sanctions against Russia and officials in Crimea. The White House stated: "the actions and policies" of the Russian government with respect to Ukraine "undermine democratic processes and institutions in Ukraine; threaten its peace, security, stability, sovereignty, and territorial integrity; and contribute to the misappropriation of its assets."

On 18 March 2014, Russia and Crimea signed a treaty of accession of the Republic of Crimea and Sevastopol in the Russian Federation, though the United Nations General Assembly voted in favor of a non-binding statement to oppose Russian annexation of the peninsula.

On July 17, 2014 Malaysia Airlines Flight 17, a Boeing 777-200, flying from to Kuala Lumpur from Amsterdam, crashed near Donetsk in Eastern Ukraine. All 283 passengers and 15 crew died. A preliminary classified U.S. intelligence analysis concluded the rebels most likely fired the missile. "Evidence indicates that the plane was shot down by a surface-to-air missile that was launched from an area that is controlled by Russian-backed separatists inside of Ukraine," Obama told reporters on July 18.

Since then Russia, despite its denials, has poured troops and equipment into Eastern Ukraine which declared its independence from the rest of the country and the central government in Kiev. According to U.S. Air Force Gen. Philip Breedlove, the Supreme Allied Commander in Europe, NATO forces have confirmed "columns of Russian equipment, primarily Russian tanks, Russian artillery, Russian air defense systems and Russian combat troops entering into Ukraine."

Russia also continues to ferment dissent in other former Soviet-bloc countries with Russian-speaking populations.

According to the State Department, Russia continues to spin a false and dangerous narrative to justify its illegal actions in Ukraine. The Russian propaganda machine continues to promote hate speech and incite violence by creating a false threat in Ukraine that does not exist. "We would not be seeing the violence and sad events that we've witnessed without this relentless stream of disinformation and Russian provocateurs fostering unrest in eastern Ukraine," said a spokesperson. Here are 10 more false claims Russia is using to justify intervention in Ukraine, with the facts that these assertions ignore or distort.

1. Russia Claims: Russian agents are not active in Ukraine.

Fact: The Ukrainian Government has arrested more than a dozen suspected Russian intelligence agents recently, many of whom were armed at the time of arrest. In the first week of April 2014, the Government of Ukraine had information that Russian GRU officers were providing individuals in Kharkiv and Donetsk with advice and instructions on conducting protests, capturing and holding government buildings, seizing weapons from the government buildings' armories, and redeploying for other violent actions. On April 12, armed pro-Russian militants seized government buildings in a coordinated and professional operation conducted in six cities in eastern Ukraine. Many were outfitted in bullet-proof vests, camouflage uniforms with insignia removed, and carrying Russian-designed weapons like AK-74s and Dragunovs. These armed units, some wearing black and orange St. George's ribbons associated with Russian Victory Day celebrations, raised Russian and separatist flags over seized buildings and have called for referendums on secession and union with Russia. These operations are strikingly similar to those used against Ukrainian facilities during Russia's illegal military intervention in Crimea in late February and its subsequent occupation.

2. Russia Claims: Pro-Russia demonstrations are comprised exclusively of Ukrainian citizens acting of their own volition, like the Maidan movement in Kyiv.

Fact: This is not the grassroots Ukrainian civic activism of the EuroMaidan movement, which grew from a handful of student protestors to hundreds of thousands of Ukrainians from all parts of the country and all walks of life. Russian internet sites openly are recruiting volunteers to travel from Russia to Ukraine and incite violence. There is evidence that many of these so-called "protesters" are paid for their participation in the violence and unrest. It is clear that these incidents are not spontaneous events, but rather part of a well-orchestrated Russian campaign of incitement, separatism, and sabotage of the Ukrainian state. Ukrainian authorities continue to arrest highly trained and well-equipped Russian provocateurs operating across the region.

3. Russia Claims: Separatist leaders in eastern Ukraine enjoy broad popular support.

Fact: The recent demonstrations in eastern Ukraine are not organic and lack wide support in the region. A large majority of Donetsk residents (65.7 percent) want to live in a united Ukraine and reject unification with Russia, according to public opinion polls conducted at the end of March by the Donetsk-based Institute of Social Research and Policy Analysis. Pro-Russian demonstrations in eastern Ukraine have been modest in size, especially compared with Maidan protests in these same cities in December, and they have gotten smaller as time has progressed.

4. Russia Claims: The situation in eastern Ukraine risks spiraling into civil war.

Fact: What is going on in eastern Ukraine would not be happening without Russian disinformation and provocateurs fostering unrest. It would not be happening if a large Russian military force were not massed on the border, destabilizing the situation through their overtly threatening presence. There simply have not been large-scale protests in the region. A small number of separatists have seized several government buildings in eastern cities like Donetsk, Luhansk, and Slovyansk, but they have failed to attract any significant popular support. Ukrainian authorities have shown remarkable restraint in their efforts to resolve the situation and only acted when provoked by armed militants and public safety was put at risk. Organization for Security and Cooperation in Europe (OSCE) observers have reported that these incidents are very localized.

5. Russia Claims: Ukrainians in Donetsk rejected the illegitimate authorities in Kyiv and established the independent "People's Republic of Donetsk."

Fact: A broad and representative collection of civil society and nongovernmental organizations in Donetsk categorically rejected the declaration of a "People's Republic of Donetsk" by the small number of separatists occupying the regional administration building. These same organizations confirmed their support for the interim government and for the sovereignty and territorial integrity of Ukraine.

6. Russia Claims: Russia ordered a "partial drawdown" of troops from the Ukrainian border.

Fact: No evidence shows significant movement of Russian forces away from the Ukrainian border. One battalion is not enough. An estimated 35,000-40,000 Russian troops remain massed along the border, in addition to approximately 25,000 troops currently in Crimea.

7. Russia Claims: *Ethnic Russians in Ukraine are under threat.*

Fact: There are no credible reports of ethnic Russians facing threats in Ukraine. An International Republican Institute poll released April 5 found that 74 percent of the Russian-speaking population in the eastern and southern regions of Ukraine said they "were not under pressure or threat because of their language." Meanwhile, in Crimea, the OSCE has raised urgent concerns for the safety of minority populations, especially ethnic Ukrainians, Crimean Tatars, and others. Sadly, the ethnic Russians most at risk are those who live in Russia and who oppose the authoritarian Putin regime. These Russians are harassed constantly and face years of imprisonment for speaking out against Putin's regular abuses of power.

8. Russia Claims: Ukraine's new government is led by radical nationalists and fascists.

Fact: The Ukrainian parliament (Rada) did not change in February. It is the same Rada that was elected by all Ukrainians, comprising all of the parties that existed prior to February's events, including former president Yanukovych's Party of Regions. The new government, approved by an overwhelming majority in the parliament -- including many members of Yanukovych's former party -- is committed to protecting the rights of all Ukrainians, including those in Crimea.

9. Russia Claims: Ethnic minorities face persecution in Ukraine from the "fascist" government in Kyiv.

Fact: Leaders of Ukraine's Jewish as well as German, Czech, and Hungarian communities have all publicly expressed their sense of safety under the new authorities in Kyiv. Moreover, many minority groups expressed fear of persecution in Russian-occupied Crimea, a concern OSCE observers in Ukraine have substantiated.

10. Russia Claims: Russia is not using energy and trade as weapons against Ukraine.

Fact: Following Russia's illegal annexation and occupation of Crimea, Russia raised the price Ukraine pays for natural gas by 80 percent in the past two weeks. In addition, it is seeking more than $11 billion in back payments following its abrogation of the 2010 Kharkiv accords. Russia's moves threaten to increase severely the economic pain faced by Ukrainian citizens and businesses. Additionally, Russia continues to restrict Ukrainian exports to Russia, which constitute a significant portion of Ukraine's export economy.

The United States and Ukraine have signed a Charter on Strategic Partnership centered on realizing and strengthening a democratic, prosperous, and secure Ukraine more closely integrated into Europe and Euro-Atlantic structures. It highlights the importance of the bilateral relationship and outlines enhanced cooperation in the areas of defense, security, economics and trade, energy security, democracy, and cultural exchanges. It also emphasizes the continued commitment of the United States to support enhanced engagement

between the North Atlantic Treaty Organization (NATO) and Ukraine. To fulfill one of the key tenets of the charter, the two countries have established the
Strategic Partnership Commission.

U.S. Assistance to Ukraine

U.S. Government assistance to Ukraine aims to support the development of
a democratic, prosperous, and secure Ukraine, fully integrated into the Euro-
Atlantic community.

Bilateral Economic Relations

The United States has granted Ukraine market economy status and termi-
nated the application of the Jackson-Vanik amendment to Ukraine, giving
Ukraine permanent normal trade relations status. The United States and
Ukraine have a bilateral investment treaty. U.S. exports to Ukraine include
coal, machinery, vehicles, agricultural products, fish and seafood, and aircraft.
U.S. imports from Ukraine include iron and steel, inorganic chemicals, oil,
iron and steel products, aircraft, and agricultural products. The U.S.-Ukraine
Council on Trade and Investment was established under the countries' agreement on trade and investment cooperation and works to increase commercial
and investment opportunities by identifying and removing impediments to
bilateral trade and investment flows.

Ukraine's Membership in International Organizations

Ukraine and the United States belong to a number of the same international organizations, including the United Nations, Euro-Atlantic Partnership
Council, Organization for Security and Cooperation in Europe, International
Monetary Fund, World Bank, and World Trade Organization. Ukraine also is
an observer to the Organization of American States. Ukraine has adopted a

"non-bloc" foreign policy, including abandonment of its formal bid for NATO membership.

Russia and Closer Ties with China

As Russia's relationship with the west has reached almost Cold War frostiness, its relationship with the East and especially China has warmed considerably. In October 2014, Putin gave a foreign policy speech described as "the most anti-American and anti-Western speech of his career."

At the same time he signaled Russia was seeking to strengthen ties with Asia. "Asia is playing an ever greater role in the world, in the economy and in politics, and there is simply no way we can afford to overlook these developments," said Putin.

"Some are saying today that Russia is supposedly turning its back on Europe ... and is looking for new business partners, above all in Asia," Putin said. "Let me say that this is absolutely not the case. Our active policy in the Asia-Pacific region began not just yesterday and not in response to sanctions, but is a policy that we have been following for a good many years now."

In May 2014 Russia and China signed a $400 billion gas contract. In November they signed memorandum of understanding that will make China Russia's largest customer for gas for the next 30 years. This at a time when European customers are seeking alternative supplies to reduce their dependence on Russian supplies.

Russia and China are also seeking to cooperate on a wide range of projects including a high-speed rail link between the Russian cities of Moscow and Kazan.

6

China

In today's world it is not the size of the army that makes a super power but the size of its economy. China's economy is booming which is why it is flexing its muscles in the South China Sea and elsewhere. It has laid claims to numerous contested territories and islands, alarming its neighbors in Japan, Taiwan, the Philippines and Malaysia. As all these countries are allied with the United States it is causing considerable concern in Washington as well.

Satellite images taken in November appear to show the Chinese building an artificial island large enough for an airstrip in the disputed area of the mineral-rich Spratly Islands in the South China Sea. A senior Chinese later confirmed the construction and said the artificial island will be as an electronic surveillance base. "There is a need for a base to support our radar system and intelligence-gathering activities," said Jin Zhirui of the Chinese Air Force Headquarters.

Analysts suggest there are two reasons for this latest Chinese activity—to discourage other nations from increasing their own military development and by this provocation, test the United States' resolve to protect its allies.

China if not already a super power, is not far from achieving super power status. The United States strives to maintain a "positive, cooperative and comprehensive relationship."

It seeks to do this by expanding areas of cooperation and addressing areas of disagreement, such as human rights. The United States "welcomes a strong, peaceful, and prosperous China playing a greater role in world affairs and seeks to advance practical cooperation with China in order to build a partnership based on mutual benefit and mutual respect."

The annual Strategic and Economic Dialogue (S&ED) has served as a unique platform to promote bilateral understanding, expand consensus, discuss differences, improve mutual trust, and increase cooperation. The strategic track of the S&ED has produced benefits for both countries through a wide range of joint projects and initiatives and expanded avenues for addressing common regional and global challenges such as proliferation concerns in Iran and North Korea, tensions between Sudan and South Sudan, climate change, environmental protection, and energy security. The United States has emphasized the need to enhance bilateral trust through increased high-level exchanges, formal dialogues, and expanded people-to-people ties. The U.S. approach to China is an integral part of reinvigorated U.S. engagement with the Asia-Pacific region.

U.S. Assistance to China

U.S. assistance programs in China focus on four principal areas: supporting efforts on environmental protection and climate-change mitigation, advancing the rule of law and human rights, assisting Tibetan communities, and addressing the threat of pandemic diseases. U.S. support for transparency and governance crosses these sectors, supporting the development of environmental law, as well as a free, fair, and accessible justice system. Programs in each of these areas are targeted, can be expanded with the addition of local Chinese resources, and directly address U.S. interests such as limiting the transmission of avian influenza, HIV/AIDS, and other diseases that pose threats to global security. Programs in Tibetan areas of China support activities that preserve the distinct Tibetan culture and promote sustainable development and environmental conservation.

Bilateral Economic Relations

The U.S. approach to its economic relations with China has two main elements: the United States seeks to fully integrate China into the global, rules-based economic and trading system and seeks to expand U.S. exporters' and investors' access to the Chinese market. Two-way trade between China and the United States has grown from $33 billion in 1992 to over $536 billion in goods in 2012. China is currently the third largest export market for U.S. goods (after Canada and Mexico), and the United States is China's largest export market. The stock of U.S. foreign direct investment (FDI) in China was $54.2 billion in 2011, down from $58.5 billion in 2010, and remained primarily in the manufacturing sector. During the economic track of the July 2013 S&ED, the two countries announced measures to strengthen macroeconomic cooperation, promote open trade and investment, enhance global cooperation and international rules, and foster financial stability and reform.

China's Membership in International Organizations

The People's Republic of China assumed the China seat at the United Nations in 1971, replacing Taiwan, and is a permanent member of the UN Security Council. Over the years, China has become increasingly active in multilateral organizations, particularly the United Nations. China and the United States work closely with the international community to address threats to global security, including North Korea and Iran's nuclear programs.

The Country

For centuries China stood as a leading civilization, outpacing the rest of the world in the arts and sciences, but in the 19th and early 20th centuries, the country was beset by civil unrest, major famines, military defeats, and foreign occupation. After World War II, the communists under MAO Zedong established an autocratic socialist system that, while ensuring China's sovereignty, imposed strict controls over everyday life and cost the lives of tens of millions of people. After 1978, MAO's successor DENG Xiaoping and other leaders focused on market-oriented economic development and by 2000 output had quadrupled. For much of the population, living standards have improved dramatically and the room for personal choice has expanded, yet political controls remain tight. Since the early 1990s, China has increased its global outreach and participation in international organizations.

Since the late 1970s China has moved from a closed, centrally planned system to a more market-oriented one that plays a major global role - in 2010 China became the world's largest exporter. Reforms began with the phasing out of collectivized agriculture, and expanded to include the gradual liberalization of prices, fiscal decentralization, increased autonomy for state enterprises, growth of the private sector, development of stock markets and a modern banking system, and opening to foreign trade and investment.

China has implemented reforms in a gradualist fashion. In recent years, China has renewed its support for state-owned enterprises in sectors considered important to "economic security," explicitly looking to foster globally competitive industries. After keeping its currency tightly linked to the US dollar for years, in July 2005 China moved to an exchange rate system that references a basket of currencies. From mid-2005 to late 2008 cumulative appreciation of the renminbi against the US dollar was more than 20%, but the exchange rate remained virtually pegged to the dollar from the onset of the global financial crisis until June 2010, when Beijing allowed resumption of a gradual appreciation and expanded the daily trading band within which the RMB is permitted to fluctuate.

The restructuring of the economy and resulting efficiency gains have contributed to a more than tenfold increase in GDP since 1978. Measured on a purchasing power parity (PPP) basis that adjusts for price differences, China in 2013 stood as the second-largest economy in the world after the US, having surpassed Japan in 2001. The dollar values of China's agricultural and industrial output each exceed those of the US; China is second to the US in the value of services it produces. Still, per capita income is below the world average.

The Chinese government faces numerous economic challenges, including: (a) reducing its high domestic savings rate and correspondingly low domestic consumption; (b) facilitating higher-wage job opportunities for the aspiring middle class, including rural migrants and increasing numbers of college graduates; (c) reducing corruption and other economic crimes; and (d) containing environmental damage and social strife related to the economy's rapid transformation. Economic development has progressed further in coastal provinces than in the interior, and by 2011 more than 250 million migrant workers and their dependents had relocated to urban areas to find work. One consequence of population control policy is that China is now one of the most rapidly aging countries in the world. Deterioration in the environment - notably air pollution, soil erosion, and the steady fall of the water table, especially in the North - is another long-term problem.

China continues to lose arable land because of erosion and economic development. The Chinese government is seeking to add energy production capacity from sources other than coal and oil, focusing on nuclear and alternative energy development. Several factors are converging to slow China's growth, including debt overhang from its credit-fueled stimulus program, industrial overcapacity, inefficient allocation of capital by state-owned banks, and the slow recovery of China's trading partners. The government's 12th Five-Year Plan, adopted in March 2011 and reiterated at the Communist Party's "Third Plenum" meeting in November 2013, emphasizes continued economic reforms and the need to increase domestic consumption in order to make the economy less dependent in the future on fixed investments, exports, and heavy industry. However, China has made only marginal progress toward these rebalancing goals. The new government of President XI Jinping has signaled a greater willingness to undertake reforms that focus on China's long-term economic health, including giving the market a more decisive role in allocating resources.

The People's Liberation Army has more than 750 million men and women available for military service (aged 16-49 years)'

Of especial concern to the United States are territorial issues, human rights and refugees and human trafficking.

There are continuing talks and confidence-building measures work toward reducing tensions over Kashmir that nonetheless remains militarized with portions under the de facto administration of China (Aksai Chin), India (Jammu and Kashmir), and Pakistan (Azad Kashmir and Northern Areas). India does not recognize Pakistan's ceding historic Kashmir lands to China in 1964 and China and India continue their security and foreign policy dialogue started in 2005 related to the dispute over most of their rugged, militarized boundary, regional nuclear proliferation, and other matters. China claims most of India's Arunachal Pradesh to the base of the Himalayas.

In the absence of any treaty describing the boundary, Bhutan and China continue negotiations to establish a common boundary alignment to resolve territorial disputes arising from substantial cartographic discrepancies, the largest of which lie in Bhutan's northwest and along the Chumbi salient. Burmese forces attempting to dig in to the largely autonomous Shan State to rout local militias tied to the drug trade, prompts local residents to periodically flee into neighboring Yunnan Province in China.

Chinese maps show an international boundary symbol off the coasts of the littoral states of the South China Seas, where China has interrupted Vietnamese hydrocarbon exploration. China asserts sovereignty over Scarborough Reef along with the Philippines and Taiwan, and over the Spratly Islands together with Malaysia, the Philippines, Taiwan, Vietnam, and Brunei.

China occupies some of the Paracel Islands also claimed by Vietnam and Taiwan. China and Taiwan continue to reject both Japan's claims to the uninhabited islands of Senkaku-shoto (Diaoyu Tai) and Japan's unilaterally declared equidistance line in the East China Sea, the site of intensive hydrocarbon exploration and exploitation. Certain islands in the Yalu and Tumen rivers are in dispute with North Korea.

North Korea and China seek to stem illegal migration to China by North Koreans, fleeing privations and oppression, by building a fence along portions of the border and imprisoning North Koreans deported by China. China and Russia have demarcated the once disputed islands at the Amur and Ussuri confluence and in the Argun River in accordance with their 2004 Agreement. Citing environmental, cultural, and social concerns, China has reconsidered construction of 13 dams on the Salween River, but energy-starved Burma, with backing from Thailand, remains intent on building five hydro-electric dams downstream despite regional and international protests.

China is a source, transit, and destination country for men, women, and children trafficked for the purposes of sexual exploitation and forced labor; the majority of trafficking in China occurs within the country's borders, there are many reports that Chinese men, women, and children may be subjected to conditions of sex trafficking and forced labor in numerous countries and territories worldwide; women and children are trafficked to China from Burma, Vietnam, Laos, Mongolia, Russia, North Korea, and even as far away as Europe and Africa for forced labor and prostitution; some Chinese adults and children are forced into prostitution and various forms of forced labor, including begging, stealing, and working in brick kilns, coal mines, and factories

China does not fully comply with the minimum standards for the elimination of trafficking and was downgraded to Tier 3 after the maximum of two consecutive annual waivers. According to the State Department he Chinese government has not demonstrated significant efforts to comprehensively prohibit and punish all forms of trafficking and to prosecute traffickers. The government also has not reported providing comprehensive victim protection services to domestic or foreign, male or female victims of trafficking. In 2013, the government released an eight-year national action plan, which includes measures to improve interagency and other internal coordination among anti-trafficking stakeholders and victim protection.

USAID

Regional Development Mission for Asia (RDMA), in Bangkok, supports programs in China across several sectors. USAID is helping China promote clean energy and reduce greenhouse gas emissions. It is working with China to improve environmental law and environmental governance. Activities also will strengthen environmental due diligence among national agencies and the private sector and reduce China's environmental footprint.

USAID assists China's efforts to develop a legal system for fair, participatory and transparent governance; as well as its efforts to introduce reforms within the justice system. RDMA's programs preserve cultural traditions and promote sustainable development and environmental conservation among ethnic Tibetans. RDMA is working to prevent the spread of HIV/AIDS and multi-drug resistant tuberculosis and is strengthening surveillance for avian influenza. In addition, USAID sent personnel and donated specialized search, rescue and recovery equipment following the 2008 Sichuan province earthquake.

Investment in China for U.S. Companies

The State Department helps facilitate U.S. investment in China through the Office of Economic and Business Affairs.

China maintains a more restrictive foreign investment regime than its major trading partners, including the United States. The flow of new Chinese direct investment into the United States eclipsed that of the United States into China, according to widely-cited estimates by the Rhodium Group, a leading private consultancy focused on U.S.-China investment. However, the total stock of U.S. investment in China remains significantly higher than the total stock of Chinese investment in the U.S., at US $70 billion compared to just US $17 billion as of the end of 2012, according to the Ministry of Commerce (MOFCOM) China Commerce Yearbook 2012 (the latest year for which China's bilateral data is available). China relies on an investment catalogue to encourage foreign investment in some sectors of the economy, while restricting or prohibiting it in many other industries. China's investment approval regime appears designed to foster economic growth but may also shield inefficient or monopolistic Chinese enterprises from competition, particularly those China is trying to cultivate as market leaders. Foreign investors cite concerns about rising costs, difficulty in finding qualified human resources, and the discretionary authority Chinese regulators have to discriminate against foreign investors, both in the establishment and operational phases.

Over the past years, there were several positive signs that China's new leaders are committed to redefining the State's role in the economy. Xi Jinping, in his first year as State president and head of the Communist Party, has worked to consolidate power and pushed for economic reform to further open the economy to private capital, including international investors in some sectors. Major developments include:

- China made a landmark decision to negotiate a high-standard bilateral investment treaty (BIT) with the United States that would be based on the U.S. model BIT approach to national treatment, which covers both the "pre-establishment" and post-establishment phases of investment, and delineates a clear "negative list" of negotiated exceptions.
- China established the Shanghai Pilot Free Trade Zone, partly to test reforms to the investment registration regime and to open previously closed sectors to foreign investment.
- At the Third Plenum meeting of the 18th Party Congress, the Chinese Communist Party unveiled an ambitious reform agenda that directs the authorities to broaden foreign investment access and underscores the leadership's commitment to allow market forces to play a "decisive" role in allocating resources and driving economic growth.

Although the Chinese Communist Party says it expects to "fulfill" the Third Plenum reform agenda by 2020, a detailed reform roadmap and reform timing is lacking for many economic sectors. Foreign investors remain concerned about discriminatory industrial policies, opaque investment approval proce-

dures used to achieve industrial policy goals and a lack of effective administrative and legal recourse if an investment approval is conditioned or denied.
Poor enforcement of intellectual property rights (IPR), the forced transfer of
technology, and lack of rule of law are additional concerns.

The United States government has raised concerns about China's investment restrictions and discriminatory policies at high levels, in bilateral fora
such as the U.S.-China Joint Commission on Commerce and Trade (JCCT), the
U.S.-China Strategic and Economic Dialogue (S&ED) and the U.S.-China Investment Forum. BIT negotiations are an additional opportunity to encourage
China's economic reforms, integrate China into a global rules-based system,
and level the playing field for U.S. businesses. The United States Government
emphasizes the need for China to open new sectors to foreign investment, increase transparency, and improve the enforcement of existing laws to protect
investors' rights. For China to achieve its ambitious economic growth goals, its
investment regime will have to change to permit greater competition across a
broader range of sectors.

The Chinese government has stated that it welcomes foreign investment.
China attracted US $118 billion in worldwide foreign direct investment (FDI)
in 2013 (latest data available), second only to the United States. China's sustained high economic growth rate and the expansion of its domestic market
help explain its attractiveness as an FDI destination. However, foreign investors often temper their optimism regarding potential investment returns with
uncertainty about China's willingness to offer a level playing field vis-à-vis
domestic competitors. In addition, foreign investors report a range of challenges related to China's current investment climate. These include industrial
policies that protect and promote state-owned and other domestic firms, equity caps and other restrictions on foreign ownership in many industries, weak
IPR protection, a lack of transparency, corruption, and an unreliable legal system.

7

Afghanistan

In September 2014 the newly elected Afghan President signed the Bilateral Security Agreement (BSA) and the NATO Status of Forces Agreements (SOFA). Both provide security to Afghans and are in the long-term best interests of Afghanistan, enabling the country and its citizens to continue to build on the gains made in the past 13 years.

The BSA provides U.S. military servicemembers the necessary legal framework to carry out the two critical missions post-2014: targeting the remnants of al-Qaida; and training, advising, and assisting the Afghan National Security Forces. And it also reflects the implementation of the Strategic Partnership Agreement the U.S. and Afghanistan signed over in May 2012.

(The *Enduring Strategic Partnership Agreement between the Islamic Republic of Afghanistan and the United States of America*, was a 10-year strategic partnership agreement (SPA) demonstrating the United States' enduring commitment to strengthen Afghanistan's sovereignty, stability, and prosperity and continue cooperation to defeat al-Qaida and its affiliates. Following the entry into force of the Agreement on July 4, 2012, President Obama designated Afghanistan a Major Non-NATO Ally (MNNA) on July 6, 2012. Afghanistan was the first country to be designated an MNNA since 2004.)

SOFA gives forces from allied and partner countries the legal protections necessary to carry out the NATO Resolute Support Mission when ISAF comes to an end at the end of 2014.

The U.S. has been involved in Afghanistan since it invaded after the September 11 attacks. President Bush demanded that the ruling group the Taliban hand over Osama bin Laden, head of Al-Qa'ida and mastermind behind the attacks. On October 7, 2001 and after the Taliban refused to extradite bin Laden, Bush launched Operation Enduring Freedom supported by the United Kingdom and later other members of the Northern Alliance. The U.S. and its allies drove the Taliban from power and most of its members as well as Al-Qa'ida fighters retreated to the mountains or took refuge in Pakistan. In December 2001 the United Nations Security Council established the International Security Assistance Force (ISAF), to oversee military operations in the country and train Afghan National Security Forces. At the Bonn Conference in December 2001, Hamid Karzai was selected to head the Afghan Interim Administration which then became the Afghan Transitional Administration. In the elections of 2004, Karzai was elected president of the country, now named the Islamic Republic of Afghanistan.

In 2003, NATO assumed leadership of ISAF, with troops from 43 countries. NATO members provided the core of the force. One portion of U.S. forces in Afghanistan operated under NATO command; the rest remained under direct U.S. command. Taliban leader Mullah Omar reorganized the movement and in 2003 launched an insurgency against the government and ISAF. The Taliban waged a guerilla war attacking Afghan politicians and officials and urban and military targets. At the same time they managed to take back control of many rural areas. Many of the Taliban and other insurgent groups had bases in Pakistan and so the U.S. started attacking them with drones. On May 2, 2011 a United Seals Navy Seals killed Osama Bin Laden who had been living in a compound in Abbotabad, Pakistan, probably with the complicity of Pakistan's intelligence agencies. In May 2012, NATO leaders agreed an exit strategy to withdraw their troops. In May 14 the U.S. announced that its troops would end combat operations by the end of 2014 although a small residual force would remain until 2016.

U.S. Assistance to Afghanistan

The United States has made a long-term commitment to help Afghanistan build a secure state with a democratic government that respects human rights. Through the Tokyo Mutual Accountability Framework, the United States and other international donors committed to providing Afghanistan $16 billion in aid through 2015 and continuing assistance at levels commensurate with the last decade through 2017. In its turn, Afghanistan committed to strengthening governance, building a legislative framework to ensure a credible, transparent and inclusive transfer of power, and making the structural changes to ensure that the government remains solvent and Afghan citizens can participate in a growing economy. The United States and others in the international community currently support Afghanistan with a broad array of assistance programs including private sector growth, capacity-building for government institutions, support to improve professionalism of security forces, programs to support civil society and respect for human rights, counter-narcotic programs, infrastructure projects, special support for the advancement of Afghan women and girls, and humanitarian relief.

The United States supports the Afghan government's goals of focusing on reintegration and reconciliation, economic development, improving relations with Afghanistan's regional partners, and steadily increasing the security capability of Afghan forces. The United States is using a bilateral incentive program and the Tokyo Mutual Accountability Framework to hold the Afghan Government accountable and to encourage it to take actions to combat corruption and improve governance and to provide better services for the people of Afghanistan, while maintaining and expanding on the important democratic reforms and advances in women's rights that have been made since 2001.

Bilateral Economic Relations

Afghanistan signed a Trade and Investment Framework Agreement with the United States in 2004. There is no Bilateral Taxation Treaty between the United

States and Afghanistan. Efforts are underway to improve the business climate, including strengthening Afghanistan's commercial regulatory and legal framework to attract foreign trade and investment, as well as to stimulate additional trade with the United States through trade capacity development. Afghanistan is also working towards membership in the World Trade Organization (WTO) by the end of 2014.

Afghanistan's Membership in International Organizations

Afghanistan and the United States belong to a number of the same international organizations, including the United Nations, International Monetary Fund, and World Bank. Afghanistan also is a Partner for Cooperation with the Organization for Security and Cooperation in Europe and is working toward accession to the WTO.

The New Silk Road

The New Silk Road initiative was first envisioned in 2011 as a means for Afghanistan to integrate further into the region by resuming traditional trading routes and reconstructing significant infrastructure links broken by decades of conflict. Today, Afghanistan and its neighbors are leading the way in key areas, creating new North-South transit and trade routes that complement vibrant East-West connections across Eurasia. The region is reducing barriers to trade, investing in each other's economies, and supporting international development and cross-border projects.

With multiple transitions underway in Afghanistan, the United States and its allies can bolster peace and stability in the region by supporting a transition to trade and helping open new markets connecting Afghanistan to Central Asia, Pakistan, India and beyond. Countries in the region know they have more to gain economically by working together than by being isolated. Promoting connectivity in a region that is the least-economically integrated in the world is challenging, but the benefits can be transformative. This is why the United States is promoting the New Silk Road initiative linking Central and South Asia in four key areas:

Regional Energy Markets: With a population of more than 1.6 billion people, South Asia's economies are growing rapidly, and South Asia's demand for inexpensive, efficient, and reliable energy is growing in turn. At the same time, Central Asia is a repository of vast energy resources – including oil, gas, and hydropower. Directing some of these resources southward from Central to South Asia, through Afghanistan, would be a win-win for the region's energy suppliers and energy users alike. The U.S. has provided:

- Support for CASA-1000 regional electricity grid, including a $15 million contribution following the March 2014 World Bank commitment of $526 million and support for the CASA Secretariat;
- More than $1.7 billion in support of energy transmission lines, hydropower plants, and associated reforms in Afghanistan since 2010; and
- Adding 1,000 megawatts to Pakistan's power grid, supplying power to more than 16 million people.

Trade and Transport: Improving trade and transit in South and Central Asia means improving the "hardware" of reliable roads, railways, bridges, and border crossing facilities. But it also means working on the "software" side, harmonizing national customs systems, bringing states into multilateral trade institutions, and getting neighbors to work together to break down institutional and bureaucratic barriers to trade. The U.S. has provided:

- More than 3,000 kilometers of roads built or rehabilitated in Afghanistan;
- Support for Kazakhstan and Afghanistan's accession to the WTO;
- Technical assistance for the passage of the 2010 Afghanistan-Pakistan Transit-Trade Agreement (APTTA), and support for the Cross-Border

Transport Agreement (CBTA) between Kyrgyzstan, Tajikistan, and Afghanistan.

Customs and Border Operations: Profitable regional trade depends in large part on speedy and efficient transit. It also depends on border security and good governance that prevents transit of weapons, drugs, and human trafficking. The United States works with regional partners to reduce border wait times, increase cooperation at key checkpoints and crossings, and prevent transit of illegal and dangerous material. With U.S. support:

- Since 2009, intraregional trade in Central Asia has increased by 49 percent;
- Since 2011, the average cost of crossing regional borders decreased by 15 percent;
- Customs procedures have been streamlined at seven Afghan border crossing points, resulting in expedited trade with average release time down from eight days in 2009 to three and a half hours in 2013, saving $38 million annually.

Businesses and People-to-People: Regional economic connectivity is more than infrastructure, border crossings, and the movement of goods and services. Sharing ideas and expansion of economic markets also creates opportunities for youth, women, and minorities and enhances regional stability and prosperity. The U.S. has:

- Funded university studies for hundreds of Afghan students across Central Asia;
- Sponsored the Central Asia-Afghanistan Women's Economic Symposium and South Asia Women's Entrepreneurship Symposium in support of thousands of women entrepreneurs and business owners;

- Organized trade delegations, meetings and conferences in Almaty, Islamabad, Kabul, Mazar-i-Sharif and Termez resulting in over $15 million in trade deals.

Rebuilding Afghanistan

The Afghanistan Investment and Reconstruction Task Force (Task Force) of the U.S. Department of Commerce facilitates and coordinates the Department's activities that are designed to help Afghanistan develop a sustainable economy. The Task Force works closely with the Department's Commercial Law Development Program and our Commercial Office in Kabul. Efforts focus on helping Afghanistan develop:

- A commercial legal environment that supports trade, investment and private sector-led growth. The task force has conducted business contracting training, providing advice on Arbitration and is creating a commercial legal initiative with the American University in Kabul.
- A more capable and competitive private sector. For example the task force is creating a Marble Center of Excellence and providing sector specific training and consulting.
- Stronger U.S.-Afghan commercial ties. The task force provides information and support for U.S. firms interested in doing business in Afghanistan, provides matchmaking and counseling for U.S. and Afghan firms, and facilitates business missions to Afghanistan i.e. a group of U.S. franchisors who visited Kabul this week.

Drug Trade

Illicit drug cultivation, production, trafficking, and consumption flourish in Afghanistan, particularly in parts of the south and southwest where instability is high and state institutions are weak or non-existent, according to the International Narcotics and Law Enforcement Affairs 2014 International Narcotics Control Strategy Report (INCSR).

More than 90 percent of poppy cultivation takes place in these regions. The UN Office of Drugs and Crime (UNODC) and the Afghan Ministry of Counter Narcotics (MCN) estimate that Afghanistan cultivated 209,000 hectares (ha) of opium poppy in 2013, with a total yield of 5,500 metric tons (MT) of raw opium. This was a 36 percent increase in cultivation and a 49 percent increase in opium production from 2012. The United States government estimates that in 2013, poppy cultivation in Afghanistan increased 10 percent to 198,000 ha, while potential opium production increased 28 percent to 5,500 MT. A symbiotic relationship exists between the insurgency and narcotics trafficking in Afghanistan. Traffickers provide weapons, funding, and other material support to the insurgency in exchange for the protection of drug trade routes, fields, laboratories, and their organizations. Some insurgent commanders engage directly in drug trafficking to finance their operations. The narcotics trade undermines governance and rule of law in all parts of the country where poppy is cultivated and traffickers operate.

Afghanistan is involved in the full narcotics production cycle, from cultivation to finished heroin to consumption. Drug traffickers trade in all forms of opiates, including unrefined opium, semi-refined morphine base, and refined heroin. Some raw opium and morphine base is trafficked to neighboring and regional countries, where it is further refined into heroin. While the vast majority of the opium and heroin produced in Afghanistan is exported, Afghanistan is also struggling to respond to a burgeoning domestic opiate addiction problem.

Afghanistan relies on assistance from the international community to implement its national counternarcotics strategy. Greater political will, increased institutional capacity, enhanced security, viable economic alternatives for farmers, and more robust efforts at all levels are required to decrease cultivation in high-cultivating provinces, maintain cultivation reductions in the rest of the country, and combat trafficking.

Drug Control Accomplishments, Policies, and Trends

The Government of Afghanistan is publicly committed to confronting the drug problem in Afghanistan, particularly focusing on what it identifies as the root causes of the drug economy including instability; poverty; unemployment; and organized crime. The Ministry of Counter Narcotics (MCN) is the lead governmental agency for developing counternarcotics policy and coordinates the activities of other governmental bodies involved in issues related to the drug trade. The Afghan government approved the new Afghan National Drug Control Strategy (NDCS) in October 2013. MCN is also working to insert counternarcotics into the activities of the entire government by "mainstreaming" counternarcotics efforts into other existing national strategies and programs.

Afghanistan has no formal extradition or mutual legal assistance arrangements with the United States. Afghanistan is a signatory to the 1988 UN Drug Convention, and the 2005 Afghan Counter Narcotics Law allows for the extradition of drug offenders to requesting countries under the 1988 UN Drug Convention. A 2013 domestic Afghan extradition law adds additional hurdles to any potential extradition process.

According to UNODC and MCN, Afghanistan cultivated 209,000 ha of opium poppy in 2013, up 36 percent from 2012. UNODC and MCN estimate that Afghan opium poppy crops in 2013 yielded 5,500 MT of raw opium, up 49 percent from 3,700 MT in 2012, a year in which yields were suppressed by unfavorable growing conditions. According to the UNODC and MCN, the number of poppy free provinces (those provinces with less than 100 ha of poppy under cultivation) decreased from 17 in 2012 to 15 in 2013 (out of a total of 34 provinces).

There is significant evidence of commercial cultivation of cannabis in Afghanistan. The UNODC and MCN's 2012 cannabis survey found that commercial cannabis cultivation in 2012 was approximately 10,000 ha, capable of producing 1,400 MT of hashish per year. The 2012 survey did not assess the number of households growing cannabis for commercial purposes, but a 2011 survey estimated that the number of cannabis producing households increased by 38 percent (65,000 households) from 2010. As with poppy, most cannabis cultivation takes place in insecure areas of the country.

Primary trafficking routes into and out of Afghanistan are through Pakistan and Iran to the Balkans, Turkey and Western Europe; through Pakistan to Africa, Asia, the Middle East, China and Iran; and through Central Asia to the Russian Federation. The United States is not a common destination for Afghan opiates. Drug laboratories within Afghanistan still process a large portion of the country's raw opium into heroin and morphine base. Traffickers illicitly import large quantities of precursor chemicals into Afghanistan; UNODC estimates that 475 MT of acetic anhydride are imported annually for manufacturing heroin.

MCN implements the U.S.-funded Good Performers Initiative (GPI) to reward provinces that successfully reduce poppy cultivation within their borders. Provinces that are determined to be poppy-free by UNODC, or where poppy cultivation has declined by 10 percent or more, receive funding for development projects proposed by provincial development councils and governors' offices. In 2012, 21 of Afghanistan's 34 provinces received $18.2 million in GPI awards, including two provinces that received special recognition awards of $500,000 each. The MCN-run Governor-Led Eradication program reimburses governors for expenses incurred for eradicating poppy fields. Eradication is verified by UNODC. In 2013, a total of 7,348 ha was eradicated, a decrease of 24 percent compared to 2012. Both the quality and efficiency of eradication improved in certain provinces, but attacks by criminals and insurgents on eradication teams resulted in 143 deaths on both sides in 2013, including civilians and security personnel. An additional 93 people were injured in such attacks.

The Criminal Justice Task Force (CJTF) is a vetted, self-contained unit that consists of investigators, prosecutors, and first instance and appellate court judges. Under Afghanistan's 2005 Counternarcotics Law, amended in 2010, the CJTF prosecutes all drug cases that reach certain thresholds (possession of two kilogram of heroin, 10 kilograms of opium or 50 kilograms of hashish or precursor chemicals) before the Counter Narcotics Tribunal. The Counter Narcotics Justice Center (CNJC) houses the Tribunal and CJTF, and is the central facility for the investigation, prosecution, and trial of major narcotics and narcotics-related corruption cases. The CNJC is considered a model of excellence within the Afghan justice system. Between March 2012 and March 2013, the CNJC primary court heard 551 cases and tried 704 suspects, involving more than 233 MT of illegal drugs (a 26 percent increase in the volume of drugs over the previous year). Those convicted receive sentences ranging from 11 to 20 years.

Afghan authorities have increasingly used their specialized counternarcotics units and the CNJC to arrest and prosecute high-value traffickers, including the arrest, prosecution, and conviction of Nimruz Provincial Police Chief Mohammad Kabir Andarabi in 2013. Andarabi was arrested on narcotics trafficking charges and sentenced to 10 years. According to U.S. Drug Enforcement Administration (DEA) figures, during the first nine months of 2013, specialized units of the Counternarcotics Police of Afghanistan (CNPA) conducted a total of 78 counternarcotics operations and seized 27.5 MT of opium, 16.7 MT of morphine, and 284 kilograms of heroin. The CNPA was established in 2003 as a specialized element of the Afghan National Police and is responsible for counternarcotics investigations and operations. The United States supports several specialized units within the CNPA, including the Sensitive Investigations Unit (SIU), the Technical Investigative Unit (TIU), and the National Interdiction Unit (NIU). These units are partnered with the DEA. The NIU is the tactical element of the CNPA and is capable of conducting independent, evidence-based interdiction operations and seizures in high threat environments. The TIU and SIU are specially vetted and trained law enforcement units. The SIU carries out complex CN and counter corruption investigations using intelligence developed by the TIU.

U.S. assistance has also supported the development of a viable command and control structure at the Afghan Customs Police, with specialized training and operational support provided by the Department of Homeland Security's Customs and Border Protection. These efforts, channeled through the Afghan government's Border Management Task Force, led to a 31 percent increase in narcotics seizures at border checkpoints over 2012.

Outside these special units, limited capacity and corruption within law enforcement institutions and the lack of CNPA's direct authority over its resources in the provinces hampers counternarcotics efforts.

The Afghan government acknowledges a growing domestic drug abuse problem, primarily involving opiates and cannabis. Funded by the United States, the Afghan National Urban Drug Use Survey released in 2012 provides a scientifically-valid prevalence rate for the country's urban population based on interviews and toxicology. The survey conservatively estimated that Afghanistan is home to 1.3 to 1.6 million drug users, one of the world's highest per capita rates. The United States is supporting a National Rural Drug Use Survey to complement the urban study and provide a national prevalence rate. Other recently conducted studies indicate that the prevalence of addiction and severity of consumption among Afghan children is the highest documented in the world.

The United States expanded funding to 76 inpatient and outpatient drug treatment centers across the country in 2013. Unfortunately, the demand for services exceeds the capacity of the centers, most of which have waiting lists for new patients. The United States also supports UNODC's global child addiction program throughout Afghanistan to develop protocols for treating opiate-addicted children, training treatment staff, and delivering services through Afghan non-governmental organizations. The current annual treatment capacity of Afghanistan's centers is more than 15,000 persons. The Government of Afghanistan is planning an expansion of its treatment system by opening new clinics across the country. Private clinics have also proliferated in recent years, although many of these do not apply evidence-based practices, discharging clients after detoxification without follow-up, thereby resulting in high relapse rates.

The United States funds a Counter Narcotics Community Engagement program (CNCE). This multi-track annual communication and outreach campaign, implemented by Sayara Strategies, aims to ensure a smooth transition of activities to the Afghan government through systematic capacity development efforts. The program focuses on discouraging poppy cultivation, preventing drug use by public awareness, and encouraging licit crop production. The United States has undertaken a vigorous public information campaign implemented by Colombo Plan, to reduce drug demand inside Afghanistan, including seeking the support of subject-matter experts and school teachers; engaging local media; and implementing an anti-drug curriculum in Afghan schools. In 2012, the U.S. government helped establish a partnership between the Colombo Plan's Preventive Drug Education program and the Afghan Premier Soccer League to spread an anti-drug message to Afghan youth. The United States also funds an Afghanistan-specific mobile preventive drug education exhibit.

As a matter of government policy, the Government of Afghanistan does not encourage or facilitate illicit drug production or distribution, nor is it involved in laundering proceeds from the sale of illicit drugs. However, many central, provincial, and district level government officials are believed to directly engage in and benefit from the drug trade. Corrupt practices range from facilitating drug activities to benefiting from drug trade revenue streams. The CJTF actively investigates and prosecutes public officials who facilitate drug trafficking under Article 21 of the Counter Narcotics Law, which criminalizes drug trafficking-related corruption. The CJTF has successfully prosecuted high ranking government officials, including members of the CNPA. According to Afghan officials, between March 2012 and March 2013, 21 public officials were prosecuted in the CJTF primary court.

National Goals, Bilateral Cooperation, and U.S. Policy Initiatives

The U.S. government maintains a counternarcotics strategy that supports Afghanistan's four counternarcotics priorities: disrupting the drug trade; developing licit agricultural livelihoods; reducing the demand for drugs; and building the capacity of the government's CN institutions. The strategy is formulated to help restore Afghanistan's licit agriculture economy, build Afghan institutional capacity, and disrupt the nexus among drugs, insurgents, and corruption.

In 2012, the United States signed agreements with the Afghan government laying the groundwork for a Kandahar Food Zone in 2013. Under the leadership of the Ministry of Counternarcotics, the Kandahar Food Zone was developed as a comprehensive, multi-pillar drug-control program that integrates elements of alternative development, law enforcement and eradication, public information and drug treatment. In July 2013, the United States awarded a $20 million, two-year program to develop the Alternative Livelihoods component of the Kandahar Food Zone. MCN has established a coordination mechanism to integrate alternative livelihoods activities with U.S.-funded Counter Narcotics Public Information, Drug Demand Reduction, and Governor-Led Eradication programs.

The estimated value of opium to the Afghan economy has remained relatively stable over the last decade. Yet Afghanistan's legal economy has grown steadily, and as a result, opiates now make up a much smaller fraction of Afghanistan's economy – from 60 percent of the GDP in 2003 to 10 percent in 2012.

For Afghanistan to enjoy future success in combating the narcotics trade it must continue to strengthen the capacity of the MCN and other ministries charged with conducting or supporting counternarcotics efforts, actively combat corruption at all levels of government, and further develop the ability of regular CNPA units to carry out operations. The Afghan government must also demonstrate the political will to challenge vested political and economic interests.

Farmers and those involved in processing and trafficking drugs must also have viable economic alternatives to involvement in the narcotics trade. Improvements in security and market access, as well as continued concentrated efforts to increase agricultural and other alternative livelihoods, will remain essential to undermining the drug economy and the insurgency in Afghanistan.

8

Korea

The reclusive, tyrannical North Korean regime continues to be a thorn in the side of the United States and its allies, particularly South Korea and Japan. The two Koreas are still in a state of war as no formal peace treaty was signed following the end of the Korean War in 1953 and their armies continue to face each other across the 38th parallel which marks the demilitarized zone between the two countries.

At the end of World War II, Korea was portioned along the 38th parallel. To the north was North Korea occupied by Soviet Russia and to the south was South Korea occupied by the U.S. and allied forces. North Korea became the Democratic People's Republic of Korea (DPRK) while the South became the Republic of Korea with a western-style democracy. In June 1950 North Korea invaded the South and over the next three years more than one million people died.

Since 1953 South Korea has prospered while North Korea has become a reclusive, poverty-stricken pariah state built around the ideology of founding President Kim Il Sung. His grandson Kim Jong Un assumed the presidency in 2011. Often described as a "hereditary dictatorship" North Korea's history of regional military provocations; proliferation of military-related items; long-range missile development; WMD programs including tests of nuclear devices in 2006, 2009, and 2013; and massive conventional armed forces are of major concern to the international community. The regime in 2013 announced a new policy calling for the simultaneous development of the North's nuclear weapons program and its economy. North Korea is backed by China but has to rely on the international community for food aid to feed its people. North Korea's People's Army is the largest in the world with more than 1.1 million active military and more than 8 million reservists. North Korea possesses nuclear weapons, but its arsenal remains limited. Various estimates put its stockpile at less than 10 plutonium warheads. Based on satellite images and defector testimonies, Amnesty International estimates that around 200,000 prisoners are held in six large political prison camps, where they are forced to work in conditions approaching slavery. Supporters of the government who deviate from the government line are subject to 'reeducation' in sections of labor camps set aside for that purpose.

North Korea's stated reunification policy is to achieve this without outside interference "through a federal structure retaining each side's leadership and systems." In June 2000, North and South Korea signed a Joint Declaration pledging to seek out a peaceful reunification but on-off talks over the years have not had any success.

According to Glyn Davies, Special Representative for North Korea Policy at the State Department, the Democratic People's Republic of Korea (DPRK) "continues to make choices contrary to the interests of its people, its neighbors, and the world community. It flagrantly violates its obligations through its continued pursuit of nuclear weapons and ballistic missiles, posing a growing threat to the United States, our friends and allies in the region, and the global nonproliferation regime.

"It devotes scarce resources to its illicit weapons programs to its massive standing army, and to elaborate vanity projects for a privileged elite – all while the vast majority of North Korea's nearly 25 million people continue to suffer. More troubling, a UN Commission of Inquiry has concluded that in many instances, the violations it found the DPRK regime to have committed over decades constitute crimes against humanity. And in the last year, the DPRK has repeatedly threatened the United States, and its neighbors, the Republic of Korea and Japan. It is increasingly a global outlier in every sense."

"We have no illusions about the nature of the regime, nor its intentions. We have refused to respond to DPRK provocations with concessions. North Korean has obtained no benefits from its bad behavior. Instead, we have tightened sanctions and consistently underscored to the DPRK that neither its occasional and tentative "charm" offensives nor its more frequent periods of aggressive behavior will lead us or the international community to accept a nuclear-armed North Korea. As we seek the negotiated complete, verifiable, and irreversible denuclearization of North Korea, we know we must keep pressure on Pyongyang or it will not give up the weapons it claims it needs. That is why our policy mix includes sanctions and traditional deterrence measures. In short, ours is a comprehensive approach that seeks to denuclearize North Korea through diplomacy while ensuring deterrence of the North Korean threat."

The State Department's policy is based on several factors including diplomacy and looks to China to support it in its efforts.

Diplomacy

The U.S. seeks a solution to the North Korea nuclear challenge through peaceful, persistent, multilateral diplomacy. The United States has offered — and continues to offer — Pyongyang an improved bilateral relationship provided it takes action to demonstrate a willingness to fulfill its denuclearization commitments and address other important concerns which are also shared by the international community. The U.S. has consistently signaled to the DPRK that the door for meaningful engagement is open while applying unilateral and multilateral pressure to steer it toward that door. Its policy has followed this dual-track approach: open to engagement when possible, but continuing to apply pressure as needed. Both elements are critical to sharpening Pyongyang's choices, demonstrating to the international community the seriousness of our commitment to a negotiated settlement of this issue, and building multilateral support for the various pressure and deterrence actions we take.

"Regrettably, the DPRK has consistently rebuffed offers for authentic and credible negotiations and instead responded with a series of provocations that have drawn widespread international condemnation and increased its isolation," said Davies. The DPRK has conducted ballistic missiles launches in direct violation of multiple UN Security Council resolutions. These followed short- and medium-range ballistic missile launches, which Pyongyang punctuated with threats to conduct additional longer-range launches and possibly a "new type" of nuclear test.

The DPRK says it is ready for "talks without preconditions." No codebook is needed to decipher North Korea's intention: seek open-ended discussion that diverts attention away from its nuclear program and to avoid committing to denuclearization. Pyongyang has been explicit on this point: it seeks acceptance as a nuclear weapons state. It wants to use Six-Party talks, as it has in the past, as cover to continue its clandestine weapons development. The U.S. is not interested in Six-Party talks that do not focus directly on steps to implement, as a first and primary order of business, North Korea's September 2005 promise to denuclearize.

Six Party Diplomacy

The Six-Party Talks (North and South Korea, U.S., China, Japan and Russia) have been dormant since the DPRK walked out and declared the process "dead" in 2008. North Korea's 2009 Taepo Dong-2 launch and nuclear test then undermined the modest progress that had been made pursuant to the September 2005 Joint Statement of the Six-Party Talks. Since then, robust diplomatic interaction with the other four parties strengthened five-party unity on the end goal of the verifiable denuclearization of the Korean Peninsula. As a result, Pyongyang hears a uniform and clear message from all five parties, strongly echoed by the international community, that it will not be accepted as a nuclear power, that it must live up to its denuclearization obligations, and that authentic and credible negotiations must be marked by concrete denuclearization steps.

None of the Five Parties insists North Korea denuclearize before returning to the negotiating table. But they have underscored the need to see an early and demonstrable commitment by the DPRK to denuclearize. This means the onus is on North Korea to take meaningful actions toward denuclearization and refrain from provocations.

Despite the DPRK's recidivism over the last half-decade, we remain committed to authentic and credible negotiations to implement the September 2005 Joint Statement of the Six-Party Talks and to bring North Korea into compliance with its international obligations through irreversible steps leading to denuclearization. But we will not engage in talks for the sake of talks and we will not compensate North Korea for the temporary absence of bad behavior. A resumption of Six-Party Talks makes sense if, and only if, there is plausible reason to believe that North Korea is prepared to negotiate seriously. North Korea knows this, but we have not yet seen signs that Pyongyang is prepared to meet its commitments and obligations to achieve the core goal of the September 2005 Joint Statement: the verifiable denuclearization of the Korean Peninsula in a peaceful manner.

The Republic of Korea is firmly at the center of diplomatic efforts. There is no daylight between Washington and Seoul on the issue of what is expected from North Korea. As President Obama emphasized during his public remarks in Seoul in April, the United States supports President Park's vision and desire for peaceful, progressive unification, as outlined in her March speech in Dresden, Germany." We hope to see Pyongyang take up President Park on her offer of an improved inter-Korean relationship. The DPRK — and the region — only stand to gain from embracing her principled vision".

The Role of China

While the U.S. believes that there is more China can do in terms of bringing necessary pressure to bear on North Korea so that it concludes it has no choice but to denuclearize, Beijing has done a great deal. As North Korea's last remaining patron, the PRC has a critical, indeed unique, role to play in addressing the North Korean nuclear challenge.

That is why North Korea remains at the top of the United States' bilateral agenda with China, and why it figured prominently in Secretary Kerry's discussions in Beijing at the U.S.-China Strategic and Economic Dialogue. The U.S. welcomes the steps the PRC has taken to signal its opposition to the DPRK's nuclear weapons program, including through its stated commitment to fully implement UN Security Council sanctions concerning North Korea. China voted in favor of two new rounds of UNSC sanctions and in September last year published a 900-item control list banning the export of many dual-use items to North Korea.

The United States and China share an interest in the peaceful denuclearization of North Korea. Beijing has agreed on what North Korea needs to do since the September 2005 Joint Statement. The U.S. is now focused on coming to agreement on the "how" and the "when" of denuclearization. China could still do more to exercise its unique levers of influence over Pyongyang and the U.S. remains in close touch with Beijing about ways they can work together to bring the DPRK to the realization that it has no other viable choice but to denuclearize.

Sanctions

The U.S. has no misconceptions about North Korea's willingness to give up its arsenal voluntarily. All of North Korea's actions over the past few years, from its nuclear tests to the amendment of its constitution to declare itself a nuclear state, signal that it has no interest in denuclearizing. America takes this threat seriously, and remains ironclad in its commitment to the defense of its allies, the Republic of Korea and Japan. Together with these allies and partners, The U.S. is working to shift Pyongyang's calculus from believing that a nuclear program is necessary for regime survival to understanding that such a program is incompatible with its national interests.

To do that, the U.S. continues to use the multilateral and other tools at its disposal to increase the cost of North Korea's illicit activities, to reduce resources earned through weapons exports that are subsequently reinvested in the WMD program, and to sharpen Pyongyang's choices. Over the past two years, the U.S. has substantially upped the cost of these activities — particularly its proliferation and weapons sales abroad — by tightening the web of sanctions around the DPRK. The U.S. continues to work with a range of partners across the international community to improve implementation of UN Security Council sanctions, particularly those that target the illicit activities of the North's diplomatic personnel and cash couriers, its banking relationships, and its procurement of dual-use items for its WMD and missile programs.

Full and transparent implementation of these resolutions by all UN member states, including China, is critical, the U.S. insists. It is working closely with the UN Security Council's DPRK sanctions committee and its Panel of Experts, like-minded partners, and others around the globe to harmonize sanctions programs and to ensure the full and transparent implementation of UNSCRs 1718, 1874, 2087, and 2094, which remain the heart of the multilateral sanctions regime. As a result, there has been greater actions taken by Member States to prevent illicit North Korea trade in arms, WMD-related material and luxury goods, most notably with the seizure by Panama of a substantial amount of military gear on the North Korean ship Chong Chon Gang. The Panel's annual report documents in detail the numerous actions that States have taken to enforce UN sanctions and prevent further DPRK proliferation. It is clear that UN sanctions are having an effect and are diminishing North Korea's ability to profit from its illicit activities.

The United States has expanded outreach to countries that have diplomatic or trade relations with North Korea to press them not to engage in military, WMD or other illicit activities banned by UN resolutions and U.S sanctions. Burma's announcement that it would end its military relationship with North Korea and comply with the UN resolutions is the best example of these efforts, which will continue. It has also designated a number of key proliferators — and the banks and other front companies that support them — pursuant to U.S. domestic sanctions authorities. The United States will continue to take steps to strengthen and bolster the existing sanctions regime, both through work in the UN context and through our own national measures.

Deterrence

The U.S.-ROK alliance, having celebrated its 60th anniversary, is stronger than ever. From day-to-day combined efforts to maintain peace and stability on the Peninsula, though Combined Forces Command, to the counter-provocation and counter-missile planning the Department of Defense and Joint Staff colleagues engage in with their South Korean counterparts, all send a strong deterrence signal to North Korea that the security it is seeking is not to be found in nuclear weapons.

Growing U.S.-ROK-Japan trilateral security cooperation also sends a powerful message of deterrence to Pyongyang, as seen most recently in the trilateral Search and Rescue Exercises, Joint Chiefs of Defense meeting between Chairman Dempsey and his counterparts in Seoul and Tokyo, the trilateral defense ministerial talks led by Secretary Hagel at the Shangri La dialogue, and State Department discussions with Korean and Japan counterparts. Other measures taken in the region to strengthen bilateral and trilateral missile defense cooperation are also inextricably tied to the larger diplomatic strategy of building and maintaining a strong diplomatic consensus opposed to a nuclear North Korea.

Human Rights

While denuclearization remains an essential focus of U.S. policy, so too, is the welfare of North Korea's nearly 25 million people, the vast majority of whom bear the brunt of their government's decision to perpetuate an unsustainable, self-impoverishing, military-first policy. As the UN Commission of Inquiry concluded in its impressive and sobering final report published in February 2014, systematic, widespread, and gross human rights violations have been and are being committed by the DPRK, its institutions, and its officials.

The U.S. government is deeply concerned about the well-being of the people of North Korea and commends the non-governmental organizations and their staffs of skilled, tough-minded, and principled men and women who work with ordinary North Koreans at the grass-roots level to improve conditions for those who are not members of the elite, residing in relative comfort on Pyongyang, said Davies. These men and women work tirelessly to feed, care for, and otherwise help sustain the ninety percent of North Koreans left to their own devices by the regime.

UN's Office of the High Commissioner for Human Rights

In March 2013 the United Nations Human Rights Council (HRC) authorized the creation of a Commission of Inquiry (COI) to examine "grave, widespread, and systematic violations of human rights" in the DPRK. This resolution, which the United States co-sponsored, reflected the international community's deepened concern about the deplorable human rights situation in the DPRK.

The independent Commission of Inquiry was chaired by Mr. Michael Kirby, former Justice of the High Court of Australia, and included Mr. Marzuki Darusman, the UN Special Rapporteur on the Human Rights Situation in the DPRK and former Attorney General of the Republic of Indonesia, and Ms. Sonia Biserko, president of the Helsinki Committee for Human Rights in Serbia and a prominent human rights activist.

The Commission held a series of public hearings in Seoul, Tokyo, London, and Washington, where it heard from North Korean refugees sharing first-hand accounts of abuse and violence they suffered, and their horrific experiences leaving their homeland. The Commission also heard from leading international experts, who described deliberate denial of access to food, gender-based violence, and numerous other human rights violations in the prison camps. The full proceedings of these hearings have since been made available on the UN web site in video and in written transcript.

At the completion of its investigation, the Commission issued a final report on February 17 of this year that concluded that systematic, widespread, and gross human rights violations have been and are being committed by the DPRK, its institutions, and its officials. The report further concluded that in many cases, these human rights violations by the DPRK government and its officials may "meet the high threshold required for proof of crimes against humanity in international law." The Commission's comprehensive 400-page report is the most detailed and devastating exposé of DPRK human rights to date, and it laid bare a brutal reality that is difficult, if not impossible, to imagine.

The Commission formally presented its final report to the UN Human Rights Council in Geneva in March of this year. After hearing from the Commission, the UN Human Rights Council—by an overwhelming vote approved a strongly-worded resolution praising the report and calling for accountability for those responsible for human rights violations. This resolution made clear that the international community has identified the DPRK as one of the worst human rights violators in the world.

This resolution—among many other things—called for the creation of a field office, or a "field-based structure," under the Office of the High Commissioner for Human Rights (OHCHR) to preserve and document evidence of atrocities committed in the DPRK and to support the future work of the Special Rapporteur on DPRK human rights issues.

At the request of the High Commissioner's office, South Korea has agreed to host this field office which will play an important role in maintaining visibility and encouraging action on the human rights situation in the DPRK.

Building on the momentum created by the UN Commission of Inquiry's report, the United States joined Australia and France in convening the UN Security Council's first-ever discussion of the human rights situation in North Korea. At this session on April 17, the Commission presented its report, and two North Korean refugees, Mr. Shin Dong Hyuk and Ms. Hyeonseo Lee spoke of their personal experiences in the DPRK before they escaped. Thirteen of the 15 members of the Security Council attended that discussion.

Council members expressed grave concern about the horrific human rights violations and crimes against humanity outlined in the Commission of Inquiry report and urged the DPRK to comply with the report's recommendations and to engage with United Nations human rights agencies. Council members emphasized the importance of accountability for human rights violations, and many expressed support for Council consideration of the Commission of Inquiry's recommendation of referral of the situation in North Korea to the International Criminal Court (ICC). They expressed support for the UN Human Rights Council's decision to extend the mandate of the Special Rapporteur on human rights in the DPRK and to establish a field-based office to strengthen monitoring and documentation of human rights abuses to ensure accountability.

In May, the United States participated in the UN Human Rights Council's Universal Periodic Review (UPR) of North Korea. The UPR is a mechanism to assess each country's human rights record, and puts all UN member-countries on the agenda of the Council for review. The UPR process provides the international community with another tool to discuss the situation in the DPRK, as well as provide recommendations to address it. Most recently, on June 18, the Special Rapporteur on DPRK human rights, Mr. Marzuki Darusman, gave his report on the human rights situation to the UN Human Rights Council.

It is clear that the DPRK is feeling growing international pressure. The mounting criticism of its human rights record has clearly struck a chord in Pyongyang, which responded by condemning the Commission's report and issuing its own reports on human rights in the United States and the Republic of Korea. Second, with a growing number of countries standing up for North Korean human rights, the DPRK has very few supporters left. At the UN Human Rights Council session in June, only a handful of countries were supportive of the DPRK—most protested the singling out of one country and did not comment on the substance of the human rights violations. The countries who defended the DPRK were among the world's worst human rights violators—Belarus, Cuba, Iran, Syria, and Zimbabwe.

China's statement at the June session was especially noteworthy. China objected to country-specific reports in general, but mainly defended itself against the criticism in both the Commission's and the Special Rapporteur's report against its refoulement of refugees from the DPRK who were attempting to escape through Chinese territory. The Chinese did not defend the DPRK's human rights record.

When the Commission of Inquiry presented its report to the UN Human Rights Council, it also released a 20-minute documentary, highlighting testimony of North Korean defectors. Because North Korea is one of the most closed societies on this planet—where internet access is reserved for a very tiny elite—ordinary North Koreans had no way to see the documentary, let alone any independent news about the abuses taking place inside their own country today. While this information blockade makes it nearly impossible for North Koreans to read the Commission's report or watch the video, there have been some recent indications that information from outside is becoming more available in North Korea.

It is still illegal to own a tunable radio that permits anything other than state-controlled information channels. However, the latest Broadcasting Board of Governors (BBG) study, a survey of 350 North Korean refugees and travelers who were interviewed outside of North Korea, found that as many as 35 percent of them had listened to foreign radio broadcasts while inside North Korea. Foreign DVDs are now being seen by even larger numbers—approximately 85 percent of those interviewed had seen foreign (South Korean) DVDs in North Korea. Additionally, some two million cell phones now permit North Koreans to at least communicate with each other on a domestic network, according to open source reports.

Given the closed nature of North Korean society, international media are among the most effective means of sharing information about the outside world with residents of the country. The U.S. government is a strong supporter of getting broadcasting of independent information about the outside world into North Korea through Radio Free Asia (RFA) and Voice of America (VOA). These efforts are important in breaking down the information barrier that the DPRK government has imposed on its own people.

The U.S. and its partners in the international community are working together community to make it clear to the DPRK that its egregious human rights violations prevent economic progress and weaken the regime. The United States has long made clear that it is open to improved relations with

North Korea if it is willing to take concrete actions to live up to its international obligations and commitments.

Ironically on November 28 DPRK issued a statement criticizing human rights abuses in the U.S. The statement followed the mass protests in Ferguson and other U.S. cities following a grand jury's decision not to bring charges against a white police officer involved in the fatal shooting an unarmed black teenager. "This is a clear proof of the real picture of the United States as tundra of human rights where extreme racial discrimination acts are openly practiced. The wrongful U.S. standards on human rights have provoked concerns all over the international community, including its allies," said the official KCNA news agency.

Protecting American Citizens

In October North Korea suddenly and unexpectedly released American Jeffrey Fowle and on November 8, 2014 it released two other U.S. citizens—Kenneth Bae and Matthew Todd Miller. These were the last Americans known to be held in North Korea.

"It's a wonderful day for them and their families," President Obama said at The White House following the release of Bae and Miller. "Obviously we are very grateful for their safe return," he added, noting the "challenging mission."

The State Department also welcomed the release of the captives, saying it was grateful for the "tireless efforts" by Director of National Intelligence James Clapper and international partners, including Protecting Power and the Swedish government, according to a statement by State Department spokeswoman Jen Psaki.

Clapper, who traveled to North Korea as a presidential envoy and accompanied Miller and Bae home, is the highest-ranking U.S. official to visit the country.

Bae, a Korean-American missionary, had been held for two years while leading a tour group. He was accused of crimes against the state and sentenced to 15 years hard labor. He was moved to a hospital last year because of failing health. Miller had been held for seven months and was serving a six year sentence for espionage. Fowle, accused of the crime of leaving a bible in a club, had been held for six months and was released under a 'special dispensation' granted by Kim Jong Un.

The releases marked a slight thaw in North Korea-U.S. relations and may have been a signal that North Korea wanted to start talks again. However, the detention of any American remains a source of deep concern for the State Department.

One of its highest priorities is the welfare and safety of American citizens abroad. North Korea will be judged not by its words but by its actions. It needs to refrain from actions that threaten the peace and stability of the Korean Peninsula and comply with its international obligations under UN Security Council resolutions to abandon all nuclear weapons and nuclear programs, among other things.

The U.S. has consistently told the DPRK that while the United States remains open to meaningful engagement, North Korea must take concrete steps to address the core concerns of the international community, from the DPRK's nuclear program to its human rights violations. Just as importantly, North Korea will also have to address its egregious human rights record. North Korea's choice is clear. Investment in its people, respect for human rights, and concrete steps toward denuclearization can lead to a path of peace, prosperity, and improved relations with the international community, including the United States. Absent these measures, North Korea will only continue to face greater and greater isolation—as well as pressure from the international community.

The State Department makes clear in its DPRK travel warning that foreign visitors may be arrested, detained, or expelled for activities that would not be considered criminal outside North Korea. The list of serious transgressions is long. It includes involvement in religious or political activities unsanctioned by the DPRK regime, unauthorized travel, and unauthorized interaction with the local population. Given the serious risks involved, it strongly recommends against all travel by U.S. citizens to North Korea.

Despite the risks, a number of tour operators—mainly run out of Beijing by Westerners—organize highly-regimented trips to North Korea, principally to Pyongyang. The State Department has warned that these tour operators cannot protect American citizens and urged all U.S. citizens contemplating travel to North Korea to understand the consequences of their decision.

The State Department's ongoing policy is to bring the DPRK to the realization that it must take the steps necessary to end its isolation, respect the human rights of its own people, honor its past commitments, and comply with its international obligations. Each outrageous act North Korea commits, discredits the DPRK's self-serving assertion that it is driven to act belligerently by others' hostility. It is increasingly clear that North Korea is developing nuclear weapons and intercontinental ballistic missiles to prolong the Kim regime and obtain material and political benefits from the international community. By creating a strategic challenge to the United States, the DPRK hopes to strengthen its narrative that the U.S. is responsible for North Korea's bad behavior and uniquely on the hook to mitigate it. It is not. North Korea is responsible for North Korean actions, and resolving the DPRK nuclear problem is a multilateral task, just as the DPRK's original aggression against the South was met with a strong response from the United Nations. Standing up to North Korea requires a sustained and concerted effort by all of the countries in the Six-Party process, and indeed the entire international community.

The DPRK leadership in Pyongyang faces ever-sharper choices. North Korea will not achieve security, economic prosperity, and integration into the international community while pursuing nuclear weapons, threatening its neighbors, trampling on international norms, abusing its own people, and refusing to fulfill its longstanding obligations and commitments.

9

Iran and Iraq

Iran

Known as Persia until 1935, Iran became an Islamic republic in 1979 after the ruling monarchy was overthrown and Shah Mohammad Reza Pahlavi was forced into exile. Conservative clerical forces led by Ayatollah Ruhollah Khomeini established a theocratic system of government with ultimate political authority vested in a learned religious scholar referred to commonly as the Supreme Leader who, according to the constitution, is accountable only to the Assembly of Experts - a popularly elected 86-member body of clerics.

US-Iranian relations became strained when a group of Iranian students seized the U.S. Embassy in Tehran in November 1979 and held embassy personnel hostages until mid-January 1981. The U.S. cut off diplomatic relations with Iran in April 1980. During the period 1980-88, Iran fought a bloody, indecisive war with Iraq that eventually expanded into the Persian Gulf and led to clashes between U.S. Navy and Iranian military forces. Iran has been designated a state sponsor of terrorism for its activities in Lebanon and elsewhere in the world and remains subject to U.S., UN, and EU economic sanctions and export controls because of its continued involvement in terrorism and concerns over possible military dimensions of its nuclear program.

Following the election of reformer Hojjat ol-Eslam Mohammad Khatami as president in 1997 and a reformist Majles (legislature) in 2000, a campaign to foster political reform in response to popular dissatisfaction was initiated. The movement floundered as conservative politicians, supported by the Supreme Leader, unelected institutions of authority like the Council of Guardians, and the security services reversed and blocked reform measures while increasing security repression. Starting with nationwide municipal elections in 2003 and continuing through Majles elections in 2004, conservatives reestablished control over Iran's elected government institutions, which culminated with the August 2005 inauguration of hardliner Mahmud Ahmadinejad as president. His controversial reelection in June 2009 sparked nationwide protests over allegations of electoral fraud. These protests were quickly suppressed, and the political opposition that arouse as a consequence of Ahmadinejad's election was repressed.

Deteriorating economic conditions due primarily to government mismanagement and international sanctions prompted at least two major economically based protests in July and October 2012, but Iran's internal security situation remained stable. President Ahmadinejad's independent streak angered regime establishment figures, including the Supreme Leader, leading to conservative opposition to his agenda for the last year of his presidency, and an alienation of his political supporters. In June 2013 Iranians elected a moderate conservative cleric, Dr. Hasan Fereidun Ruhani to the presidency. He is a long-time senior member in the regime, but has made promises of reforming society and Iran's foreign policy.

Nuclear Program

The UN Security Council has passed a number of resolutions calling for Iran to suspend its uranium enrichment and reprocessing activities and comply with its IAEA obligations and responsibilities, but in November 2013 the five permanent members, plus Germany, (P5+1) signed a joint plan with Iran to provide the country with incremental relief from international pressure for positive steps toward transparency of their nuclear program.

In response to Iran's continued illicit nuclear activities, the United States and other countries have imposed unprecedented sanctions to censure Iran and prevent its further progress in prohibited nuclear activities, as well as to persuade Tehran to address the international community's concerns about its nuclear program. Acting both through the United Nations Security Council and regional or national authorities, the United States, the member states of the European Union, Japan, the Republic of Korea, Canada, Australia, Norway, Switzerland, and others have put in place a strong, inter-locking matrix of sanctions measures relating to Iran's nuclear, missile, energy, shipping, transportation, and financial sectors.

These measures are designed: (1) to block the transfer of weapons, components, technology, and dual-use items to Iran's prohibited nuclear and missile programs; (2) to target select sectors of the Iranian economy relevant to its proliferation activities; and (3) to induce Iran to engage constructively, through discussions with the United States, China, France, Germany, the United Kingdom, and Russia in the "E3+3 process," to fulfill its nonproliferation obligations. These nations have made clear that Iran's full compliance with its international nuclear obligations would open the door to its receiving treatment as a normal non-nuclear-weapon state under The Nonproliferation Treaty and sanctions being lifted.

The United States has imposed restrictions on activities with Iran under various legal authorities since 1979, following the seizure of the U.S. Embassy in Tehran. The most recent statute, the Iran Threat Reduction and Syria Human Rights Act (ITRSHRA), added new measures and procedures to the 1996 Iran Sanctions Act (ISA). The ISA authorizes sanctions on businesses or individuals engaging in certain commercial transactions in Iran.

The Department of State's Office of Economic Sanctions Policy and Implementation is responsible for enforcing and implementing a number of U.S. sanctions programs that restrict access to the United States for companies that engage in certain commercial activities in Iran, in particular the Iran Sanctions Act (ISA), the Comprehensive Iran Sanctions, Accountability, and Divestment Act (CISADA), Iran Threat Reduction and Syria Human Rights Act (ITRSHRA), Executive Order 13590, and Executive Order 13622.

The U.S. Government, through executive orders issued by the President as well as congressional legislation, prohibits nearly all trade and investment with Iran by U.S. persons, but maintains broad authorizations and exceptions that allow for the sale of food, medicine, and medical devices by U.S. persons or from the United States to Iran. Sanctions have been imposed on Iran because of its sponsorship of terrorism, its refusal to comply with international obligations on its nuclear program, and its human rights violations.

The Department of Treasury also plays a primary role in enforcing sanctions against Iran.

On November 24, 2014 it was agreed that theP5+1 talks in Vienna over Iran's nuclear program should be extended for seven months as there had been "real and substantial progress" with new ideas brought to the table.

Speaking in Vienna after the decision to extend the talks, Secretary Kerry said:

> I want to thank the United Nations and my colleagues from the United Kingdom, Germany, France, Russia, China, and the EU, and especially my good friend Baroness Cathy Ashton, whose partnership has been absolutely invaluable throughout this process and who has done a terrific job of helping to bring people together and define the process. I also want to take this opportunity to thank Foreign Minister Javad Zarif. The Iranian foreign minister has worked hard and he has worked diligently. He has approached to these negotiations in good faith and with seriousness of purpose, and that's what it takes to try to resolve the kind of difficult issues here.
>
> Now we have worked long and hard not just over these past days but for months in order to achieve a comprehensive agreement that addresses international concerns about Iran's nuclear program. This takes time. The stakes are high and the issues are complicated and technical, and each decision affects other decisions. There's always an interrelationship, and each decision also deeply affects international security and national interests.
>
> It also takes time to do this because we don't want just any agreement. We want the right agreement. Time and again, from the day that he took office,

President Obama has been crystal clear that we must ensure that Iran does not acquire a nuclear weapon, period. And this is not specific to one country; it's the policy of many countries in the world to reduce the numbers of nuclear weapons that exist today and not to allow new ones. And we are engaged in that struggle in many places. And the fact is that even Russia and the United States, who have the largest number, are working hard to reduce that number and to reduce the potential of fissionable nuclear material being available to any additional entity in the world.

President Obama has been just as clear that the best way to do this is through diplomacy, through a comprehensive and durable agreement that all parties can agree to, that all parties are committed to upholding, and whose implementation is not based on trust but on intensive verification. And that is not just because diplomacy is the preferred course; it is also the most effective course.

Diplomacy is also difficult. These talks aren't going to suddenly get easier just because we extend them. They're tough and they've been tough and they're going to stay tough. If it were easier, if views on both sides weren't as deeply held as they are, then we'd have reached a final agreement months or even years ago. But in these last days in Vienna, we have made real and substantial progress, and we have seen new ideas surface. And that is why we are jointly – the P5+1, six nations and Iran – extending these talks for seven months with the very specific goal of finishing the political agreement within four months and with the understanding that we will go to work immediately, meet again very shortly. And if we can do it sooner, we want to do it sooner.

At the end of four months, we have not agreed on the major – if we have not agreed on the major elements by that point in time and there is no clear path, we can revisit how we then want to choose to proceed.

Now we believe a comprehensive deal that addresses the world's concerns is possible. It is desirable. And at this point, we have developed a clearer understanding of what that kind of deal could look like, but there are still some significant points of disagreement, and they have to be worked through.

Now I want to underscore that even as the negotiations continue towards a comprehensive deal, the world is safer than it was just one year ago. It is safer than we were before we agreed on the Joint Plan of Action, which was the interim agreement.

One year ago, Iran's nuclear program was rushing full speed toward larger stockpiles, greater uranium enrichment capacity, the production of weapons-grade plutonium, and ever shorter breakout time. Today, Iran has halted progress on its nuclear program and it has rolled it back for the first time in a decade.

A year ago, Iran had about 200 kilograms of 20 percent enriched uranium in a form that could be quickly enriched into a weapons-grade level. Today, Iran has no such 20 percent enriched uranium – zero, none – and they have diluted or converted every ounce that they had and suspended all uranium enrichment above 5 percent.

A year ago, Iran was making steady progress on the Arak reactor, which, if it had become operational, would have provided Iran with a plutonium path to a nuclear weapon. Today, progress on Arak, as it is known, is frozen in place.

A year ago, inspectors had limited access to Iran's nuclear program. Today, IAEA inspectors have daily access to Iran's enrichment facilities and a far deeper understanding of Iran's program. They have been able to learn things about Iran's centrifuge production, uranium mines, and other facilities that are important to building trust. That's how you build trust, and that's why Iran made the decision to do it. And they've been able to verify that Iran is indeed living up to its JPOA commitments.

All of these steps by Iran and the limited sanctions relief that the international community provided in return are important building blocks to lay the foundation for a comprehensive agreement and they begin to build confidence among nations.

A year ago, we had no idea whether or not real progress could be made through these talks. We only knew that we had a responsibility to try. Today, we are closer to a deal that would make the entire world, especially our allies and partners in Israel and in the Gulf, safer and more secure.

Is it possible that in the end we just won't arrive at a workable agreement? Absolutely. We are certainly not going to sit at the negotiating table forever, absent measurable progress. But given how far we have come over the past year and particularly in the last few days, this is not certainly the time to get up and walk away. These issues are enormously complex. They require a lot of tough political decisions and they require very rigorous technical analysis of concepts. It takes time to work through the possible solutions that can effectively accomplish our goals and that give the leaders of all countries confidence in the decisions that they are being asked to make.

So our experts will meet again very soon. In fact, we will have a meeting in December as soon as possible in order to continue this work and to drive this process as hard as we can. And as the parties continue to negotiate, all of the current restraints on the nuclear program in Iran will remain in place.

Now, let me make it clear: Our goal in these negotiations is not a mystery. It is not a political goal. It is not an ideological goal. It is a practical goal, a goal of common sense, and it is achievable. The United States and our EU and P5+1 partners – the UK, France, Germany, Russia, and China, a group of nations that doesn't always see eye to eye – agree unanimously about what a viable agreement would need to look like.

First and foremost, the viable agreement would have to close off all of the pathways for Iran to get fissile material for a nuclear weapon. A viable agreement would have to include a new level of transparency and verification beyond the expanded access that we've had under the JPOA. And as these conditions are met, a viable agreement would also include for Iran relief from the international nuclear-related sanctions that help to bring them to the table to negotiate in the first place.

And because of the nature of these talks, we should not – and I emphasize we will not – in the days ahead discuss the details of the negotiations. And we're doing that simply to preserve the space to be able to make the choices that lie ahead. But I can tell you that progress was indeed made on some of the most vexing challenges that we face, and we now see the path toward potentially resolving some issues that have been intractable.

I want to also emphasize: This agreement, like any agreement, regarding security particularly, cannot be based on trust because trust can't be built overnight. Instead, the agreement has to be based on verification, on measures that serve to build confidence over time. And I want to make it even further clear to everybody here we really want this to work – but not at the cost of just anything. We want to reach a comprehensive deal and we want it to work for everybody. And we want the people of Iran to get the economic relief that they seek and to be able to rejoin the international community.

We want to terminate the sanctions. Yes, we want to terminate the sanctions which were put in place to get us to these negotiations and ultimately to be able to bring about a deal. But the world – and I underscore this – not just the United States, not just the P5+1 – the world still has serious questions about Iran's nuclear program. And for the sanctions to be terminated, we need Iran to take concrete, verifiable steps to answer those questions. That's the bottom line.

And for my friends in the United States Congress, with whom I spent almost 30 years in the United States Senate, I would say that together, we have been through some tough policy deliberations. I had the responsibility of chairing the Foreign Relations Committee when we put the sanctions regime in place that has helped us get this far. I believe in the institution and the critical role that the Senate has to play, and the House. We have stayed in close consultation throughout this process, and we will continue to do so. And we look for your support for this extension and for continued talks.

And I would say to those who are skeptical, those who wonder whether we should rush ahead down a different course, I believe the United States and our partners have earned the benefit of the doubt at this point. Many were quick to say that the Joint Plan of Action would be violated; it wouldn't hold up, it would be shredded. Many said that Iran would not hold up its end of the bargain. Many said that the sanctions regime would collapse. But guess what? The interim agreement wasn't violated. Iran has held up its end of the bargain, and the sanctions regime has remained intact.

My friends, we have the time in the next weeks and months to try and get this right. And because of that, we should continue to exercise the judgment and the patience to defend our interests, uphold our core principles, maintain our sense of urgency that this issue deserves, and keep open the road to a peaceful resolution. That's what we decided to do here today. I am convinced it is the right decision, made on the basis of what we have done over the course of these last days, and on the prospects of what we could achieve if we can reach a comprehensive agreement.

Israel and Iran

The Iran nation has never recognized Israel and it "will never ever recognize it", President Ahmadinejad said in July 2008. In August 2012 Ayatollah Ahmad Khatami called for "annihilation of the Zionist regime."

As a result, Israel has vowed to do everything possible to sabotage Iran's nuclear program. While Iran insists the program is for purely peaceful purposes, the Israeli's and the U.S. believe the real motive is to develop nuclear weapons which would change the balance of power in the Middle East and beyond.

In November 2003 Israeli defence minister Shaul Mofaz said,"Under no circumstances would Israel be able to tolerate nuclear weapons in Iranian possession." In 2005 it was claimed that Israeli Prime Minister Ariel Sharon had ordered plans to be drawn up to attack uranium enrichment plants in Iran. He said, "Israel - and not only Israel - cannot accept a nuclear Iran. We have the ability to deal with this and we're making all the necessary preparations to be ready for such a situation."

Israel has repeatedly said it is prepared to take unilateral action to destroy Iran's nuclear program while Iran in turn, continues to supply Israel's enemies and advocates the complete destruction of Israel.

On 22 September 2012, General Mohammad Ali Jafari, the commander of the Iranian Revolutionary Guards, said that a war with Israel would soon break out, during which Iran would eradicate Israel, which he referred to as a "cancerous tumor."

Iran openly supports Israel's arch enemy Hezbollah in Lebanon and during the 2006 war between Lebanon and Israel Iran's elite Revolutionary Guards fought alongside Hezbollah fighters in Lebanon and assisted them in firing rockets into Israel. The Israeli air force has carried out several attacks on Iranian arms shipments being smuggled to Hamas and Hezbollah, both designated terrorist groups, via road and sea and Israel is also thought to be behind a wave of assassinations that targeted Iranian nuclear scientists in 2010.

In June 2010 Iran's nuclear program was hit by a computer worm called Stuxnet which had been developed in the U.S. and Israel. It is estimated that as many as 1,000 centrifuges were damaged after being affected by the worm in the Natanz enrichment plant

Iraq

Formerly part of the Ottoman Empire, Iraq was occupied by Britain during the course of World War I; in 1920, it was declared a League of Nations mandate under UK administration. In stages over the next dozen years, Iraq attained its independence as a kingdom in 1932.

A "republic" was proclaimed in 1958, but in actuality a series of strongmen ruled the country until 2003. The last was Saddam Husain. Territorial disputes with Iran led to an inconclusive and costly eight-year war (1980-88). In August 1990, Iraq seized Kuwait but was expelled by U.S.-led, UN coalition forces during the Gulf War of January-February 1991. Following Kuwait's liberation, the UN Security Council (UNSC) required Iraq to scrap all weapons of mass destruction and long-range missiles and to allow UN verification inspections. Continued Iraqi noncompliance with UNSC resolutions over a period of 12 years led to the U.S.-led invasion of Iraq in March 2003 and the ouster of the Saddam Husain regime. U.S. forces remained in Iraq under a UNSC mandate through 2009 and under a bilateral security agreement thereafter, helping to provide security and to train and mentor Iraqi security forces.

In October 2005, Iraqis approved a constitution in a national referendum and, pursuant to this document, elected a 275-member Council of Representatives (COR) in December 2005. The COR approved most cabinet ministers in May 2006, marking the transition to Iraq's first constitutional government in nearly a half century. In January 2009 and April 2013, Iraq held elections for provincial councils in all governorates except for the three governorates comprising the Kurdistan Regional Government and Kirkuk Governorate. Iraq held a national legislative election in March 2010 - choosing 325 legislators in an expanded COR - and, after nine months of deadlock the COR approved the new government in December 2010. Nearly nine years after the start of the Second Gulf War in Iraq, U.S. military operations there ended in mid-December 2011.

Since then Iraq began to move closer politically to Iran with the Shiites in central control and the Sunnis largely ignored by the government. That led to resentment which allowed al Qa'ida to establish itself again in Sunni areas. Backed by wealthy supporters in Kuwait, Saudi Arabia and other Gulf States, al Qa'ida and then ISIS was able to establish bases then take over large tracts of land including major cities before spreading into Syria.

In September 2014 Iraqi lawmakers approved a new government with Haider al-Abadi named Prime Minister and former Prime Minister Nuri al-Maliki named one of the three vice presidents. The new government, formed after intensive pressure from the U.S. does attempt to represent Sunni, Shiite and Kurdish factions. Secretary Kerry described the new government as "unquestionably a major milestone. It has the potential to unite all of Iraq's diverse communities."

Attempting to accommodate all three communities, reconciling the considerable differences between them and at the same time, fighting the ISIS insurgency will be a massive task.

U.S. Reconstruction in Iraq

The U.S. has to date spent more than $60.45 billion on reconstructing Iraq. Of this amount up to $8 billion cannot be accounted for but is thought to have been stolen or corruptly obtained. According to the Special Inspector General for Iraq Construction, reconstruction efforts have been plagued by "poor management, mishandling of reconstruction funds, inadequate coordination with Iraqis and widespread attacks on construction sites and contractors."

10

Embassy Protection

Embassies and consulates serve as the front door for U.S. diplomacy. The safety and security they provide to our personnel are the first priority, but they must also reflect our national values of openness and ingenuity. In addition, embassies and consulates must exemplify the best of American architecture, environmental stewardship, and innovation. Championing excellent design and efficient technologies benefits both the American taxpayer and those overseas we seek to serve.

—Secretary Kerry, November 2013

The U.S. has almost 300 embassies, consulates and diplomatic missions worldwide. They serve several purposes. They are able to establish close relations with the host country and further diplomatic, commercial, economic and even military ties. They serve as a flagship of America's global influence and reach and they offer services and support to U.S. citizens, both business and tourist, visiting that country.

The downside to this is that U.S. embassies and other institutions can become ready targets for attack if relations between the U.S. and the host country deteriorate i.e. the Iran hostage crisis in 1979 and the Benghazi crisis 2012 (see below). Embassies can also be attacked by terrorist groups seeking symbolic targets even if those groups are not associated with the host country.

As a result security is of critical importance. In September 2014, President Obama directed all U.S. diplomatic posts to review their security "to protect American personnel, facilities and interests, including those of private citizens and businesses."

Benghazi Attack

On the evening of September 11, 2012 Islamic militants attacked the American diplomatic compound in Benghazi, Libya, killing U.S. Ambassador J. Christopher Stevens and U.S. Foreign Service Information Management Officer Sean Smith. Stevens was the first U.S. Ambassador killed on duty since 1979. A second CIA compound about a mile away was then targeted resulting in the deaths of two CIA contractors, Glen Doherty and Tyrone Woods, both former Navy SEALS, with ten others injured.

The attacks led to an immediate tightening of security at U.S. embassies, consulates and military facilities worldwide and demands for an inquiry at home.

The State Department was criticized for not providing additional security before the attack and afterwards for issuing incorrect statements about the reasons for it. It was first reported that the attacks were the result of a "spontaneous protest" to an anti-Muslim 14-miinute video that had been uploaded to YouTube.

In his press briefing on September 14, White House Press Secretary Jay Carney told reporters that "we don't have and did not have concrete evidence to suggest that this [the Benghazi attack] was not in reaction to the film."

"There was no intelligence that in any way could have been acted on to prevent these attacks. He said that a report that "suggested that there was intelligence that was available prior to this that led us to believe that this facility would be attacked, is false. We have no information to suggest that it was a preplanned attack. The unrest we've seen around the region has been in reaction to a video that Muslims, many Muslims find offensive. And while the violence is reprehensible and unjustified, it is not a reaction to the 9/11 anniversary that we know of, or to U.S. policy."

On September 16, the U.S. Ambassador to the U.N. Susan Rice appeared on five major interview shows to discuss the attacks. Prior to her appearance, Rice was provided with "talking points" from a CIA memo, which stated:

> The currently available information suggests that the demonstrations in Benghazi were spontaneously inspired by the protests at the U.S. Embassy in Cairo and evolved into a direct assault against the U.S. diplomatic post in Benghazi and subsequently its annex. There are indications that extremists participated in the violent demonstrations.
>
> This assessment may change as additional information is collected and analyzed and as currently available information continues to be evaluated. The investigation is ongoing, and the U.S. government is working with Libyan authorities to bring to justice those responsible for the deaths of U.S. citizens.

Relying on these talking points, Rice stated:

> Based on the best information we have to date, what our assessment is as of the present is in fact what began spontaneously in Benghazi as a reaction to what had transpired some hours earlier in Cairo where, of course, as you know, there was a violent protest outside of our embassy—sparked by this hateful video. But soon after that spontaneous protest began outside of our consulate in Benghazi, we believe that it looks like extremist elements, individuals, joined in that-- in that effort with heavy weapons of the sort that are, unfortunately, readily now available in Libya post-revolution. And that it spun from there into something much, much more violent."
>
> We do not—we do not have information at present that leads us to conclude that this was premeditated or preplanned. I think it's clear that there were extremist elements that joined in and escalated the violence. Whether they were al Qaeda affiliates, whether they were Libyan-based extremists or al Qaeda itself I think is one of the things we'll have to determine.

It later became known that the attacks had been premeditated and were carried out by Ansar al-Sharia, listed by the U.S. State Department as a terror organization. The U.S. government in later statements acknowledged that Benghazi had been a premeditated terrorist attack but the initial confusion was enough to get many leading Republicans to talk about a cover-up and demand investigations.

Since then there have been investigations into the attack carried out by the Federal Bureau of Investigations, Senate Select Committee on Intelligence and Five House Committees – Armed Services Foreign Affairs, Intelligence, Judiciary and Oversight ad Government Reform.

The State Department's Accountability Review Board which reported in December, 2012, did criticize State Department officials for ignoring requests for more security and safety upgrades and for failing to adapt security procedures to a deteriorating security environment.

"Systemic failures and leadership and management deficiencies at senior levels within two bureaus of the State Department ... resulted in a special mission security posture that was inadequate for Benghazi and grossly inadequate to deal with the attack that took place," said the unclassified version of the report

The House Intelligence Committee report, released on November 21, 2014, concluded "there was no deliberate wrongdoing by the Obama administration in the 2012 attack on the U.S. Consulate in Benghazi, Libya, and that news briefing given by the administration reflected the conflicting intelligence assessments in the days immediately following the crisis."

Not content with the reports, Republicans in the House announced a new special committee on Benghazi under the chair of Rep. Trey Gowdy, with its first public hearings in December. Gowdy promised a "robust investigative plan" while Democrats and the President attacked the committee as a political stunt.

Buildings

Located within the Department of State, the Bureau of Overseas Buildings Operations (OBO) is responsible for the buildings that house America's overseas embassies, consulates and missions. OBO conducts much of its work using domestic contractors who handle the building of new embassies. Since the 1998 bombings of American embassies in east Africa, the federal government has conducted the largest construction effort in US diplomatic history to upgrade diplomatic posts and secure them against terrorist attacks. Problems have arisen, however, in the course of several high-profile embassy projects, including the sprawling new complex in Baghdad, Iraq.

Over the past 30 years, American diplomatic outposts have been at the center of some major events in American foreign relations. On November 4, 1979, Iranian militants stormed the United States Embassy in Tehran and took approximately 70 Americans captive. The terrorist act triggered the most profound crisis of the Jimmy Carter presidency, contributing greatly to his only serving one term in the White House.

In 1982 the US State Department found itself embarrassed by revelations that a significant portion of its brand new, half-completed embassy in Moscow was filled with eavesdropping equipment planted by Soviet spies, rendering the facility useless (it was subsequently torn down and rebuilt).

The following year terrorists destroyed the U.S. embassy in Beirut, Lebanon, by exploding a van carrying 2,000-pounds of explosives outside the seven-story building. The bombing killed 63, including 17 Americans.

In August 1998, an even greater attack on U.S. embassies took place in Kenya and Tanzania as twin car-bombings killed 224 people including 43 State Department employees. The attacks in east Africa prompted the federal government to reevaluate the security of its diplomatic outposts by convening a group of experts, the Overseas Presence Advisory Panel, which issued its report in 1999. The findings of the "America's Overseas Presence in the 21st Century" led to an unprecedented building program to fortify US diplomatic outposts throughout the world.

After assessing the state of US diplomatic facilities overseas, the State Department determined that more than 85% of embassies, missions and consulates did not meet security standards and were vulnerable to terrorist attacks. This prompted the implementation of a $21 billion program to replace 201 insecure and dilapidated diplomatic buildings.

Up until 2009 the State Department had a Standard Embassy Design (SED) for all diplomatic buildings anywhere in the world. The SED laid out the process to plan, design, and construct new embassy compounds. It consisted of a series of documents, including site and building plans, specifications, design criteria, an application manual describing its adaptation for a specific project, and contract requirements. The aim of the SED was to speed up construction and reduce the cost and enable the State Department to provide new facilities to greater number of diplomatic posts in a shorter period of time.

Since then the OBO had adopted new design criteria. The building must still provide safe, secure and functional facilities that represent the U.S. government to the host nation and support the staff in the achievement of U.S. foreign policy objections. The facilities now also must represent American values and the best in American architecture, design, engineering, technology, sustainability, art, culture and construction execution.

The new, sprawling self-sufficient embassy in Baghdad is the largest of its kind in the world – a complex of 21 buildings on 104 acres – employing some 5,500 Americans and Iraqis. The cost is estimated at $1 billion.

Staff

The Chief of Mission (COM) is responsible for developing and implementing security policies and programs that provide for the protection of all U.S. Government personnel (including accompanying dependents) on official duty abroad. This mission is executed through the Bureau of Diplomatic Security (DS). Personal and facility protection are the most critical elements of the DS mission abroad as they directly impact upon the Department's ability to carry out its foreign policy. With terrorist organizations and coalitions operating across international borders, the threat of terrorism against U.S. interests remains great. Therefore, any U.S. mission overseas can be a target even if identified as being in a low-threat environment.

As a result, DS is more dedicated than ever to its mission of providing a secure living and working environment for our Foreign Service colleagues as they implement foreign policy and promote U.S. interests around the world. Nearly 800 DS special agents serve in regional security offices at over 250 posts worldwide. The DS special agents, also called regional security officers (RSOs) when serving abroad, manage security programs and also provide the first line of defense for our personnel, their families, U.S. diplomatic missions, and national security information. RSOs serve as the primary advisor to the COM on all security matters by developing and implementing security programs that shield U.S. missions and residences overseas from physical and technical attack.

RSOs, in concert with other U.S. Government agencies represented at post, formulate plans to deal with various emergency contingencies, including defining emergency management responsibilities for incidents ranging from hostage taking to evacuations. Often, in times of crisis and political instability, RSOs rely on the U.S. military for assistance. Unified commands have the capability to supply post with combat-equipped troops, e.g., Fleet Anti-Terrorism Security Teams (FAST), to augment post security requirements.

RSOs are the primary liaison with foreign police and security services overseas in support of U.S. law enforcement initiatives and investigations. Much of the investigative and law enforcement liaison work accomplished by RSOs abroad is on behalf of other federal, state, and local agencies. DS has achieved noteworthy success in locating and apprehending hundreds of wanted fugitives who have fled the United States.

RSOs also provide unclassified security briefings and other professional security advice to U.S. businesses, academia, faith-based groups, and nongovernmental organizations as part of the Overseas Security Advisory Council (OSAC) Country Program, which has as its primary goal an effective security communication network.

RSOs face a tremendous challenge in implementing a mission's security program, and it cannot be handled alone. In the challenge to safeguard our personnel and sensitive information overseas, DS security engineering officers (SEOs) augment the efforts of the security office. SEOs are the primary developers and implementers of technical security policy and regulations. They design or develop, implement, and manage security equipment programs at our missions abroad. In a constantly evolving technical environment, SEOs are responsible for detecting and preventing loss of sensitive information from technical espionage.

In addition to SEOs, RSOs depend upon Marine Security Guards, U.S. Navy Seabees, surveillance detection teams, local guards, cleared American guards, local investigators, host government officials, and other DS elements domestically and abroad to provide assistance in combating criminal, intelligence, and terrorist threats against U.S. interests worldwide. These entities play a crucial role in the DS security efforts overseas.

At the highest threat posts, RSOs may often require further security assistance. In those instances, DS dispatches Mobile Security Teams from Washington to conduct training for embassy personnel, their dependents, and local guards in protective tactics such as attack recognition, self-defense, hostage survival, and defensive driving. These teams also provide emergency security support to overseas posts, including protective security for COMs, surveillance detection operations, and assistance with post evacuations. In cases where the host country is either unable or unwilling to provide necessary security for the conduct of American diplomacy, specially trained DS special agents lead contractor-provided personal protection teams and guard services in areas of ongoing conflict.

Following the bombings of the U.S. Embassies in Dar es Salaam (Tanzania) and Nairobi (Kenya) in 1998, security countermeasures for our U.S. missions overseas took on greater importance, and this continues today.

International Travel and Health

A major duty of U.S. Embassies and consulates is to assist citizens who become seriously ill or injured abroad. Consular officers from the U.S. embassy or consulate can assist in locating appropriate medical services and informing family or friends. If necessary, a consular officer can also assist in the transfer of funds from the United States. However, payment of hospital and other expenses is the patient's responsibility.

Another duty of the State Department is to issue travel warnings and alerts. Travel Warnings are issued when the State Department wants you to consider very carefully whether you should go to a country at all. Examples of reasons for issuing a Travel Warning might include unstable government, civil war, ongoing intense crime or violence, or frequent terrorist attacks. The State Department wants you to know the risks of traveling to these places and to strongly consider not going to them at all. Travel Warnings remain in place until the situation changes; some have been in effect for years.

Travel alerts are generally for short-term events you should know about when planning travel to a country. Examples of reasons for issuing a Travel Alert might include an election season that is bound to have many strikes, demonstrations, or disturbances; a health alert like an outbreak of H1N1; or evidence of an elevated risk of terrorist attacks. When these short-term events are over, the Travel Alert is cancelled.

Ebola

The Ebola outbreak in West Africa is an example of how the State Department and other agencies work together to protect U.S. citizens traveling to and from high risk areas. In the case of Ebola it was necessary to implement additional protection for travelers entering the United States after visiting these affected areas.

The Department of State has issued a Travel Alert for parts of West Africa because of Ebola Virus Disease (EVD).

The Department of Homeland Security requires that all persons traveling to the United States from the West African countries of Liberia, Sierra Leone, Guinea, and Mali must enter the U.S. through New York's Kennedy, Newark's Liberty, Washington's Dulles, Chicago's O'Hare, and Atlanta's Hartsfield-Jackson airports and undergo EVD screening.

Passengers traveling from Liberia, Sierra Leone, Guinea, and Mali who were not originally passing through one of these airports must rebook their flights to make entry through one of the listed airports.

Due to an outbreak of EVD in Liberia, Sierra Leone, and Guinea, the Centers for Disease Control and Prevention (CDC) issued Level 3 Travel Warnings for those three countries advising against non-essential travel and provided guidance to reduce the potential for spread of EVD. The CDC Level 2 Travel Alert for Nigeria was removed because Nigeria has been declared Ebola free.

The World Health Organization (WHO) and CDC have also published and provided interim guidance to public health authorities, airlines, and other partners in West Africa for evaluating risk of exposure of persons coming from countries affected by EVD. Measures can include screening, medical evaluation, movement restrictions up to 21 days, and infection control precautions. Travelers who exhibit symptoms indicative of possible Ebola infection may be prevented from boarding and restricted from traveling for the 21-day period. Please note neither the Department of State's Bureau of Consular Affairs nor the U.S. Embassy have authority over quarantine issues and cannot prevent a U.S. citizen from being quarantined should local health authorities require it. For questions about quarantine, please visit the CDC website that addresses quarantine and isolation issues.

The cost for a medical evacuation is very expensive. The State department encourages U.S. citizens travelling to Ebola-affected countries to purchase travel insurance that includes medical evacuation for EVD. Policy holders should confirm the availability of medical care and evacuation services at their travel destinations prior to travel.

Some local, regional, and international air carriers have curtailed or temporarily suspended service to or from Ebola-affected countries. U.S. citizens planning travel to or from these countries, in accordance with the CDC Health Travel Warnings and Health Travel Alert, should contact their airline to verify seat availability, confirm departure schedules, inquire about screening procedures, and be aware of other airline options.

The Department is aware that some countries have put in place procedures relating to the travel of individuals from the affected countries, including complete travel bans. Changes to existing procedures may occur with little or no notice. Please consult your airline or the embassy of your destination country for additional information.

The State Department strongly recommends that U.S. citizens traveling or residing abroad enroll in the Department of State's Smart Traveler Enrollment Program (STEP). STEP enrollment allows you to receive the Department's safety and security updates, and makes it easier for the nearest U.S. embassy or U.S. consulate to contact you in an emergency. If you do not have Internet access, enroll directly with the nearest U.S. embassy or consulate.

The CDC has provided interim guidance to public health authorities, airlines, and other partners for evaluating risk of exposure of persons coming from countries affected by Ebola. Neither the Bureau of Consular Affairs nor the Embassy deals with quarantine issues and cannot prevent a U.S. citizen from being quarantined should local health authorities require it.

Handling Emergencies

Lost or Stolen Passport

You will have to replace the passport before returning to the United States. Contact the nearest U.S. embassy or consulate for assistance. Ask to speak to the Consular Section to report your passport lost or stolen. If you have been the victim of a serious crime, be sure to tell a consular officer about it as soon as possible so that the appropriate assistance can be provided. If you are scheduled to leave the foreign country shortly, provide consular staff with the details of your travel. Every effort to assist you quickly will be made including directing you to where you can obtain a photo for your replacement passport. In most cases, you will need to get a passport photo prior to your arrival at the consular section.

Medical Emergencies

If you or a U.S. citizen loved one become seriously ill or injured abroad, a consular officer from the U.S. embassy or consulate can assist in locating appropriate medical services and informing your family or friends. If necessary, a consular officer can also assist in the transfer of funds from the United States. However, payment of hospital and other expenses is the patient's responsibility. You can find local medical and emergency information at the website of the U.S. embassy or consulate near the ill or injured person. Find it online at usembassy.gov.

Before you go abroad, learn what medical services your health insurance will cover overseas. If your health insurance policy provides coverage outside the United States, REMEMBER to carry both your insurance policy identity card as proof of such insurance and a claim form. Although many health insurance companies will pay "customary and reasonable" hospital costs abroad, very few will pay for your medical evacuation back to the United States. Medical evacuation can easily cost $10,000 and up, depending on your location and medical condition. You are NOT covered by Medicare abroad.

Victims of Crime

The State Department is committed to assisting U.S. citizens who become victims of crime while abroad. It helps in two ways:

- Overseas: consular officers, agents, and staff work with crime victims and help them with the local police and medical systems.

- In the United States: our office of Overseas Citizens Services will stay in touch with family members in the United States, and help provide U.S.-based resources for the victim when possible.

When a U.S. citizen is the victim of a crime overseas, he or she may suffer from physical, emotional or financial injuries. It can be more difficult because the victim may be in unfamiliar surroundings, and may not know the local language or customs. Consular officers, consular agents, and local employees at overseas posts know local government agencies and resources in the country where they work.

Arrest and Detention

One of the highest priorities of the Department of State and U.S. embassies and consulates abroad is to provide assistance to U.S. citizens incarcerated abroad.

The Department of State is committed to ensuring fair and humane treatment for U.S. citizens imprisoned overseas. It stands ready to assist incarcerated citizens and their families within the limits of our authority in accordance with international law, domestic and foreign law.

Avoid getting arrested overseas by:

- Following the laws and regulations of the country you are visiting or living in.
- Learning about laws there which might be different from the laws in the United States. We provide some information for each country on our Country Specific pages. For further information on laws within the foreign country before you go, contact that country's nearest embassy or consulate within the United States.

If you are arrested overseas or know a U.S. citizen who is:

- Ask the prison authorities to notify the U.S. embassy or consulate
- You may also wish to reach out to the closest U.S. embassy or consulate to let us know of arrest.

Consular Assistance to U.S. Prisoners. When a U.S. citizen is arrested overseas, he or she may be initially confused and disoriented. It can be more difficult because the prisoner is in unfamiliar surroundings, and may not know the local language, customs, or legal system.

The local embassy or consulate can:

- Provide a list of local attorneys who speak English
- Contact family, friends, or employers of the detained U.S. citizen with their written permission
- Visit the detained U.S. citizen regularly and provide reading materials and vitamin supplements, where appropriate
- Help ensure that prison officials are providing appropriate medical care for you
- Provide a general overview of the local criminal justice process
- Inform the detainee of local and U.S.-based resources to assist victims of crime that may be available to them
- If they would like, ensuring that prison officials are permitting visits with a member of the clergy of the religion of your choice
- Establish an OCS Trust so friends and family can transfer funds to imprisoned U.S. citizens, when permissible under prison regulations

It cannot:

- Get U.S. citizens out of jail overseas
- State to a court that anyone is guilty or innocent
- Provide legal advice or represent U.S. citizens in court overseas
- Serve as official interpreters or translators
- Pay legal, medical, or other fees for U.S. citizens overseas

Missing Persons

If you are concerned about a U.S. citizen relative or friend who is traveling or living abroad, you can call 1-888-407-4747. Embassies and Consulates abroad can use the information you provide to try to locate the individual and pass on your message. They check also with local authorities in the foreign country to see if there is any report of a U.S. citizen hospitalized, arrested, or otherwise unable to communicate with those looking for them. If necessary, it may personally search hotels, airports, hospitals, or even prisons. The more information that you can provide about the person you are concerned about, the better the chances are of finding him or her.

The information that can be shared with you about these searches is sometimes impacted by the "Privacy Act." A U.S. law called the Privacy Act is designed to protect the privacy rights of U.S. citizens. The Act states that information may not be revealed regarding a U.S. citizen's location, welfare, intentions, or problems to anyone, including the citizen's family members and Congressional representatives, without the written consent of that individual. Although this law may occasionally cause distress to concerned families, it must be complied with if the individual has asked that information about him or her not be shared. However, exceptions can be made for the health and safety of the individual and when minors are involved. A consular officer can explain how the Privacy Act might impact your specific case.

Often, U.S. citizens abroad forget to contact their families on a regular basis due to time differences, busy schedules, irregular access to email, or difficulty making international phone calls. In most cases, worried family members eventually hear from their relative abroad, although it may take several days after you contact them before they are able to respond. It is also a good idea to discuss communication plans with friends and relatives before they travel; agree on how frequently they'll be in touch and whether it will be by phone or email. Make sure they leave contact information and when possible, a copy of their itinerary. These details will also help in trying to locate them if it becomes necessary.

Death Abroad

When an U.S. citizen dies abroad, the Bureau of Consular Affairs assists the family and friends during this difficult time. The Bureau will locate and inform the next-of-kin of the U.S. citizen's death and provide information on how to make arrangements for local burial or return of the remains to the United States. The disposition of remains is subject to U.S. law, local laws of the country where the individual died, U.S. and foreign customs requirements, and the foreign country facilities, which are often vastly different from those in the United States.

The Bureau of Consular Affairs assists the next-of-kin to convey instructions to the appropriate offices within the foreign country, and provides information to the family on how to transmit the necessary private funds to cover the costs overseas. The Department of State has no funds to assist in the return of remains or ashes of U.S. citizens who die abroad. Upon issuance of a local death certificate, the nearest embassy or consulate may prepare a Consular Report of the Death of an American Abroad. Copies of that report are provided to the next-of-kin or legal representative and may be used in U.S. courts to settle estate matters.

A U.S. consular officer overseas has statutory responsibility for the personal estate of a U.S. citizen who dies abroad if the deceased has no legal representative or next-of-kin in the country where the death occurred, subject to local law. In that situation the consular officer takes possession of personal effects, such as jewelry, personal documents and papers, and clothing. The officer prepares an inventory of the personal effects and then carries out instructions from the legal representative or next-of-kin concerning the effects.

Natural Disasters

Earthquakes, hurricanes, and tsunamis are only some of the natural disasters threatening the safety of U.S. citizens abroad. When natural disasters occur abroad, the Department of State and U.S. embassies and consulates in the affected country stand ready around the clock to locate and assist U.S. citizens in need.

Difficult choices and decisions must be made during an evacuation, and the Department of State stands ready to assist U.S. citizens; however pets usually cannot be accommodated on an evacuation flight. Whenever possible, you should make arrangements for someone in country to take care of your pets.

Part III: Appendices

Secretaries of State

Thomas Jefferson (1790-1793)

Thomas Jefferson served as the first Secretary of State from March 22, 1790, to December 31, 1793. Jefferson brought remarkable talents to a long career guiding U.S. foreign affairs. He successfully balanced the country's relatively weak geopolitical position and his fear of expansive federal powers with his desire for U.S. territorial and commercial expansion.

Jefferson was born into the Virginia planter elite. He graduated from the College of William & Mary in 1762, studied law, and was admitted to the Virginia bar in 1767. He was elected to the Virginia House of Burgesses in 1769 and served until the British dissolved the House in 1774. He was a leading activist in the U.S. independence movement and in 1773, a founding member of Virginia's Committee of Correspondence, which disseminated anti-British views. In 1774, he published A Summary View of the Rights of British America.

Jefferson was elected as a Delegate to the Second Continental Congress in 1775, and, in 1776 when he was thirty-three years of age, he drafted the Declaration of Independence. During the Revolutionary War, Jefferson returned to Virginia and served as a Delegate (1776-1779) and then as Governor (1779 and 1780). He served as a Delegate to the Confederation Congress from 1783 to 1784 and played a major role in shaping federal land policy. Jefferson joined John

Adams and Benjamin Franklin in Paris in 1784 to negotiate commercial treaties with European powers. The following year, he succeeded Franklin as Minister to France (1785-1789) before becoming Secretary of State.

A founder of the Democratic-Republican Party, Jefferson was elected Vice President in 1796 and served two terms as President (1801-1809).

Jefferson made enormous contributions to U.S. diplomacy. While Minister to France, he negotiated a commercial treaty with Prussia (1785) and the Consular Convention with France (1788). As Secretary of State, Jefferson's approach to foreign affairs was limited by Washington's preference for neutrality regarding the war between Britain and France. Jefferson favored closer ties to France, who had supported the United States during the Revolutionary War. Tension within Washington's cabinet—notably with Secretary of the Treasury Alexander Hamilton, who favored an assertive central government—prompted Jefferson's resignation.

As President, Jefferson's interest in territorial expansion was satisfied by Napoleon Bonaparte's 1803 offer to sell the Louisiana Territory for 15 million dollars. The purchase solved the longstanding dispute over navigation rights on the Mississippi River, and doubled the size of the country.

Jefferson waged a foreign war, from 1801 to 1805, when he sent U.S. warships to force the Barbary States to cease harassing U.S. shipping. War between France and Great Britain and those states' infringement of U.S. neutrality inspired Jefferson to push for the 1807 Embargo Act, which prohibited U.S. shipping. Unfortunately, the embargo crippled the U.S. economy and left the nation ill-prepared for the war with Great Britain that would eventually arrive in 1812.

Edmund Jennings Randolph (1794-1795)

Edmund Jennings Randolph succeeded Thomas Jefferson as Secretary of State on January 2, 1794. Randolph resigned on August 20, 1795, following a struggle to maintain a policy of neutrality in the war between Great Britain and Revolutionary France and accusations of corruption by the Federalists in President George Washington's cabinet.

As Secretary of State, Randolph faced many of the same challenges that his predecessor, Thomas Jefferson, had attempted to address. Randolph managed the settlement of the Citizen Genêt Affair. He prompted a resumption of talks with Spain and assisted in the negotiations of the 1795 Treaty of San Lorenzo, which opened the Mississippi River to U.S. navigation and fixed the boundaries between Spanish possessions and the United States.

Randolph attempted to continue Jefferson's efforts to maintain close relations with France and minimize Alexander Hamilton's influence over President Washington. However, Washington chose to endorse Jay's Treaty, an agreement that secured commercial ties with Great Britain. Randolph, along with the Senate, strongly objected to provisions that would disrupt the trade of neutral countries, particularly U.S. shipping to France. Political intrigue against Randolph ended his term as Secretary of State. Hoping to neutralize Randolph's opposition to the favorable Jay Treaty, the British Government provided his opponents in Washington's Cabinet with documents written by French Minister Jean Antoine Joseph Fauchet that had been intercepted by the British Navy. The documents were innocuous, yet Federalists in the Cabinet claimed they proved that Randolph had disclosed confidential information and solicited a bribe. Randolph was innocent, but his standing with Washington was permanently weakened. He resigned in 1795.

Timothy Pickering (1795-1800)

Timothy Pickering was appointed by President George Washington as ad interim Secretary of State on August 20, 1795, and elevated to the position of Secretary of State on December 10, 1795. President John Adams dismissed him on May 12, 1800.

Before appointing him Secretary of State, President Washington sent Pickering on special missions during the 1790s to negotiate with the Northeastern Indian tribes and to dissuade them from allying with Northwestern tribes. Pickering signed the 1794 Treaty of Canandaigua with the Iroquois League, a confederacy of six nations. In the agreement, the U.S. Government recognized the League's sovereignty over a sizable territory within New York State and offered payments, including an annual allowance, in exchange for a peace agreement and the right of passage through Iroquois Territory for U.S. citizens.

Pickering became Secretary of State in a controversial manner, and controversy would characterize his tenure. He manipulated an end to the tenure of his predecessor, Edmund Randolph, largely because of Randolph's opposition to the 1794 Jay Treaty. Pickering produced a slanted translation of French documents that had been intercepted by the British Navy and informed President Washington that they proved Randolph's traitorous behavior.

Once appointed as Secretary of State, Pickering followed a pro-British agenda and did not share Presidents Washington's and Adams' qualms about political entanglements with warring European powers. The ratification of the Jay Treaty worsened U.S.-French relations due to its preferential treatment of Great Britain. France's hostile reaction to the treaty—including the decision not to receive a U.S. Minister and the seizure of U.S. merchant ships caught trading with Britain—encouraged Pickering's pro-British stance. He opposed Adams' decision to send a delegation to negotiate with France. The XYZ Affair (1797-1798) propelled Pickering's desire to ally with Great Britain in a full-scale war with France.

When Adams reopened negotiations with France late in 1798 seeking to end the Quasi-War with France, Pickering stepped up his protests. He conspired to place pro-British Alexander Hamilton as a Major General in the Army, hoping to establish a large permanent army. Pickering also attempted to hinder Adams' efforts to explore options for peace with France. Pickering's public attacks on the President eventually drove Adams to request his resignation. Pickering refused to resign and was subsequently dismissed by Adams.

John Marshall (1800-1801)

President John Adams nominated John Marshall to be Secretary of State on May 12, 1800, the same day that Adams dismissed Timothy Pickering. The U.S. Senate confirmed Marshall as Secretary of State the next day. He served as

Secretary of State from June 6, 1800, until February 4, 1801, and then as *ad interim* Secretary of State until March 4, 1801.

Marshall began his diplomatic career as one of the three envoys appointed by President Adams to negotiate with French Foreign Minister Talleyrand in 1797. The mission failed, resulting in the XYZ Affair and the Quasi-War with France. Nonetheless, Marshall's conduct and reporting about the scandal turned a diplomatic failure into a personal triumph as his reputation soared at home.

As Secretary of State, Marshall was less partisan and more loyal to President Adams than Pickering had been. Adams entrusted Marshall with considerable authority over foreign affairs, particularly so after Adams departed the newly established national capital at Washington for an eight-month stay in Massachusetts. Marshall's deference to Adams further defined the position of the Secretary of State as a political subordinate of the President rather than the independent office that Pickering had imagined.

Secretary Marshall reasserted a policy of nonalignment regarding the European powers during a critical period. He split with other Federalists, such as Alexander Hamilton, and supported ongoing efforts to negotiate with France following the humiliating XYZ Affair. He backed the Convention of 1800 between the United States and France, which finally ended the undeclared naval war between the two countries. In dealing with Britain, Marshall protested the British Navy's unlawful seizure of U.S. shipping and impressment of U.S. seaman as well as the British courts' tolerance of piracy against U.S. merchant vessels. Recognizing the limitations of U.S. naval power, Marshall begrudgingly approved ongoing payments to the Barbary pirates who continued to raid U.S. merchant vessels. He also experienced frustration when negotiating with the Spanish who disregarded U.S. neutrality rights and protested against U.S. support for anti-colonial uprisings in Spanish America.

James Madison (1801-1809)

James Madison was appointed Secretary of State by President Thomas Jefferson on March 5, 1801. He entered duty on May 2, 1801, and served until

March 3, 1809. He had already made invaluable contributions to the establishment of the federal government before starting a long career in diplomacy.

Madison's foreign policies were guided by his republican ideals and his faith in the strength of the expanding U.S. economy. As Secretary of State, he cooperated closely with President Jefferson who kept close control over key decisions. Together they organized the negotiations with France that led to the 1803 Louisiana Purchase. Despite concerted effort, however, they could not convince the Spanish to sell West Florida.

As President, Madison annexed West Florida through intrigue and force in 1810. Madison also supported Jefferson's decision to fight a naval war against the Barbary Pirates. The Napoleonic Wars presented a dire foreign policy challenge when both France and Britain began violating U.S. neutrality rights. Particularly disturbed by the British impressment of U.S. sailors, Jefferson and Madison sought to conclude a new treaty with Britain that would protect U.S. trading rights and ban impressment. Unable to achieve these concessions, they adopted a policy to pressure the European powers through economic restrictions.

A series of acts aimed to display foreign dependence on the U.S. economy followed, including the Embargo Act of 1807 and the Non-Intercourse Act of 1809. The restrictions spurred smuggling by U.S. merchants, failed to sway European policies, and disrupted U.S. trade, especially when European powers reciprocated with trade limitations. Madison's struggle to stop British violations of U.S. neutrality culminated after his election to the Presidency when the two nations entered the War of 1812. Madison's hopes to gain Canadian territory through military victories were never realized due to the political stalemate that followed major losses on the battlefield.

Robert Smith (1809-1811)

Robert Smith served as Secretary of State under President James Madison from March 6, 1809, until April 1, 1811. Smith's controversial appointment and clashes with Madison influenced his service as Secretary of State.

Smith's difficult relationship with President James Madison began upon his appointment as Secretary of State. Madison's first choice for the position was Albert Gallatin, Secretary of the Treasury. However, Smith's supporters in the Senate, including his brother Samuel Smith, balked at the selection of foreign-born Gallatin and advanced Robert Smith.

When Smith assumed the position of Secretary of State, Madison and Gallatin were poised to undermine his authority and seek his ouster. By remaining close to Madison's rivals in the Senate, Smith ensured a continuing climate of disfavor. Madison, who had served as Secretary of State for eight years, did not trust Smith's competence in the position and redrafted many of Smith's diplomatic notes.

Smith's major diplomatic mission to improve relations with Great Britain proved a failure. Advised by Madison, Smith entered negotiations with David M. Erskine, the British Minister at Washington. The two intended to stabilize relations between the United States and Britain by restoring neutral trading rights during the Napoleonic War.

Unfortunately, Erskine overstretched his authority, offered too many concessions, and failed to convey British Foreign Minister George Canning's central requirement for an agreement: that the United States agree not to trade with the French for the duration of Britain's war with France. This omission doomed the 1809 Smith-Erskine Agreement, which stipulated a cancellation of the British Orders in Council respecting the United States and the opening of U.S. trade with Britain. Canning informed the House of Commons that Erskine had violated his instructions and that the agreement would not be upheld. When Madison and Smith finally read Canning's instructions to Erskine, they concluded that Canning had never intended to reach a settlement. Frustration over the agreement's failure helped propel the two countries into the War of 1812.

In March 1811 Gallatin asked Madison to dismiss Smith from the Cabinet and threatened to otherwise resign. Madison consented and offered Smith the post of Minister to Russia, hoping to quash Smith's future chances at high office.

Smith refused the mission and retaliated in a published address, hoping to topple the Madison Administration. However, like Edmund Randolph who had criticized President George Washington, Smith was unable to tarnish the public prestige of the Presidency. He resigned on April 1, 1811, and did not return to government service.

James Monroe (1811-1817)

James Monroe was appointed by President James Madison as Secretary of State on April 2, 1811. Monroe assumed duty on April 6, 1811, and served until March 3, 1817, with a brief period from October 1, 1814, to February 28, 1815, as *ad interim* Secretary of State. Monroe had a prestigious military career before embarking upon a distinguished career in public service.

Monroe conducted numerous diplomatic missions addressing the most critical international threats facing his generation. President George Washington appointed Monroe Minister to France in 1794. Jay's Treaty frustrated Monroe's efforts to retain cordial relations with the French Government and he was recalled in 1796.

Monroe returned to France in 1803 on a successful mission to assist Robert Livingston with the Louisiana Purchase negotiations. Monroe also served as Minister to Britain from 1803 until 1807, a period complicated by disputes over U.S. neutrality rights. In 1805 Monroe traveled to Spain, intending to win recognition of the U.S. possession of West Florida. The United States claimed the territory as part of the Louisiana Purchase, but Monroe could not gain the consent of the Spanish Government.

Monroe joined with Special Commissioner William Pinkney in 1806 in the effort to halt British impressment of U.S. sailors and to secure neutral trading rights. The proposed Monroe-Pinkney Treaty, however, failed to address impressments, and President Jefferson therefore declined to forward the treaty to the Senate.

While serving as Secretary of State in 1811, Monroe became convinced that a declaration of war against Great Britain was the best option to change offensive British policies. Along with Madison, Monroe encouraged Congress to issue a war declaration, which came on June 17, 1812. Monroe skillfully managed the expansion of the U.S. military occupation of Florida and served as acting Secretary of War during the War of 1812.

Although there would be no clear victor, the United States emerged from the war with enhanced international prestige. As President, Monroe's main diplomatic challenges stemmed from the recession of the Spanish Empire in the Americas and Russian Tsar Alexander's hopes to populate the Oregon Coast. Monroe responded effectively. In 1819 he skillfully managed the total Acquisition of Florida.

Along with his influential Secretary of State John Quincy Adams, Monroe issued the Monroe Doctrine, which forewarned the imperial European powers against interfering in the affairs of the newly independent Latin American states or potential U.S. territories in the Western hemisphere. Adhering to the intellectual underpinnings of the doctrine, Monroe granted diplomatic recognition to newly-independent Latin American republics.

John Quincy Adams (1817-1825)

John Quincy Adams was appointed Secretary of State by President James Monroe on March 5, 1817. He served from September 22, 1817, until March 3, 1825. Adams enjoyed unique training in diplomacy and became one of the most influential diplomats in U.S. history.

Adams' unsurpassed diplomatic career addressed the major foreign policy challenges of his time. President George Washington appointed him U.S. Minister Resident to the Netherlands in 1794. After serving three years in the Netherlands, Adams became U.S. Minister Resident to Prussia from 1797 to 1801, appointed this time by his father.

President James Madison appointed Adams U.S. Minister to Russia in 1809, and Adams served until 1814. He duly reported on Napoleon's failed invasion, among other events. Adams headed the Commission that negotiated the Treaty of Ghent in 1814, which ended the War of 1812 with Great Britain. His placement as U.S. Minister to Great Britain from 1815 to 1817 insured that he would be central to the ongoing efforts to improve Anglo-American relations.

He concluded the Commercial Convention of 1815, which included a mutual import non-discrimination measure that would serve as a model for future trade agreements.

Adams helped start negotiations to disarm the Great Lakes that culminated in the Rush-Bagot Pact of 1817. He also guided the progress of the Convention of 1818, which set the boundary between the United States and western British North America (later Canada) at the Rocky Mountains and stipulated joint occupation of the Oregon Country, among other issues.

As Secretary of State, Adams' views about territorial expansion guided President Monroe's policies. Adams' brilliant diplomacy with Spain, which led to the Adams-Onís Treaty of 1819, was largely responsible for the Acquisition of Florida and the U.S. assumption of Spain's claim to the Oregon Country. Adams worked to delay U.S. support of the new Latin American republics until the treaty was ratified.

By 1822, however, he supported President Monroe's recognition of several new republics. The following year, Monroe announced the Monroe Doctrine, which reflected many of Adams' views, particularly his insistence that the proclamation be unilateral. Adams also achieved a favorable convention with Russia in 1824 that recognized the U.S. claim to the Oregon Country.

Foreign affairs were not central to Adams' presidential term. As a Representative from Massachusetts, however, Adams ended his great drive to expand the territory of the United States. His disapproval of the expansion of slavery led him to oppose the annexation of Texas and the war with Mexico. Alternatively, Adams supported President James K. Polk's efforts to annex the Oregon Country. Adams believed that slavery would not reach Oregon and that the coastal territory would benefit foreign trade.

Henry Clay (1825-1829)

Henry Clay was appointed Secretary of State by President John Quincy Adams on March 7, 1825. Clay entered his duties on the same day and served until March 3, 1829. Famous as the "Great Pacificator" for his contributions to domestic policy, he emphasized economic development in his diplomacy.

Clay's appointment as Secretary of State stirred controversy. His bid for the Presidency in the election of 1824 ended with no clear majority for any candidate. Clay lent his support to John Quincy Adams instead of Andrew Jackson, thereby violating the instructions of the Kentucky legislature. Adams was then selected as President by the House of Representatives.

Due to the informal precedent that the Secretary of State would eventually assume the presidency, Jackson supporters portrayed Clay's subsequent appointment as Secretary of State as a "corrupt bargain." Nonetheless, Clay had diplomatic experience and an agenda to pursue as Secretary of State.

He had served on the Peace Commission following the War of 1812 that negotiated the Treaty of Ghent with Great Britain in 1814. As a Commissioner, Clay pressed to prevent the British from gaining free navigation on the Mississippi River. Clay based his foreign policy plan on the so-called "American System," emphasizing federal support of national economic development. To this end, Clay achieved a number of important successes as Secretary of State.

Clay oversaw the settlement of twelve commercial treaties, more than all earlier administrations, and developed economic ties with the newly independent Latin American republics. The British Government agreed to pay an indemnity for slaves freed during the War of 1812.

Clay's political negotiations, however, produced ample frustration. The Government of Mexico opted to expel Clay's minister, Joel Poinsett, after Poinsett offered to purchase Texas. Furthermore, U.S. delegates arrived too late to attend an important diplomatic event in Latin America, the Inter-American Congress at Panama in 1826.

Another disappointment came when Clay failed to settle continuing boundary disputes with Great Britain. In 1827 the United States and Great Britain merely agreed to the joint occupation of Oregon. Despite such setbacks and the remaining bitterness over Clay's appointment as Secretary of State, Clay's emphasis upon U.S. economic expansionism would prove to be a harbinger of modern U.S. diplomacy.

Martin Van Buren (1829-1831)

Martin Van Buren was appointed Secretary of State by President Andrew Jackson on March 6, 1829. Van Buren served in that capacity from March 28, 1829, to March 23, 1831. He was an astute career politician who approached foreign affairs with caution.

Jackson provided Van Buren an entrée to foreign affairs. Jackson selected Van Buren as Secretary of State as a reward for Van Buren's efforts to deliver the New York vote to Jackson.

As President, Jackson was hesitant to relinquish control over foreign policy decisions or political appointments. Over time, Van Buren's ability to provide informed advice about domestic policies, including the Indian Removal Act of 1830, won him a place in Jackson's circle of closest advisers.

Van Buren's tenure as Secretary of State included a number of successes. Working with Jackson, he reached a settlement with Great Britain to allow trade with the British West Indies. They also secured a settlement with France, gaining reparations for property seized during the Napoleonic Wars. In addition, they settled a commercial treaty with the Ottoman Empire that granted U.S. traders access to the Black Sea.

However, Jackson and Van Buren encountered a number of difficult challenges. They were unable to settle the Maine-New Brunswick boundary dispute with Great Britain, or advance the U.S. claim to the Oregon territory. They failed to establish a commercial treaty with Russia and could not persuade Mexico to sell Texas.

Van Buren resigned as Secretary of State due to a split within Jackson's Cabinet in which Vice President John C. Calhoun led a dissenting group of Cabinet members. Jackson acquiesced and made a recess appointment to place Van Buren as U.S. Minister to Great Britain in 1831.

While in Great Britain, Van Buren worked to expand the U.S. consular presence in British manufacturing centers. His progress was cut short when the Senate rejected his nomination in January of 1832.

Van Buren returned to the United States and entered presidential politics, first as Jackson's Vice President and then as President. While serving as chief executive, Van Buren proceeded cautiously regarding two major foreign policy crises.

He worked to diffuse a potential breach with Great Britain when Maine farmers attacked across the northern border and when Canadians burned the U.S. vessel Caroline in the Niagara River. Van Buren was also wary of worsening U.S. relations with Mexico. He declined to support the U.S. annexation of Texas, which would have added a slave state to the Union.

Edward Livingston (1831-1833)

Edward Livingston was appointed Secretary of State by President Andrew Jackson on May 24, 1831. Livingston entered duty on the same day. His tenure as Secretary of State ended on May 29, 1833. Livingston brought considerable legal expertise to the office but operated under strict presidential constraints upon his authority.

President Jackson asked for the resignation of his entire cabinet in 1831 in order to neutralize his feud with Vice President John Calhoun and Calhoun's supporters within the cabinet. Jackson appointed Livingston as Secretary of State upon the advice of outgoing Secretary of State Martin Van Buren.

Like his predecessor, Livingston would have to pay deference to President Jackson regarding foreign policy. Livingston's authority was actually broader regarding domestic affairs. Notably, he rewrote Jackson's famous Nullification Proclamation of 1832, which responded to a crisis over states' authority to nullify federal law.

Livingston inherited a number of unresolved—and challenging—diplomatic projects. He could not settle the dispute over the northeast boundary despite his considerable efforts to sway the British and U.S. citizens in Maine. He focused on the ratification of a major commercial treaty with France, but the French Government delayed action on the agreement.

Livingston also struggled with Britain's interest in suppressing slavery, protesting the British Government's decision not to return U.S. slaves who reached British soil.

Finally, he oversaw failed efforts to reach a settlement with the Mexican Government regarding Texas. Although U.S. negotiators did advance commercial agreements with Naples, Muscat, Russia, Siam, and Turkey during his tenure, Livingston had little to do with their progress.

Livingston was more involved with political disturbances in the Western Hemisphere. He followed an uneven approach regarding the Monroe Doctrine. In 1832 New Granada withdrew a commercial treaty with the United States at Britain's urging. In response, Livingston called upon the Monroe Doctrine, establishing the commercial element of the doctrine.

In contrast, he declined to invoke the doctrine when Britain seized the Falkland Islands in 1833, ousting the Argentine Government to reaffirm a prior territorial claim.

On the day of Livingston's resignation as Secretary of State, President Jackson appointed him U.S. Minister to France. During his stay in France from 1833 to 1835, Livingston employed his diplomatic skill and his appreciation of French culture to help bring into force the French Spoliation Claims Treaty, which addressed decades-old claims over the seizure of U.S. vessels and cargo. While delays infuriated President Jackson, the settlement finally came in 1836, shortly after Livingston's departure and death.

Louis McLane (1833-1834)

Louis McLane was appointed Secretary of State by President Andrew Jackson on May 29, 1833. McLane entered duty on the same day and left the position on June 30, 1834. He was an able administrator who eventually clashed with President Jackson over foreign policy.

While serving as Minister to Great Britain, McLane conducted the 1831 negotiations over an important agreement that allowed U.S. trade with the British West Indies. This breakthrough resolved a dispute dating back to the John Jay Treaty, which was ratified in 1795.

As Secretary of State, McLane's central achievement was a successful reorganization of the Department of State's staff into distinct bureaus. His main foreign policy success was an arrangement with the Spanish Government that settled U.S. claims for property seized by Spain during the Napoleonic Wars.

McLane quickly encountered the tough issues that had frustrated his predecessors Martin Van Buren and Edward Livingston. Namely, the northeast boundary dispute with Great Britain still proved to be intractable. The Mexican claims and boundary issues also remained unsettled.

Finally, McLane's efforts to resolve the longstanding dispute with France over the damages inflicted upon U.S. foreign commerce during the Napoleonic Wars led to the end of his tenure as Secretary of State. A treaty had been signed in 1831, but the French Government refused to issue the payments stipulated therein. McLane supported a policy of reprisal against French exports. When President Jackson decided against reprisals, McLane opted to resign.

McLane eventually returned to diplomacy in 1845 when President James K. Polk appointed him U.S. Minister to Great Britain. His hopes to negotiate the Oregon Territory boundary were disappointed when the talks instead commenced in Washington.

John Forsyth (1834-1841)

John Forsyth was appointed Secretary of State by President Andrew Jackson on June 27, 1834. He entered duty on July 1, 1834, and completed his tenure on March 3, 1841, during the administration of President Martin Van Buren. Forsyth faithfully served two Presidents who both held close control over foreign policy.

When he became Secretary of State, Forsyth brought with him some prior experience with foreign affairs. As U.S. Minister to Spain, he assisted in securing the ratification of the 1819 Adams-Onís Treaty, which ceded Spain's claim to East and West Florida. His open criticism of the Spanish Government, however, earned him an official rebuke.

While a U.S. Congressmen, Forsyth was a leading proponent of Indian removal, the withdrawal of U.S. recognition of tribal sovereignty, and the numerous Indian Treaties. President Jackson appointed Forsyth Secretary of

State as a reward for political support and consistently ensured that Forsyth followed his lead on foreign policy. Together, they finally concluded the long-standing controversy over the damages inflicted by France upon U.S. foreign commerce during the Napoleonic Wars.

In 1834 Jackson urged Congress to pass legislation to seize French property unless the French Government released the payments stipulated in an 1831 settlement treaty. Jackson's bellicose stance convinced the French Government to sever relations with the United States. However, a clarification by Jackson—that he had not intended to insult France—ended the impasse and the payments began. The French Government committed to a $5 million payment to settle outstanding U.S. claims and the U.S. Government reduced the import duty on French wines.

Forsyth also cautiously coordinated with President Jackson on the U.S. recognition of the independent Republic of Texas in 1837.

Under Van Buren's presidency, Forsyth supported the President's decision against annexing Texas. Forsyth also backed Van Buren's calm approach to the dispute with Great Britain over the U.S.-Canadian border, which was complicated by the aggressive stance of the Maine State Government. Forsyth also issued strong statements denying British claims to the right to search U.S. vessels for slaves off the African coast. Finally, Forsyth labored in vain to diffuse the controversy stirred by the *Amistad* case of 1839. Ultimately, the Supreme Court held against the Van Buren administration's position, and the African slaves were returned to Sierra Leone in 1842.

Daniel Webster (1841-1843)

Webster was appointed Secretary of State by President William Henry Harrison on March 5, 1841. He entered duty the next day and completed his tenure on May 8, 1843, during the administration of President John Tyler.

Webster returned to the position when he was appointed by President Millard Fillmore on July 22, 1850. Webster officially entered duty as Secretary of State for his second tenure on July 23, 1850, and left the position on October 24, 1852.

During his two tenures as Secretary of State, Webster focused his considerable legal talents on strengthening the U.S. Government and expanding foreign trade.

Webster's major task during his first appointment as Secretary of State was to negotiate a number of longstanding disputes with Great Britain. He helped achieve the landmark Anglo-American Webster-Ashburton Treaty of 1842. The treaty settled the Maine boundary, increased U.S. involvement in suppressing the African slave trade, and included an extradition clause that would become a model for future treaties. The agreement also ushered in an era of rapprochement between the two nations, allowing the U.S. Government to focus on westward expansion.

Webster extended diplomatic protection to U.S. missionaries abroad, and he arrogated the Monroe Doctrine to the Hawaiian Islands.

He resigned from the Secretaryship in 1843 due to financial difficulties and a disagreement with President Tyler over the annexation of Texas, a move stridently opposed by Webster.

After President Fillmore brought Webster back as Secretary of State in 1850, Webster dedicated significant attention to domestic affairs such as the Compromise of 1850 and the Fugitive Slave Law.

Undiplomatically, he created a rift with the Austrian Empire with his so-called Hülseman note (named for J.G. Hülseman the Austrian Chargé to the United States). Webster intended to explain U.S. support for Hungarian independence, but his note starkly criticized European monarchism.

In somewhat of a contrast, he later defended the Spanish Crown's right to protect its Cuban colony against U.S. filibustering expeditions.

Webster continued to take steps toward improving Anglo-American relations. He successfully advised the British Government to cede its protectorates and some geographical claims in Central America. However, he found no success with the Mexican Government, which blocked the U.S.-backed construction of a railway across the Isthmus of Tehuantepec.

Webster died while serving as Secretary of State and working on a number of prescient matters, including the drive to expand U.S. trade in Asia.

Abel Parker Upshur (1843-1844)

Abel Parker Upshur was appointed *ad interim* Secretary of State by President John Tyler on June 24, 1843. On July 24, 1843, Tyler appointed Upshur Secretary of State, and he entered duty on the same day. His term ended on February 28, 1844, the day he died.

As Secretary of the Navy, Upshur believed in the vital role the Department played in securing the nation's interests. He worked to expand the Navy, outfit it with modernized warships and reform its administration. His tenure there provided him the necessary foreign policy experience to make the transition to the Department of State in 1843 at the request of President Tyler, a lifelong friend.

Tyler implored a hesitant Upshur to take the position, appealing to his interest in expanding the nation westward. As Secretary of State, Upshur's diplomacy set in motion territorial expansion that did not come to fruition until after his death.

He single-mindedly pursued this goal and reopened negotiations for the eventual Annexation of Texas in 1845. Pro-slavery and wary of British influence in the Southwest, like President Tyler, Upshur believed it was in the United States' best interest to annex Texas as a slave-holding state.

He also worked to settle a prolonged border dispute with Great Britain over the Oregon Territory, resulting in the Oregon Treaty of 1846.

John Caldwell Calhoun (1844-1845)

John Caldwell Calhoun was appointed Secretary of State by President John Tyler on March 6, 1844. Calhoun entered duty on April 1, 1844, and left the position on March 10, 1845. A former U.S. Representative, U.S. Senator, Secretary of War and Vice President, Calhoun served as Secretary of State for less than one year before returning to his position in the U.S. Senate, where he served until his death in 1850.

Calhoun entered office as Secretary of State not at the behest of President Tyler, but of Henry Wise, a mutual associate who had all but promised him the position. Tyler accepted the proposition and named Calhoun to his Cabinet with the assurance that its newest member would carry out the directives of his predecessor, namely the Annexation of Texas.

One of Calhoun's first acts as Secretary of State was to submit a treaty of annexation to the Senate. The 1844 treaty had been largely crafted by President Tyler and the former Secretary Upshur, but it was Calhoun's vociferous and controversial support of slavery in Texas that was blamed for its defeat in Congress. He continued to press for annexation of a pro-slavery Texas, which deeply troubled President Tyler, the incumbent in that year's election who hoped to downplay sectional differences and unite, rather than divide, the nation over the issue of annexation.

When President Polk was elected on a pro-expansionist platform, sitting President Tyler recommended annexation by a joint resolution of Congress, which passed days before he left office in 1845.

Calhoun also worked to resolve territorial disputes to the north, opening negotiations on a settlement with the British over the Oregon Territory. The U.S. also signed the Treaty of Wangxia, its first commercial treaty with China, during Calhoun's tenure. President Polk chose not to retain Calhoun as Secretary of State, and the South Carolinian returned to the Senate, where he served until his death five years later.

James Buchanan (1845-1849)

James Buchanan was appointed Secretary of State by President James K. Polk on March 6, 1845. Buchanan entered duty on March 10, 1845, and left the position on March 7, 1849. After an unsuccessful bid for the Democratic presidential nomination in 1852, Buchanan secured the nomination in 1856 and was elected President. He served one term, from 1857 to 1861.

Both President Polk and Secretary Buchanan believed in Manifest Destiny and were strong proponents of U.S. westward expansion.

In addition to supporting U.S. efforts to annex Texas, Buchanan was charged with negotiating a settlement on the boundary dispute with Great

Britain over the Oregon Territory. Like the 1848 treaty with Mexico that would soon follow, the 1846 Oregon Treaty fell short of a full territorial concession.

Outgoing President Tyler successfully pushed for the Annexation of Texas by a congressional joint resolution just before leaving office, an effort supported by Buchanan. Annexation prompted the Mexican-American War and resulted in the 1848 Treaty of Guadalupe Hidalgo. The treaty brought the United States significant territorial expansion, yet Buchanan opposed its outcome and believed that Baja and the northern provinces of Mexico should have been included.

Polk directed most aspects of U.S. foreign policy during his presidency, allowing Buchanan little control. Buchanan felt this lack of power intensely and communicated his discontent to close friends and associates. Nevertheless, he served as Secretary of State until the end of the Polk Administration.

After serving as Secretary of State, Buchanan attempted to win the Presidency in 1852 but failed. Instead, he served as Minister to Great Britain from 1853 to 1856, where he drafted the Ostend Manifesto with other U.S. diplomats. His absence during the sectional schism of the Democratic Party allowed him to win that party's nomination and subsequently the Presidency in 1856.

John Middleton Clayton (1849-1850)

John Middleton Clayton was appointed Secretary of State by President Zachary Taylor on March 7, 1849, and entered duty the next day. He resigned the position on July 22, 1850, shortly after President Taylor died and Millard Fillmore assumed the Presidency. Clayton served during a difficult administration and suffered frequent criticism despite the fact that he wielded little influence under Taylor.

Clayton's tenure as Secretary of State was marked by war scares with France and Portugal, opposition from both houses of Congress, and troubled diplomacy. Clayton pushed for a strict adherence to the Monroe Doctrine, and managed to keep British influence in abeyance.

They key achievement of the Taylor administration was the Clayton-Bulwer Treaty over building a proposed Anglo-American canal through the Central

American Republic of Nicaragua. The canal never went beyond the planning stages, however, and was supplanted by the canal in Panama. Upon the death of President Taylor in July of 1850, Clayton immediately resigned his position.

Daniel Webster (1850-1852)

Webster was appointed Secretary of State by President William Henry Harrison on March 5, 1841. He entered duty the next day and completed his tenure on May 8, 1843, during the administration of President John Tyler.

Webster returned to the position when he was appointed by President Millard Fillmore on July 22, 1850. Webster officially entered duty as Secretary of State for his second tenure on July 23, 1850, and left the position on October 24, 1852.

During his two tenures as Secretary of State, Webster focused his considerable legal talents on strengthening the U.S. Government and expanding foreign trade.

Webster's major task during his first appointment as Secretary of State was to negotiate a number of longstanding disputes with Great Britain. He helped achieve the landmark Anglo-American Webster-Ashburton Treaty of 1842. The treaty settled the Maine boundary, increased U.S. involvement in suppressing the African slave trade, and included an extradition clause that would become a model for future treaties. The agreement also ushered in an era of rapprochement between the two nations, allowing the U.S. Government to focus on westward expansion.

Webster extended diplomatic protection to U.S. missionaries abroad, and he arrogated the Monroe Doctrine to the Hawaiian Islands.

He resigned from the Secretaryship in 1843 due to financial difficulties and a disagreement with President Tyler over the annexation of Texas, a move stridently opposed by Webster.

After President Fillmore brought Webster back as Secretary of State in 1850, Webster dedicated significant attention to domestic affairs such as the Compromise of 1850 and the Fugitive Slave Law.

Undiplomatically, he created a rift with the Austrian Empire with his so-called Hülseman note (named for J.G. Hülseman the Austrian Chargé to the United States). Webster intended to explain U.S. support for Hungarian independence, but his note starkly criticized European monarchism.

In somewhat of a contrast, he later defended the Spanish Crown's right to protect its Cuban colony against U.S. filibustering expeditions.

Webster continued to take steps toward improving Anglo-American relations. He successfully advised the British Government to cede its protectorates and some geographical claims in Central America. However, he found no success with the Mexican Government, which blocked the U.S.-backed construction of a railway across the Isthmus of Tehuantepec.

Webster died while serving as Secretary of State and working on a number of prescient matters, including the drive to expand U.S. trade in Asia.

Edward Everett (1852-1853)

Edward Everett was appointed Secretary of State by President Millard Fillmore on November 6, 1852, and entered into duty on the same day. Although President Fillmore appointed Everett to succeed Daniel Webster, Everett was sworn in after Fillmore was defeated in his reelection bid, and served in the position for only four months, ending his service on March 3, 1853.

As Webster's successor, Everett had a relatively unremarkable and very short tenure. One of Everett's first acts as Secretary was to draft a formal letter to the Emperor of Japan for the Perry Expedition, which facilitated Japanese trade with the West.

He was also charged with dispelling a potential diplomatic crisis with Peru over territorial claims to guano-rich Lobos Island.

The highlight of Everett's short-lived tenure was his contribution to shaping U.S. policy toward Cuba. Great Britain and France had proposed a tripartite guarantee of Spanish sovereignty over Cuba in 1852. Everett rejected the proposal, responding firmly that Cuba was to remain a U.S. matter and that the United States maintained its aversion to "entangling alliances."

A respected orator and writer, Everett won praise for his apt expression of deep-rooted U.S. principles in foreign policy matters. When the new administration under Franklin Pierce began in March of 1853, Everett's term as Secretary of State ended.

Upon his departure from the Department of State, he was immediately elected Senator from his home state of Massachusetts.

William Learned Marcy (1853-1857)

William Learned Marcy was appointed Secretary of State by President Franklin Pierce on March 7, 1853, and entered into duty the following day. Marcy served until March 6, 1857.

Marcy came to the position of Secretary of State with little foreign policy experience. He had never traveled outside of the United States, but was valued for his pragmatism and judgment.

During his four-year tenure, Marcy negotiated many treaties including the prominent 1853 Gadsden Treaty, which added nearly 30,000 square miles to the United States and made possible a transcontinental railroad.

Interest in territorial expansion shifted from the American Southwest to the Caribbean as the United States became increasingly involved in the question of Cuba's sovereignty. Marcy oversaw the drafting of the Ostend Manifesto, a document that detailed the reasons for a proposed U.S. acquisition of Cuba. The Manifesto was released to the public but was later rescinded after its issuance embarrassed the Pierce administration and met with international criticism over the expansion of U.S. slavery.

The following year, Marcy negotiated a treaty with Great Britain over reciprocal fishing rights in Canada. Marcy served the duration of the Pierce presidency, until March 1857. Four months later, he unexpectedly died in New York.

Lewis Cass (1857-1860)

Lewis Cass was appointed Secretary of State by President James Buchanan on March 6, 1857, and assumed office the same day. He served until December 14, 1860.

President Buchanan appointed Cass Secretary of State with hopes he would unify the Democratic Party then riddled with sectional tensions.

An experienced diplomat and former Secretary of State, President Buchanan aggressively directed foreign policy. Two focal points of the Buchanan administration were Latin America and Great Britain. Internal dissension from antislavery proponents, sparked in part by the attempt to purchase Cuba from Spain, often thwarted Buchanan's foreign policy plans. Attempts to purchase more territory from Mexico were also frustrated by an increasingly divided Congress and disinterest on the part of Mexican leaders.

Nonetheless, Cass successfully negotiated a final settlement of the Clayton-Bulwer Treaty with the British Government. The treaty limited both U.S. and British control throughout Latin America. The British also relinquished their claim to the right to search U.S. vessels under Cass's tenure.

With the election of Abraham Lincoln and the rise of the new Republican Party, Cass began to voice his long-held disagreements with the Buchanan administration, specifically his protests related to sectional differences. Cass tendered his resignation in the last days of 1860.

Jeremiah Sullivan Black (1860-1861)

Jeremiah Sullivan Black served as Attorney General in President James Buchanan's Cabinet until December 17, 1860, when he was chosen to succeed Lewis Cass as Secretary of State after Cass's sudden resignation. He entered into duty on December 19, 1860, and served for the duration of the Buchanan administration, leaving office on March 5, 1861.

The most pressing issue for the Buchanan administration in late 1860 was the threat of secession by the Confederate States. That December, President

Buchanan declared the act of secession unconstitutional, based partly on former Attorney General Black's legal arguments.

The new Secretary of State stood vehemently against secession, but also felt it was unconstitutional for the Union to force a state to remain. Black's role as trusted adviser to the President changed little with his new appointment. With domestic political affairs in crisis, little attention was paid to international affairs during Black's three-month commission.

One of the last acts of Black's short tenure as head of the Department of State was undoubtedly his most important. On February 28, 1861, he instructed U.S. diplomatic representatives abroad to caution their respective governments against recognition of the Confederacy.

When President Lincoln was inaugurated in March of 1861, Black left office at odds with his fellow Democrats. He was appointed Reporter to the U.S. Supreme Court in 1861, a respectable, albeit lower office than he had held previously. Following a long and distinguished career in public service, Black returned to his private law practice in his home state of Pennsylvania, where he remained until his death in 1883.

William Henry Seward (1861-1869)

William Henry Seward was appointed Secretary of State by Abraham Lincoln on March 5, 1861, and served until March 4, 1869. Seward carefully managed international affairs during the Civil War and also negotiated the 1867 purchase of Alaska.

Along with other political leaders, Seward unsuccessfully negotiated to resolve the secession crisis during the winter of 1861. Once in Lincoln's Cabinet, Seward anticipated that he would wield a strong influence over foreign policy. However, he underestimated Lincoln's interest in foreign affairs.

Although Seward was willing to consider war against European powers should they prove too friendly toward the Confederacy, Lincoln overruled Seward on this point. Seward thus focused most of his efforts on preventing foreign recognition of the Confederacy.

Seward sent U.S. agents to Europe to publicly lobby for the Union cause, but early in his tenure a diplomatic crisis arose when the U.S. Navy arrested Confederate envoys headed for Europe. Despite public support in favor of their detention, Seward agreed to release the envoys to avoid the threat of war with Great Britain.

Seward also faced difficulties in encouraging foreign governments to curtail the smuggling of goods and war materiel, as well as the construction of Confederate warships. Seward worked with the U.S. Minister in London, Charles Francis Adams, to put an end to the building of these ships. The British Government failed to prevent the launch of the CSS Alabama and CSS Florida, but the subsequent embarrassment caused officials to more strictly enforce British neutrality and prevented the building of further Confederate ships on British soil.

After the Civil War ended with a Union victory, Seward pursued negotiations to expand U.S. territory. He resumed discussions to purchase Russian Alaska, which resulted in the 1867 Alaska Purchase. Seward also attempted, unsuccessfully, to acquire territory elsewhere, as negotiations to acquire the Virgin Islands, part of the Dominican Republic, as well as several other small islands in the Caribbean failed. However, the U.S. Navy occupied Midway Atoll in 1867.

Seward also involved the United States in Mexican affairs from 1865 to 1867, by supporting the anti-French forces in defeating Austrian archduke Maximilian, whom the French had installed as Emperor of Mexico in 1862.

Seward continued to serve as Secretary of State under Lincoln's successor, Andrew Johnson. As as a Republican moderate, however, Seward found himself at odds with Johnson and other conservatives in the Cabinet, while radicals in Congress distrusted him for his continued loyalty to Johnson. Despite congressional hostility toward Seward, Congress still approved the purchase of Alaska.

Elihu Benjamin Washburne (1869-1869)

Elihu Benjamin Washburne was appointed by President Ulysses S. Grant as Secretary of State, and his commission was issued on March 5, 1869. Grant's appointment was intended as a personal yet temporary means to honor Washburne while Grant restructured his Cabinet, and thus Washburne resigned on March 10 to make way for his replacement. However, Washburne remained at his post until the arrival of his successor, Hamilton Fish, on March 16, 1869.

Washburne was born in Livermore, Maine in 1816. He attended Harvard Law School, and settled in Galena, Illinois in 1840, where he practiced law.

He was elected to Congress in 1853 as a Whig, but soon joined the new Republican Party. Washburne became well-known for his efforts to promote fiscal discipline and also rose to prominence as a leader of the Radical Republicans.

In 1869, incoming President Ulysses S. Grant selected Washburne to be Secretary of State. However, Grant came under investigation by the Senate for his attempt to appoint department store owner A.T. Stewart as Secretary of the Treasury, as key Senators were concerned about possible conflicts of interest in the appointment. Consequently, Grant was forced to restructure his Cabinet. Grant therefore appointed Washburne as Secretary of State as a temporary measure, with the agreement that Washburne was not to make any appointments or key decisions during his brief tenure. After serving as a placeholder from March 5 to 16, he was replaced by Hamilton Fish.

As a consolation, Grant appointed Washburne U.S. Minister to France, where he served until 1877. Washburne was a contender for the Republican candidacy for the Presidency in 1876 and 1880, but failed to win the party's nomination. Thereafter, he retired from politics and wrote his memoirs, which were published in 1887.

As Washburne's tenure as Secretary of State was remarkably short, his main influence on U.S. foreign policy came during his tenure as U.S. Minister to France. Washburne's term in Paris covered a tumultuous time in French history, as he served during the Franco-Prussian War and the violent suppression of the Paris Commune.

At the time of his arrival in the spring of 1869, he expected the post to be relatively undemanding. However, on July 19, 1870, France declared war on the German state of Prussia, and the North German states subsequently joined the war on the Prussian side, igniting the Franco-Prussian War.

During the war, Washburne assumed the duties of protecting North German citizens and property. He also had to deal with the inconsistent policies of the French Government, which alternately wanted to draft German residents of France and expel all Germans from France. Prussian victories led to the collapse of Emperor Napoleon III's government, the birth of the Third French Republic, and then to punitive peace terms.

When the new government placed disproportionate financial demands on Parisian renters to pay war indemnities to the newly constituted German Empire, Parisians rose up in a left-wing revolt known as the Paris Commune. Washburne was again caught by surprise, and although he personally did not sympathize with the Communards, he believed that his presence in Paris was crucial as U.S. citizens living there needed assistance.

While other diplomats left the city, Washburne remained to facilitate the departure of foreigners from the embattled city and to prevent Commune forces from enlisting foreigners into compulsory service. Washburne also visited imprisoned Americans and identified American bodies. Lastly, he acted as an intermediary between the Vatican and the Commune to try to exchange the imprisoned archbishop of Paris, but the archbishop was executed on May 23, as the Commune itself was on the brink of being crushed by the French Government.

Following the collapse of the Commune, Washburne continued to serve as U.S. Minister to France until 1877.

Hamilton Fish (1869-1877)

Hamilton Fish was appointed Secretary of State by President Ulysses S. Grant on March 11, 1869, and began his duties on March 16. Fish served until March 11, 1877.

Upon becoming Secretary of State, Fish first faced the challenges related to the unpopular Johnson-Clarendon Convention, an agreement made to resolve Civil War disputes over issues such as the British-built Confederate warship Alabama. On April 13, 1869, the Senate overwhelmingly rejected the Convention.

U.S. attempts to continue to press claims stemming from British recognition of the Confederacy's belligerent status were hampered by the possibility that the United States had considered granting the same status to anti-Spanish rebels in Cuba.

The Americas were central to Fish's foreign policy. Working with President Grant, he tried unsuccessfully to acquire new territory in the Dominican Republic, as well as the lands controlled by Hudson's Bay Company, which the British Government instead sold to Canada in 1870.

In 1868, a revolt against Spanish rule began in Cuba that became known as the Ten Years' War. In the United States, Spanish attempts to crush the insurgency aroused strong public sympathy for Cubans. Fish worked closely with Senator Charles Sumner to formulate a policy on the Cuban situation. They recommended and finally convinced Grant not to recognize Cuban rebels as belligerents in an effort to protect American commerce and maintain peace with Spain.

Over the next several years, incidents involving Spanish attempts to suppress the rebellion in Cuba led to diplomatic tensions. Fish eventually began to pressure Spanish officials to consider granting Cuban independence and ending slavery on the island. The Spanish Government did neither during Fish's tenure.

Eventually, on February 4, 1877, U.S. Minister Caleb Cushing signed a protocol with Spanish Foreign Minister Fernando Calderón, in which Spain agreed to greater due process for U.S. citizens in Cuba.

Later in Fish's tenure as Secretary of State, he faced Indian raids and poor law enforcement along the border with Mexico, an issue which would escalate under Fish's successor William Evarts.

William Maxwell Evarts (1877-1881)

William Evarts was appointed Secretary of State by President Rutherford B. Hayes on March 7, 1877, and began serving as Secretary on March 12. Evarts served until March 7, 1881.

As a federal prosecutor, Evarts addressed international issues including investigations of possible filibustering expeditions into Central America. These investigations eventually led to the detention of the ship *Cleopatra*, which was part of Narciso López's expedition against Cuba.

During the Civil War, Evarts became involved in the early prosecution of Confederate privateers. He was also dispatched on a mission to convince the British Government to enforce neutrality regulations more strictly in an effort to cut off assistance to the Confederacy. Evarts visited France to advocate for the Union cause and attempted to dissuade the French Government from permitting the construction of Confederate warships. Evarts also served as an arbitrator in the Alabama claims.

When Evarts became Secretary of State, he grappled with the decision of whether or not to recognize the new Mexican government led by Porfirio Díaz. Previously, the United States had followed a policy of recognizing Mexican governments as they came into effective control of Mexico, but Evarts decided to act differently. He placed several conditions on his recognition of the Díaz government, most importantly the right of U.S. troops to cross the Mexican border in pursuit of Indian raiders.

Díaz's government responded with a condemnation of the demands and moved troops to the border. War seemed possible, particularly since Diaz's opposition accused him of a potential willingness to bow to U.S. pressure. Under the threat of congressional investigation, Evarts backed down and extended recognition, but did not withdraw the order allowing pursuit across the border until 1880.

Evarts also faced domestic challenges from anti-immigration supporters on the West Coast, who began to make stronger demands that Chinese immigrants be prevented from entering the United States despite the provisions of the 1868 Burlingame-Seward Treaty.

In 1880, Evarts sent a committee to negotiate with the Chinese Government in an effort to secure Chinese endorsement of restrictions on immigration. Chinese officials were unwilling to allow an outright ban, but were willing to agree to limits. Evarts also unsuccessfully attempted to negotiate peace between Chile, Peru and Bolivia during the War of the Pacific.

James Gillespie Blaine (1881-1881)

James G. Blaine served two terms as Secretary of State. He was first appointed by U.S. President James A. Garfield, serving from March 7, 1881, until December 18, 1881, and was again appointed by U.S. President Benjamin Harrison, serving from March 5, 1889, until his resignation on June 4, 1892.

Once in office as Secretary of State, Blaine encouraged peaceful relations within the Americas, and also advocated for American commercial expansion and increased naval power. Blaine negotiated for the release of U.S. citizens who had been arrested and confined without trial in Ireland as part of a British crackdown on Irish nationalist rent boycotts.

Blaine unsuccessfully attempted to negotiate peace between Peru, Bolivia and Chile, all engaged in the War of the Pacific from 1879 to 1883. He also attempted to arbitrate a border dispute between Mexico and Guatemala. Blaine's overtures were cut short on September 19, 1881, by the death of President Garfield, who had been shot two months before on July 2. Blaine remained in office through December 18 while Chester A. Arthur, the new president, selected a replacement for him.

Under President Harrison, Blaine's first challenge was to counter German expansion in Samoa, where the United States competed for influence. The agreement reached in 1889 between the United States, Germany and the United Kingdom did not resolve the tensions between those countries, but further eroded Samoan sovereignty. During this term, Blaine attempted to negotiate a disagreement over Canadian fur seal hunting rights in the Bering Sea. He also faced controversies over the lynching of Italian citizens in New Orleans in 1891 and an attack on U.S. sailors in Valparaiso, Chile.

Blaine oversaw the Pan-American Conference, which had been organized by his predecessor, Thomas Francis Bayard. The conference covered trade, communication and legal issues, and eventually led to the establishment of the Pan-American Union.

Blaine resigned from his post on June 4, 1892. His resignation caught everyone, including President Harrison, by surprise. Although Blaine was a candidate for the 1892 Republican nomination, his poor health meant that he was not considered seriously. Blaine's health declined sharply after his resignation, and he died not long afterward on January 27, 1893.

Frederick Theodore Frelinghuysen (1881-1885)

Frederick Theodore Frelinghuysen was appointed Secretary of State by President Chester A. Arthur and served from December 19, 1881, to March 5, 1885.

As Secretary of State, Frelinghuysen inherited a number of diplomatic issues from his predecessor, James G. Blaine. He continued Blaine's unsuccessful attempts to mediate peace negotiations between Peru, Bolivia, and Chile. Frelinghuysen appointed Cornelius A. Logan as Minister to Chile. Logan mediated the 1883 peace agreement between Chile and Peru, terminating the War of the Pacific with the Treaty of Ancón on October 23, 1883. Despite the achievement of peace, diplomatic blunders in Chile and Peru and Bolivia's territorial losses remained an ongoing source of tension between the United States and South America.

Against President Arthur's wishes, Frelinghuysen canceled the Pan-American Conference that Blaine had organized before his departure. Arthur brought the issue before Congress, which took no action, and the invitations for the conference were withdrawn. Frelinghuysen remained concerned that past U.S. actions had encouraged negative attitudes towards U.S. power and suspicion of possible intervention. He also remained wary of being drawn into mediating disputes between neighbors. These concerns prompted the U.S. Government to refuse to arbitrate in the emerging boundary dispute between Venezuela and Britain over Guyana's western border.

Concerned about European construction in the Panama Canal, Frelinghuysen unsuccessfully attempted to renegotiate the 1850 Clayton-Bulwer Treaty with Great Britain. He negotiated an 1884 treaty with Nicaragua granting the United States exclusive rights to construct and control a transoceanic canal—terms which directly contradicted the Clayton-Bulwer Treaty. The U.S. Senate failed to ratify the treaty.

In addition to his efforts in Latin America, Frelinghuysen also instructed delegates to the 1884 Berlin Conference, where German leader Otto von Bismarck sought to mediate the European scramble for Africa. Frelinghuysen also oversaw and approved Rear Admiral Robert Shufeldt's attempt to secure a treaty with Korea. Frelinghuysen served as Secretary of State until the end of Arthur's term and died shortly afterwards in Newark, New Jersey, on May 20, 1885.

Thomas Francis Bayard (1885-1889)

President Grover Cleveland appointed Thomas Francis Bayard as Secretary of State on March 6, 1885. Bayard served from March 7 to the end of Cleveland's first term, leaving office on March 4, 1889.

As Secretary of State, Bayard moved away from patronage appointments, choosing instead to appoint diplomats known for their skill and expertise rather than their political loyalty. However, controversy soon erupted when the Italian and Austro-Hungarian Governments rejected his appointment of Anthony M. Keiley as Minister.

In foreign affairs, Bayard intervened in the ongoing disputes over U.S. fishing rights in Canada and Newfoundland. Following the expiration of an 1871 agreement, the U.S. Government had attempted to negotiate a treaty with Canada and Great Britain in early 1888. However, the hunting of fur seals in the Bering Sea had become a contentious issue, and relations were further complicated by an unclear land and sea boundary division between Alaska and Canada. The U.S. Senate ultimately rejected the terms of the treaty. Bayard continued to pursue negotiations with the British Government, but the issue would not be resolved until a 1903 treaty.

In addition to addressing fishing rights, Bayard also focused on Pacific affairs. In 1887, he oversaw the Senate's ratification of the renewal of a reciprocity treaty with Hawaii. That same year he hosted the inconclusive Washington Conference intended to de-escalate tensions between Germany, Great Britain, and the United States in competition for influence over Samoa. As Secretary, Bayard was also interested in increasing Japanese autonomy. Richard B. Hubbard, U.S. Minister to Japan, signed an agreement in 1889 with Japanese Minister of Foreign Affairs, Marquis Okuma Shigenobu, which provided for the gradual abolition of extraterritorial privileges for U.S. citizens living in Japan. However, Bayard acquiesced to British occupation of the Geomun-do Islands, despite Korean pleas for U.S. assistance under the terms of an 1883 treaty that had been negotiated by U.S. Envoy Robert W. Shufeldt.

After his tenure as Secretary of State, Bayard served as U.S. Ambassador to the United Kingdom. As Ambassador, Bayard became involved in the Venezuela-Guyana boundary dispute. His public, pro-British pronouncements placed him at odds with then Secretary of State, Richard Olney, and President Grover Cleveland. Bayard remained as Minister until the end of Cleveland's second term in 1897.

Bayard retired, and died in Dedham, Massachusetts on September 28, 1898.

James Gillespie Blaine (1889-1892)

James G. Blaine served two terms as Secretary of State. He was first appointed by U.S. President James A. Garfield, serving from March 7, 1881, until December 18, 1881, and was again appointed by U.S. President Benjamin Harrison, serving from March 5, 1889, until his resignation on June 4, 1892.

Once in office as Secretary of State, Blaine encouraged peaceful relations within the Americas, and also advocated for American commercial expansion and increased naval power. Blaine negotiated for the release of U.S. citizens who had been arrested and confined without trial in Ireland as part of a British crackdown on Irish nationalist rent boycotts.

Blaine unsuccessfully attempted to negotiate peace between Peru, Bolivia and Chile, all engaged in the War of the Pacific from 1879 to 1883. He also attempted to arbitrate a border dispute between Mexico and Guatemala. Blaine's overtures were cut short on September 19, 1881, by the death of President Garfield, who had been shot two months before on July 2. Blaine remained in office through December 18 while Chester A. Arthur, the new president, selected a replacement for him.

Under President Harrison, Blaine's first challenge was to counter German expansion in Samoa, where the United States competed for influence. The agreement reached in 1889 between the United States, Germany and the United Kingdom did not resolve the tensions between those countries, but further eroded Samoan sovereignty. During this term, Blaine attempted to negotiate a disagreement over Canadian fur seal hunting rights in the Bering Sea. He also faced controversies over the lynching of Italian citizens in New Orleans in 1891 and an attack on U.S. sailors in Valparaiso, Chile.

Blaine oversaw the Pan-American Conference, which had been organized by his predecessor, Thomas Francis Bayard. The conference covered trade, communication and legal issues, and eventually led to the establishment of the Pan-American Union.

Blaine resigned from his post on June 4, 1892. His resignation caught everyone, including President Harrison, by surprise. Although Blaine was a candidate for the 1892 Republican nomination, his poor health meant that he was not considered seriously. Blaine's health declined sharply after his resignation, and he died not long afterward on January 27, 1893.

John Watson Foster (1892-1893)

President Benjamin Harrison appointed John Watson Foster as Secretary of State on June 29, 1892. Foster assumed his duties on that day and served until February 23, 1893.

Foster served as Minister to Mexico during the rise to power of Porfirio Díaz in 1876. Foster supported recognition of Díaz's rule, but was overruled by then Secretary of State, William Evarts. As the tensions rose between the two countries, Foster testified before Congress, carefully advocating recognition without appearing to undermine Evarts or President Rutherford B. Hayes. In the end, Foster was able to secure recognition for the new Mexican government. While serving in Mexico, Foster also began the negotiations to resolve U.S.-Mexico border troubles that eventually led to an 1882 agreement.

As Minister to Russia, Foster's most pressing duty was to advocate for the rights of Jewish U.S. citizens living there. As Minister to Spain, Foster secured a reciprocal trade agreement for the Spanish colonies of Cuba and Puerto Rico in 1885, but the U.S. Senate rejected the agreement.

While serving as legal counsel to foreign legations in Washington, following his post in Spain, Foster provided legal representation for the Chinese Government seeking redress for an anti-immigration riot that killed twenty-eight Chinese laborers in Rock Springs, Wyoming in 1885. Foster also advocated on behalf of the Chinese Government during negotiations to overcome the exclusion of Chinese immigration to the United States and would continue to represent the Chinese Government in later years.

Foster became Secretary of State in 1892 and served for the remaining eight months of Harrison's administration. Foster had already forged a close working relationship with Harrison, as he was involved in negotiations for numerous trade agreements in the Western Hemisphere, and continued to be as Secretary of State.

As Secretary, Foster also attempted to counter British attempts at imperial expansion in Samoa and the Mosquito Coast. Foster also worked to negotiate a 99-year lease for a naval base in the Dominican Republic, but financial demands by the Dominican Government made Congress unwilling to approve the lease.

Foster instructed U.S. representatives at the International Monetary Conference in Brussels to advocate for a fixed rate of exchange between silver and gold, but the conference came to no agreement on precious metal issues. Foster also unsuccessfully attempted to annex the Kingdom of Hawaii.

After leaving office in 1893, Foster represented the United States in international arbitration regarding seal hunting rights in the Bering Sea and before the Alaskan Boundary Tribunal in the 1890s. At the time of his death on November 15, 1917, Foster's son-in-law Robert Lansing was serving as Secretary of State. Foster was also the grandfather of future Secretary John Foster Dulles.

Walter Quintin Gresham (1893-1895)

President Grover Cleveland nominated Walter Quintin Gresham to be Secretary of State on March 6, 1893, and Gresham entered into duty on March 7. Gresham died in office on May 28, 1895.

As soon as he assumed his position as Secretary of State, Gresham began investigating the circumstances surrounding the failed U.S. attempt to annex Hawaii under his predecessor, John W. Foster. Gresham's investigation showed the direct involvement of U.S. diplomats in the overthrow of Queen Liliuokalani. On the advice of Attorney General Richard Olney, President Cleveland decided to withdraw the treaty of annexation before the Senate. Since the Queen's overthrow was essentially a coup by pro-American sugar planters intent on eliminating Native Hawaiian political power, Cleveland hoped to restore Liliuokalni to power. However, the Senate declined to give Cleveland the authority to do so.

Gresham also worked to counter British influence in the Americas, citing the Monroe Doctrine as his guiding principle. He warned Julian Pauncefote, the British Ambassador to the United States, against British involvement in an 1895 royalist Brazilian coup attempt. However, when the Nicaraguan President José Zelaya attempted to exert a Nicaraguan claim to the Mosquito Coast in 1894, Gresham worked in concert with the British Government to ensure the continued commercial privileges of resident Americans in the region. The U.S. Government would later intervene to remove Zelaya from power in 1911.

In addition to his attention to Western Hemisphere concerns, Gresham encountered ongoing problems regarding the status and treatment of U.S. citizens in the Ottoman Empire. The Ottoman Government, at times, refused re-entry of emigrants who had become U.S. citizens. Gresham found that his attempts to secure rights for U.S. citizens, particularly during a time of Turkish-Armenian tensions, were rebuffed by Sultan Abdulhamid II. Gresham tried to walk a fine line between doing what was possible for U.S. citizens in the empire, while continuing a policy of non-intervention in European affairs, particularly those concerning the internal affairs of the Great Powers. This sensitive position led Gresham to reject calls by missionaries for a U.S. naval base in Smyrna.

Gresham's tenure as Secretary of State was cut short by his unexpected death on May 28, 1895 in Washington, D.C. Owing to the suddenness of his death, President Cleveland did not appoint a replacement until June 8.

Richard Olney (1895-1897)

President Grover Cleveland appointed Richard Olney as Secretary of State on June 8, 1895. Olney began duty on June 10, 1895, and served until March 5, 1897.

Olney came to the Department of State at a time when a Cuban revolt against Spanish rule in Cuba was gaining strength. As the Spanish Government attempted to suppress the rebellion, Olney faced public pressure to intervene. The U.S. Government tried to halt shipments from Cuban sympathizers and exiles from Key West and other U.S. ports. Tensions over Cuba would eventually ignite the Spanish-American War the year after Olney left office in 1898.

Olney played a significant role in mediating the boundary dispute between Venezuela and the British colony of Guyana. The dispute stemmed from the historically vague definition of the Venezuela-Guyana border, which had never been delineated during the colonial period.

In 1893, Venezuela publicly pressed its claims and hoped for arbitration. Hoping to secure assistance by invoking the Monroe Doctrine, José Andrade, Venezuelan Minister to the United States, brought the issue to the U.S. Department of State, and President Cleveland mentioned the issue in his 1894 message to Congress.

In February of 1895, Congress passed a resolution favoring U.S. arbitration. Although his predecessor, Walter Gresham, was less interested in pursuing the issue, Olney believed it was important to enhance national prestige and to capitalize on U.S. popular resentment of British power. At issue was not British reluctance to arbitrate, but British refusal to accept Venezuelan border demands as a possible outcome of the arbitration.

The situation began to change when renewed Anglo-German tensions pushed the Venezuela boundary dispute off the front pages of British newspapers. British policymakers began to favor maintaining good relations with the other Great Powers as British diplomacy suffered increasing international isolation.

Lord Salisbury decided that conciliation would be expedient and authorized British Ambassador to the United States, Julian Pauncefote, to negotiate an arbitration treaty. Olney and Pauncefote signed a treaty on February 2, 1897, which subjected the Venezuela-Guyana border to U.S. arbitration, allowing full Venezuelan claims to be considered in the arbitration process. The resulting arbitration, decided in October of 1899, awarded territory to Venezuela.

Olney left office at the end of Cleveland's second administration, and resumed practicing law, although he continued to write about international relations. In 1904, Olney was a candidate for the Democratic nomination for President. He declined the Ambassadorship to Great Britain in 1914, citing his age. Olney died on April 8, 1917.

John Sherman (1897-1898)

John Sherman was appointed Secretary of State in President William McKinley's Cabinet, a position in which he served from March 6, 1897, until April 27, 1898. Sherman resigned his position days after the outbreak of the Spanish-American War.

Sherman's tenure as Secretary of State was marked by the tension between him, President McKinley, and Assistant Secretary of State William R. Day.

Sherman had been offered the position largely to free up a Senate seat for Mark Hanna, a supporter and friend of the President. Unfortunately for the President, Sherman often diverged from the President's foreign policy agenda and became increasingly vocal in his criticism of the McKinley administration.

As a result, the President and other members of the Cabinet soon ostracized Secretary of State Sherman, allowing Sherman's subordinates to negotiate many foreign policy decisions.

Relations between Sherman and the McKinley administration became so tense that Assistant Secretary Day often replaced Sherman at Cabinet meetings, an obvious affront to the Secretary.

Day negotiated the annexation of Hawaii, as well as U.S. policy towards Spain as the two nations were on the brink of war.

Sherman did wield influence when it came to upholding the U.S. interpretation of most-favored-nation treatment in matters relating to international trade. He also worked to secure U.S. commercial concessions in China; many of his policies would become part of the Open Door Policy at the turn of the century. Despite his influence on issues of international commerce, Sherman's weak position in the Cabinet meant that he was unable to press his opposition to U.S. acquisition of Cuba and his objection to war with Spain.

Sherman finally resigned in protest four days into the Spanish-American War in 1898. His bitterness toward President McKinley and his administration continued until his death in 1900.

William Rufus Day (1898-1898)

William Rufus Day was appointed Secretary of State in President William McKinley's Cabinet on April 26, 1898. He entered into duty on April 28, 1898, and served until September 16, 1898.

Day assumed the position of Secretary of State just a few days after the start of the Spanish-American War. Although he was not known to be an especially skilled diplomat, Day worked tirelessly to secure the neutrality of Europe during the war. The Spanish-American War dominated his tenure, as well as the annexation of Hawaii.

Day had agreed only to take the position of Secretary of State until the end of the war, and submitted his resignation shortly after the peace treaty with Spain was signed in 1898. As the U.S. representative to the peace conference in Paris, Day successfully negotiated with Spain the ceding of Cuba, Guam, the Philippines, and Puerto Rice to the United States for $20 million.

President McKinley's foreign policy aims were largely carried out by Day with little conflict. Day's only objection in the Spanish-American War peace settlement was the annexation of the Philippines, yet he honored McKinley's wishes.

After resigning as Secretary of State, he transferred his duties to John Hay. Shortly after, Day returned to the legal profession. President McKinley appointed Day judge to the Sixth Circuit Court of Appeals. He served there until 1903, when President Roosevelt nominated him Associate Justice of the U.S. Supreme Court.

Day enjoyed a long and distinguished career in the Supreme Court, serving nearly 20 years. He resigned due to failing health in 1922. Justice Day died the following year.

John Milton Hay (1898-1905)

John Milton Hay was appointed Secretary of State in President William McKinley's Cabinet on September 30, 1898, and entered into duty the same day. He continued in office under President Theodore Roosevelt following McKinley's assassination in 1901 and served until his death in office on July 1, 1905.

Hay had a significant influence on the direction of U.S. foreign policy while serving in President McKinley's Cabinet. He faced the aftermath of the Spanish-American War and the annexation of the Philippine Islands, which amplified U.S. interest in Asia.

As Secretary of State, Hay was a proponent of increased trade through the "Open Door" policy. He worked to encourage stability in China and to counteract the rising nationalism that threatened foreign interests in China, which included the challenge of the Boxer Rebellion of 1900.

As Secretary, Hay also secured the settlement of the Alaska-Canada boundary controversy. When President McKinley was assassinated, Hay stayed on as Secretary of State to serve under President Theodore Roosevelt. Roosevelt and Hay had few policy differences, although the new President wielded greater influence over foreign policy than his predecessor.

Hay helped secure, by treaty, the right for the United States to construct and defend the Panama Canal in 1903.

Although he suffered from deteriorating health, Hay played an active role in the Roosevelt administration during the last two years of his tenure. He died in office in 1905.

Elihu Root (1905-1909)

Elihu Root was appointed Secretary of State following the death of John Hay. He entered into duty on July 19, 1905, and served until January 27, 1909.

An isolationist, Root differed from President Roosevelt when it came to U.S. involvement in other nations' crises. Root's first notable act as Secretary of State was a goodwill tour through Latin America, where he worked to ease tensions in Cuba over the Platt Amendment and in Colombia over the role the United States played in Panamanian independence at the outset of the construction of the Canal.

The most pressing diplomatic issue that faced the United States when Root entered into duty was a dispute between France and Germany over interests in Morocco, which was resolved in 1907. Despite his reluctance to involve the United States in issues in which it had limited interests, Root negotiated arbitration treaties with 24 nations. Root was awarded the Nobel Peace Prize in 1912 (several years after he was Secretary of State) for his work on international arbitration.

Root also worked to reorganize the Department of State in unprecedented ways. Root sought to professionalize the Foreign Service and Consular Service and created the first Foreign Service Exam. He instituted new methods of recordkeeping in the Department, devised a system of rotating members of the diplomatic service to give them greater experience, and organized the Department by geographic regions. These reforms would ultimately prove to be more enduring than Root's contributions to foreign policy.

Robert Bacon (1909-1909)

Robert Bacon was appointed Secretary of State January 27, 1909, and entered into duty the same day. Bacon had served as Assistant Secretary of State under Elihu Root prior to his appointment. He served only 37 days as Secretary of State, until March 5, 1909, when President Theodore Roosevelt left office.

Bacon's business savvy aided his diplomatic efforts as he worked diligently to ratify treaties between Colombia, Panama and the United States regarding the Panama Canal. Bacon's appointment as Secretary of State for the remainder of Roosevelt's term was mostly due to his friendship with the President. However, he used that month wisely, successfully passing the treaties through the Senate.

Bacon also convened an environmental conference between the North American states, to discuss conservation of natural resources on the continent. Bacon's diplomatic skill was recognized by his successor, Secretary of State Philander Knox, who appointed Bacon as Ambassador to France.

Years later, Bacon served under General Pershing during World War One. His military service at an advanced age put a general strain on Bacon's health, and he died in 1919, shortly after returning to the United States.

Philander Chase Knox (1909-1913)

President William Howard Taft appointed Pennsylvania Senator Philander Chase Knox as Secretary of State on March 6, 1909. Following his unsuccessful bid for the Republican presidential nomination the previous year, Knox resigned his seat in the U.S. Senate and entered into duty that same day.

As Secretary of State, Knox tightly controlled U.S. foreign policy. He reorganized the Department of State into regional divisions, maximizing expertise acquired by those in the Foreign Service. Knox extended the merit system of selection and promotion from the Consular Service to the Diplomatic Service.

Knox continued the Open Door Policy of his predecessors and pursued an even more aggressive role in encouraging and protecting U.S. investments abroad.

His emphasis on trade to promote democracy and stability became known as "Dollar Diplomacy." The United States first initiated this policy in Asia, but it became the core of U.S. foreign policy in Latin America. Interventions in the Caribbean and Central America were based on the theory that democratic governments would lead to free markets and open trade.

Knox also successfully negotiated the Bering Sea controversy during his time as Secretary. The treaty, designed to put an end to the devastating slaughter of seals, was signed by the United States, Great Britain, Japan and Russia in 1911.

After President Taft lost his second presidential bid in 1912, Knox resigned his position and returned to Pittsburgh. He continued to practice law until he returned to the U.S. Senate in 1916, where he led the fight against the Treaty of Versailles and the League of Nations after World War One.

Knox served in the Senate until his death in 1921.

William Jennings Bryan (1913-1915)

President Woodrow Wilson appointed William Jennings Bryan Secretary of State on March 5, 1913. He entered into duty the same day and served as Secretary until his resignation on June 9, 1915.

Bryan's major accomplishment as Secretary was his negotiation of peace treaties that pledged the 30 signatories to refrain from hostilities during arbitration of disputes. He also negotiated the Bryan–Chamorro Treaty in 1914 (ratified by the Senate in 1916), which permitted the United States the latitude to construct an isthmian canal across Nicaragua and secured rights to build naval bases at the Gulf of Fonseca and on the Corn Islands.

Bryan's position on the rights of neutrals during wartime placed him at odds with President Wilson. Declaring U.S. neutrality following the outbreak of World War I in August 1914, Wilson adhered to traditional concepts governing the recognition of blockades, neutral transport of contraband goods, and travel of civilians to belligerent nations on combatant ships. Bryan asserted that technological innovations such as submarines had altered the nature of international law and made it impossible to protect U.S. citizens traveling into a war zone, and he attempted to persuade Wilson to prohibit such travel.

The German practice of unrestricted submarine warfare, which Wilson perceived as a violation of the rights of neutrals, resulted in the sinking of the British passenger liner Lusitania in May 1915 and the deaths of 128 U.S. citizens. Wilson responded by sending the German Government a strongly worded protest note affirming the right of neutrals to transit on the high seas. Bryan insisted that Wilson send a similar protest to Britain for its violations of neutral rights, an act the president rejected. Wilson's dispatch of a second note demanding an end to German submarine warfare prompted Bryan to resign on June 9, 1915.

Following his resignation, Bryan continued to write and lecture and opposed Clarence Darrow as counsel in the Scopes trial. Bryan died on July 26, 1925.

Robert Lansing (1915-1920)

Robert Lansing served as Secretary of State from June 24, 1915, until February 13, 1920. Lansing's background in international law afforded him a wealth of foreign relations experience, which influenced his tenure at the Department of State. His most important achievements included his oversight of U.S. foreign policy during the First World War and his negotiation of a major agreement between the United States and Japan.

Lansing's influence on U.S. diplomacy extended beyond his tenure as Secretary of State due to the important role he played in helping to settle a number of high-profile international disputes. This influence only grew once Lansing became Secretary.

While Secretary he was faced with the significant foreign policy challenges related to the U.S. position in the First World War. Initially, Lansing advocated benevolent neutrality in the European conflict and strongly protested British blockades and contraband practices, while advocating for the principles of the freedom of the seas and the rights of neutral nations. Lansing eventually came to favor U.S. participation in the war and accompanied President Woodrow Wilson to Europe as one of the lead U.S. negotiators at the Paris Peace Conference in 1919.

As Secretary of State, Lansing also signed the Treaty of 1916 for the purchase of the Danish West Indies and the Lansing-Ishii Agreement of 1917 with Japan--a pledge between the United States and Japan to uphold the Open Door Policy in China, while recognizing that Japan had special interests in China.

Lansing is also credited with establishing the Diplomatic Security Service, having hired the Department of State's first special agents, who were assigned to observe Central Power activities in the United States before and during the First World War. Due to disagreements over the League of Nations and President Wilson's inability to perform his presidential duties following a stroke, Lansing resigned on February 13, 1920.

Bainbridge Colby (1920-1921)

President Woodrow Wilson appointed Bainbridge Colby as his third Secretary of State on March 23, 1920. He was confirmed by the Senate and entered into duty the same day. Colby served until the end of the Wilson administration, leaving office on March 4, 1921.

President Wilson and Secretary of State Colby shared many of the same views on the conduct of U.S. foreign policy. However, Colby entered office during the challenging last years of the Wilson administration.

Despite Colby's efforts, the Senate refused to ratify the Versailles Treaty following World War One and contested U.S. membership in Wilson's League of Nations.

Colby experienced more success in his approach towards the new government of the Soviet Union. He formulated a non-recognition policy toward the Soviet Union based on its promotion of international communism and the threat it posed to existing governments.

Closer to home, Colby successfully negotiated recognition and normal diplomatic relations with the Mexican Government following the Mexican Revolution. He toured Latin America on behalf of the President, promoting hemispheric cooperation.

Audiences warmly received the Secretary of State and approved of his willingness to publicly discuss the merits of the Monroe Doctrine. Colby convincingly argued that the doctrine was not imperialistic, but rather promoted democracy throughout Latin America.

Colby left office at the end of the Wilson administration in 1921 and returned to private practice. Colby died on April 11, 1950.

Charles Evans Hughes (1921-1925)

Charles Evans Hughes served as Secretary of State from March 5, 1921, to March 5, 1925, during the administration of President Warren Harding. He continued as Secretary after Harding's death in office, but resigned at the beginning of President Calvin Coolidge's full term.

Hughes came to the office of Secretary of State at a moment of transition in U.S. politics. President Wilson's internationalist ideas, grounded in his wartime Fourteen Points and his advocacy of a new League of Nations designed to prevent future wars, had been discredited in the United States during the peace negotiations at the end of World War I. Although President Wilson had successfully negotiated the Treaty of Versailles, ending the war and establishing the League, the U.S. Senate had refused to ratify the treaty in 1920, and President Wilson had been unwilling to compromise in order to secure its passage.

President Harding was elected in part because of his call for a return to "normalcy," and as a result Hughes implemented a foreign policy that pursued only the most limited connection to the League or the principles of collective security laid out during the Wilson administration.

Hughes increased U.S. prestige in Latin America by arbitrating disputes between countries in the Western Hemisphere, and during his tenure, the United States recognized the new government in Mexico and compensated Colombia for the 1903 Panamanian revolt, which the United States had supported. He also directed the Washington Naval Conference of 1921-22, which resulted in the Five-Power Treaty, setting the ratio of naval strength among the five largest naval powers.

At the same time, he signed several agreements with the Japanese limiting the deployments of Japanese and U.S. military forces in the Pacific Ocean. He also ended the state of war with Germany with the Treaty of Berlin.

As Secretary of State, Hughes also worked to improve morale and increase the level of talent in the Department of State by supporting the 1924 Foreign Service Act ("Rogers Act,"), which would eventually result in a professional, highly-trained Foreign Service.

Frank Billings Kellogg (1925-1929)

Frank Billings Kellogg served as Secretary of State during the full term of President Calvin Coolidge from 1925 until 1929, after serving as the U.S. Ambassador to the United Kingdom. He served from March 5, 1925, to March 28, 1929.

Even before he became Secretary of State, Kellogg had great influence. As Ambassador to the United Kingdom, he influenced U.S. foreign policy, especially regarding the issue of German reparations to the Allies, as outlined in the Treaty of Versailles. Kellogg was one of several important negotiators of the 1924 Dawes Plan, a serious attempt to modify the burden of German reparations payments to France, Belgium, and the United Kingdom.

Once Secretary, he took part in the unsuccessful follow-up to the 1921 Washington Naval Conference, the Geneva Conference of 1927. He also encountered anti-Americanism at the Western Hemisphere conference in 1928. However, he was successful in negotiating a settlement between Chile and Peru regarding the Tacna-Arica border dispute and negotiating a treaty of arbitration with the Republic of Mexico. He also negotiated or signed nearly 80 other treaties with European and Western Hemisphere states, breaking the record set by William Jennings Bryan.

Kellogg's most lasting achievement, for which he received the Nobel Peace Prize in 1929, was the negotiation of the Kellogg-Briand Pact. This multilateral pact negotiated between 1927 and 1928 with Aristide Briand, the French Foreign Minister, began as a French proposal for a mutual security pact and evolved into a treaty renouncing war as an instrument of national policy. It was ratified overwhelmingly by the U.S. Senate in 1929, despite criticism that it could never be an effective deterrent to war.

Henry Lewis Stimson (1929-1933)

Henry Lewis Stimson served as Secretary of State in President Herbert Hoover's Cabinet from March 28, 1929, until March 4, 1933.

Stimson succeeded Frank Kellogg as Secretary of State only a few days after the U.S. Senate had ratified the Kellogg-Briand Pact. He attempted during his tenure to save that pact, but commented in 1933 that "the situation in the world seemed to me like the unfolding of a great Greek tragedy, where we could see the march of events and know what ought to be done, but seemed to be powerless to prevent its marching to its grim conclusion."

He headed the U.S. delegation to the London Naval Conference in 1930, which succeeded in limiting the naval race among the largest naval powers, although Japan would withdraw from the agreement in 1935. He also led the U.S. delegation to the Geneva Disarmament Conference in 1932.

Upon Japan's occupation of Manchuria in 1931, Stimson articulated what later became known as the "Stimson Doctrine," that the United States would recognize no diminution of U.S. treaty rights brought about by aggression. He also attempted, unsuccessfully, to limit the economic effects of war debts, but was thwarted by the U.S. Congress' adoption of the Hawley-Smoot Tariff.

Cordell Hull (1933-1944)

Cordell Hull was appointed Secretary of State by President Franklin D. Roosevelt on March 4, 1933, and served until November 20, 1944. Hull holds the distinction of being the longest-serving U.S. Secretary of State.

As Secretary of State, Hull's role in U.S. foreign policymaking was greatly circumscribed by President Roosevelt. Hull nonetheless achieved prominence as an advocate of trade liberalization, closer relations with Latin America, and a postwar multinational institution to promote peace and security.

Although President Roosevelt typically represented the United States at the major conferences with Allied leaders during the Second World War, Hull took the lead in attempting to delay war with Japan following its invasion of China. He was also a strong supporter of President Roosevelt's "Good Neighbor" policy and became the first sitting Secretary of State to attend the International Conference of American States (precursor to the Organization of American States). At the December 1933 meeting in Montevideo, Uruguay, he announced that the U.S. Government would henceforth observe a policy of "non-intervention" in the affairs of its neighbors in the Western Hemisphere.

His greatest contribution to the postwar world came within the realm of international trade. As a firm believer in Woodrow Wilson's vision of liberal internationalism, Hull believed that free trade promoted international peace and prosperity. He considered high tariff barriers a pressing issue that had contributed to the economic decline leading to the Great Depression and the rise of fascism.

In 1934, Hull helped secure the passage of the Reciprocal Trade Agreements Act (RTAA), which gave the President the authority to personally negotiate bilateral tariff reductions.

Hull also championed the creation of the United Nations. For his efforts in creating the United Nations, Hull was honored with the Nobel Peace Prize in 1945.

Cordell Hull resigned as Secretary for health reasons on November 30, 1944, but served as a delegate to the United Nations Conference in San Francisco in 1945. He died in Washington, D.C., on July 23, 1955.

Edward Reilly Stettinius (1944-1945)

Edward Reilly Stettinius, Jr. served as Secretary of State from December 1, 1944, until June 27, 1945, under Presidents Franklin Delano Roosevelt and Harry S. Truman. As Secretary of State, he oversaw the end of the Second World War in Europe and the creation of the United Nations.

Stettinius came to the position of Secretary of State with a great deal of foreign policy experience. His roles in war production and national defense and his work as chief Lend-Lease administrator and Special Assistant to the President had prepared him for the challenges of being chief diplomat.

As Secretary of State, Stettinius accompanied President Roosevelt to the Yalta Conference in February of 1945, where they met with British Prime Minister Winston Churchill and Soviet Premier Joseph Stalin to discuss issues such as the Pacific War with Japan, the future political status of Eastern Europe, and what should be done with Germany following its surrender.

Stettinius also chaired the United States delegation to the United Nations Conference, held in San Francisco from April 25 to June 26, 1945, which brought together delegates from 50 Allied nations to create the United Nations.

He resigned his position as Secretary of State on June 27, 1945, to become the first U.S. Ambassador to the United Nations, a post which he held until resigning in June 1946 over what he saw as President Truman's refusal to use the United Nations forum to resolve growing Soviet-American tensions.

Stettinius continued his interest in international issues after his resignation as U.S. Ambassador to the United Nations by heading the Liberia Company, which partnered U.S. financiers with the Liberian Government to provide funds for Liberia's development.

James Francis Byrnes (1945-1947)

James Francis Byrnes was appointed Secretary of State by President Harry S. Truman on July 3, 1945, and entered duty on the same day. He left office on January 21, 1947. Byrnes led the Department of State during the significant transition from World War II to the Cold War.

A skilled policymaker, Byrnes spent much of his time outside of Washington meeting with foreign leaders. President Truman was uncertain of his own aptitude in matters of foreign policy and thus placed a great deal of confidence in Secretary Byrnes.

Within days of his appointment, Byrnes accompanied President Truman to the Potsdam Conference, a critical turning point in U.S.-Soviet relations. He continued to negotiate the rapidly fraying post-war alliance at conferences in London and Moscow.

Byrnes increasingly wielded less control over U.S. foreign policy as disagreements arose with President Truman over how forceful the country should be against the increasingly uncooperative Soviet Union.

The Secretary was a proponent of using the newly-developed atomic bomb against Japan, and under his advice, two atomic bombs were detonated over Japan in August of 1945. It was also during Byrnes' tenure as Secretary of State that George Kennan authored his famous 1946 "Long Telegram," advocating a change in policy towards the Soviets. President Truman and Secretary Byrnes implemented these changes swiftly, laying the foundations for the early Cold War.

Byrnes resigned his position on January 21, 1947, and continued to practice law. In 1951 he was elected Governor of South Carolina and served one term. James Byrnes died in 1972.

George Catlett Marshall (1947-1949)

George Catlett Marshall was nominated as Secretary of State by President Harry S. Truman on January 8, 1947, and was confirmed unanimously by the Senate. Marshall entered on duty on January 21, 1947, and served as Secretary of State until January 20, 1949.

Following Marshall's resignation as Chief of Staff, President Truman relied heavily on Marshall's expertise to navigate postwar diplomacy. Marshall's first assignment was to lead a special mission to China in late 1945 to mediate the conflict between the Nationalists and the Communists. Although this mission was ultimately unsuccessful, Marshall's tenure as Secretary of State was marked by several notable achievements.

In 1947 and 1948, Marshall led the effort to formulate and secure congressional support for the massive aid package to Western Europe that would become known as the Marshall Plan. The United States also negotiated the Inter-

American Treaty of Reciprocal Assistance and the North Atlantic Treaty Organization under Secretary Marshall. Although Marshall typically served President Truman without objection, he did strongly disagree with Truman on the recognition of the State of Israel.

Marshall resigned as Secretary of State in 1949 and became president of the American Red Cross. However, he returned to the Truman Cabinet as Secretary of Defense in 1950 and served briefly in that capacity until 1951. Marshall died in 1959 after receiving the Nobel Peace Prize in 1953 for his work to restore Europe's economy in the post-World War II period.

Dean Gooderham Acheson (1949-1953)

Dean Gooderham Acheson served as Secretary of State from January 21, 1949, through January 20, 1953, and exerted significant influence on U.S. foreign policy during his tenure.

As Secretary of State, Acheson played an important role in shaping U.S. policy during the early Cold War. Acheson enjoyed a good working relationship with President Harry S. Truman, who often allowed Acheson to be the first official to speak on record about U.S. foreign policy decisions.

Although Acheson supported the containment of communism and the tenets of the Truman Doctrine, he was also a realist who recognized that the Soviet Union was not only an ideological opponent, but also a viable global power that had to be viewed as a serious geopolitical challenge to U.S. interests. This belief shaped Acheson's approach to the many foreign policy challenges that faced the United States during his tenure.

Chief among these was the question of what to do with Germany and how to prevent future Soviet influence there. To this end, Acheson supported the formation of the North Atlantic Treaty Organization (NATO) in 1949, a defensive alliance geared to counter the Soviet threat to Europe while ensuring that the western part of Germany was tied firmly to the West.

Although Europe was Acheson's primary focus, he also faced questions related to international control of atomic weapons; the fall of mainland China to the Communist forces of Mao Zedong and the retreat of the U.S.-backed Nationalists to Taiwan; the rebuilding of Japan as a cornerstone of U.S. policy in East Asia; the Korean War; and Soviet designs on Yugoslavia, the Middle East, and Asia.

Senator Joseph McCarthy ultimately singled Acheson out for "losing" China to the communists.

Acheson continued to have influence on U.S. foreign policy after leaving the Department of State. During the Kennedy administration, Acheson sat on the Executive Committee created to address the Cuban Missile Crisis.

Later in the decade, Acheson served as an advisor to the Lyndon B. Johnson administration for how to disengage from the war in Vietnam. Acheson died at the age of 78 in 1971.

John Foster Dulles (1953-1959)

John Foster Dulles was appointed Secretary of State by President Dwight Eisenhower on January 21, 1953. Dulles served for much of the decade, leaving an indelible mark upon U.S. foreign policy that included close cooperation between the Department of State and the Central Intelligence Agency as well as a focus upon international mutual security agreements designed to contain communism.

President Dwight D. Eisenhower appointed Dulles as his Secretary of State on January 21, 1953. During the 1950s, Dulles and Eisenhower forged a strong friendship that granted the Secretary of State direct and unprecedented access to the President. Furthermore, Dulles's time as Secretary was marked by a general consensus in U.S. policy that peace could be maintained through the containment of communism. This consensus allowed Dulles and Eisenhower to secure international mutual security agreements while at the same time reducing the number of troops in the U.S. military and the production of conventional weapons. Dulles also enjoyed the close cooperation of the Central Intelligence Agency, which was run by his brother, Allen Dulles.

Dulles confronted many foreign policy challenges during his tenure including the integration of Europe, escalation of the crisis in Indochina, U.S. response to the Hungarian Revolution, and the Suez Canal crisis of 1956. Despite being diagnosed with advanced stage cancer in the immediate aftermath of the Suez Crisis, Dulles returned to work in Foggy Bottom. One of his last directives was the formulation of the Eisenhower Doctrine in response to the Suez Crisis. (The Eisenhower Doctrine was an expression of the key tenets of Dulles's foreign policy views: containment and international mutual security agreements reinforced by economic aid.)

Dulles was also the first Secretary of State to be directly accessible to the media and to hold the first Department press conferences.

Poor health forced Dulles to resign his position at the Department of State in April of 1959, only weeks before his death on May 24, 1959.

Christian Archibald Herter (1959-1961)

Christian A. Herter was appointed Secretary of State on April 22, 1959, and remained in that position until the end of the Dwight D. Eisenhower administration on January 20, 1961. Whether working for the U.S. Government or in the private sector, Herter dedicated much of his adult life to serving his country and shaping its role in world affairs.

Herter played an active role in U.S. diplomacy throughout his life, whether he was working for the Department of State or the U.S. House of Representatives. While in Congress, a report that was written in a committee he chaired initiated proposals that led to President Harry Truman's Marshall Plan, in which the United States gave $13 billion in reconstruction aid to Europe following the Second World War.

Along with scholar George Camp Keiser, Herter founded the Middle East Institute in 1947, and he also served on the board of trustees of the World Peace Foundation. As Under Secretary of State and Secretary of State, Herter helped oversee U.S. diplomacy during the 1958 invasion of Lebanon, the 1958 Taiwan Strait Crisis, and the U-2 incident in 1960.

Herter's role in the international arena did not end with the Eisenhower administration. He also served as a trade negotiator in the administrations of both John F. Kennedy and Lyndon B. Johnson.

David Dean Rusk (1961-1969)

David Dean Rusk served as Secretary of State under Presidents John F. Kennedy and Lyndon Baines Johnson. Rusk entered into duty as Secretary on January 21, 1961, and resigned on January 20, 1969.

Rusk asserted that the Secretary of State served at the pleasure of the President. As such, the Secretary's role reflected that of an advisor who would preside over policy debates, offer informed views, and endorse the President's decisions.

Rusk subverted his own misgivings about the failed 1961 Cuban Bay of Pigs invasion and closed ranks around Kennedy. From his own perspective, Rusk perceived the world of the 1960s as caught up in "revolutionary changes"—notably the establishment of new nations—and believed that U.S. foreign policy should provide emerging nations with technical and humanitarian assistance to speed these nations along the path toward modernity and democracy.

Rusk also advocated a "dignified diplomacy," emphasizing civility and communication between the United States and the Soviet Union. Rusk's diplomatic orientation and his ability to evaluate and judge competing points of view defused tensions during the October 1962 Cuban Missile Crisis and contributed toward the successful negotiation of the Limited Nuclear Test Ban Treaty in August 1963.

Although he favored a gradualist approach to U.S. involvement in Vietnam—in order to maintain the U.S. obligation to Vietnam under SEATO—his support of President Lyndon Johnson's war policy exposed him to public criticism.

Rusk ended his tenure as Secretary on January 20, 1969. He was appointed the Samuel H. Sibley Professor of International Law at the University of Georgia (1970–1984), established the Dean Rusk Center for International and Comparative Law, and completed a memoir, with the assistance of his son Richard Rusk, entitled As I Saw It. Rusk died on December 20, 1994.

William Pierce Rogers (1969-1973)

William Pierce Rogers served as President Richard M. Nixon's Secretary of State from January 22, 1969, until September 3, 1973. Although often overshadowed by the Assistant to the President for National Security Affairs and his own successor, Henry Kissinger, Rogers proved to be an accomplished administrator and diplomat.

As Secretary of State, Rogers promoted a cease-fire in the Middle East in 1970, which lasted until the 1973 war, dealt with problems of security and cooperation in Europe, signed the 1973 Vietnam peace agreement, and brought the State Department into the electronic age by ordering the installation of a computerized system to store diplomatic documents and information.

Rogers is best known for his efforts to broker a lasting peace settlement between Israel, its Arab neighbors, and the Palestinian refugees. In a December 9, 1969 speech Rogers unveiled what would later become known as the "Rogers Plan," calling for collective action on the part of the United States, the Soviet Union, the United Kingdom, and France to implement U.N. Resolution 242, which ended the Third Arab-Israeli War. Ultimately, none of the concerned parties were able to agree on a suitable framework for implementing Rogers' initiative, thereby leading to the outbreak of the Fourth Arab-Israeli War in October 1973.

Rogers' successor, Dr. Henry Kissinger, did, however, begin the process of securing a negotiated Israeli withdrawal from the Sinai in 1974 as a result of the "shuttle diplomacy" that ended the October War.

Henry A. (Heinz Alfred) Kissinger (1973-1977)

Henry Alfred Kissinger was appointed Secretary of State on September 21 by President Richard M. Nixon and served in the position from September 23, 1973 to January 20, 1977. With his appointment, he became the first person ever to serve as both Secretary of State and National Security Adviser, a position he had held since President Nixon was sworn into office on January 20, 1969.

However, on November 3, 1975, President Gerald R. Ford removed him from his National Security Adviser position while keeping him as Secretary of State.

Kissinger entered the State Department just two weeks before Egypt and Syria launched a surprise attack on Israel. The October War of 1973 played a major role in shaping Kissinger's tenure as Secretary. First, he worked to ensure Israel received an airlift of U.S. military supplies. This airlift helped Israel turn the war in Israel's favor, and it also led members of the Organization of Petroleum Exporting Countries (OPEC) to initiate an oil embargo against the United States. After the implementation of a United Nation's sponsored cease-fire, Kissinger began a series of "shuttle diplomacy" missions, in which he traveled between various Middle East capitals to reach disengagement agreements between the enemy combatants. These efforts produced an agreement in January 1974 between Egypt and Israel and in May 1974 between Syria and Israel. Additionally, Kissinger's efforts contributed to OPEC's decision to lift the embargo.

On August 9, 1974, the Watergate scandal compelled President Nixon to resign, but Kissinger stayed on in his dual roles under President Gerald Ford. Kissinger helped Ford acclimate to the international scene and both men worked to continue policies implemented by Nixon and Kissinger previously, including détente with the Soviet Union, establishing relations with the People's Republic of China, and negotiations in the Middle East.

Kissinger also played a major role in the negotiations leading to the August 1975 Helsinki Accord, an agreement signed by 35 countries and addressing many issues that promised to improve relations between East and West. In September 1975, Kissinger helped conclude a second disengagement agreement between Egypt and Israel that moved both countries closer to a peace agreement.

Kissinger's tenure as Secretary comprised many controversial issues, including his role in influencing U.S. policies towards countries such as Chile and Angola. Additionally, he engaged in new international issues such as law of the sea, which became more prominent for U.S. foreign policy in the decades ahead.

Cyrus Roberts Vance (1977-1980)

Cyrus Roberts Vance was appointed Secretary of State by President Jimmy Carter on January 21, 1977. He entered his position on January 23 and resigned on April 28, 1980 in protest over President Carter's decision to attempt a military rescue of American hostages in Iran.

Vance emphasized negotiations over military confrontation during his tenure as Secretary of State and shared with President Carter a belief that human rights should be a central tenet of U.S. diplomacy. Within his first months of entering office, Vance worked diligently on arms control issues with the Soviet Union and sought a comprehensive peace agreement between Israel and its Arab neighbors.

Although his initial efforts bore no immediate fruit, over the course of the next two years, Vance helped negotiate the Panama Canal Treaty, which would relinquish U.S. control of the canal zone; the Israel-Egypt Peace Treaty, the first peace treaty between Israel and an Arab neighbor; the restoration of full diplomatic relations with China; and a settlement among political factions in Zimbabwe that allowed for majority rule.

In 1979, Vance grew frustrated as President Carter appeared to move toward more confrontational policies, disregarding Vance's advice on several issues, including how to handle the political crisis in Iran that led to the Shah's ouster and the creation of the Islamic Republic of Iran. During this political turmoil, Iranian student militants seized the American Embassy and took its staff hostage. After President Carter ordered a rescue attempt to free the hostages in the spring of 1980, an attempt that ultimately failed, Vance decided to resign because he believed a military operation would be in vain and would damage the negotiations he had been working on to win the release of the hostages.

Although Vance returned to private law practice, he frequently found himself drawn back into a foreign policy role and served on several diplomatic missions, most notably as the United Nations Special Envoy to Bosnia in 1993. Vance died in early 2002.

Edmund Sixtus Muskie (1980-1981)

Edmund Sixtus Muskie served as President Jimmy Carter's Secretary of State from May 8, 1980 until January 18, 1981. A long-time U.S. Senator from Maine, Muskie was tapped to serve as Carter's second Secretary of State after the resignation of Cyrus Vance following the failed rescue of the American hostages in Iran.

Following the resignation of Cyrus Vance, President Carter envisioned Muskie's role as more of a senior statesman and spokesman for the Administration, while leaving the everyday management of the Department of State to Deputy Secretary Warren Christopher.

In the nine months Muskie served as Secretary of State, he conducted the first high-level meeting with the Soviet government after its December 1979 invasion of Afghanistan. During these negotiations, Secretary Muskie unsuccessfully attempted to secure the withdrawal of Soviet forces from Afghanistan.

Muskie also assisted President Carter in the implementation of the "Carter Doctrine," which aimed to limit Soviet expansion into the Middle East and Persian Gulf. Finally, under Muskie's leadership, the State Department negotiated the release of the remaining American hostages held by Iran.

Alexander Meigs Haig (1981-1982)

Alexander Meigs Haig, Jr. was appointed Secretary of State by President Ronald Reagan and assumed the office on January 22, 1981. He served a relatively short time in office, facing many challenging situations before stepping down on July 5, 1982.

As Secretary of State, Haig had hoped to restore the Department of State to the dominant position in foreign policy-making that it had lost during previous administrations. However, the United States faced many challenges during the time that Haig served as Secretary of State, including the Soviet presence in Afghanistan, the Solidarity movement in Poland, disputes with the People's Republic of China over trade and Taiwan, escalating tensions between the

United Kingdom and Argentina, and a new round of conflict between Israel, Lebanon, and Syria. He also had to deal with the intra-government turmoil that followed in the wake of the attempted assassination of President Reagan.

Haig did have some diplomatic successes, particularly in regards to relations with China, where he forged a balance that both stabilized relations with the PRC and allowed for the continuation of arms sales to the government on Taiwan.

He also strengthened the NATO alliance and helped to re-orient the focus of U.S. foreign policy back toward the Soviet Union, both of which reflected the overall foreign policy priorities of the Reagan Administration.

Nevertheless, his efforts to broker diplomatic resolutions to the disputes over the Falkland Islands and in the Middle East did not succeed. Throughout his tenure as Secretary, Haig was overshadowed in foreign policy matters by other members of the Administration and was thus unable to fully control the Administration's diplomatic process. He resigned from office after only 18 months.

George Pratt Shultz (1982-1989)

George Shultz was named as Secretary of State by President Ronald Reagan on June 25, 1982. Following confirmation by the Senate, he assumed the office of Secretary on July 16, and he remained in that position until January 20, 1989.

As Secretary of State, Shultz played a crucial role in guiding U.S. diplomacy during his lengthy six and a half year tenure in office. Upon his confirmation, he inherited a number of foreign policy challenges, including war in Lebanon, delicate negotiations with the People's Republic of China and the Government on Taiwan, and a ratcheting up of Cold War tensions with the Soviet Union.

Over the next several years, Shultz focused U.S. diplomatic efforts on resolving the conflict in the Middle East, defusing trade disputes with Japan, managing increasingly tense relationships with several Latin American nations, and crafting U.S. responses to the rise of Mikhail Gorbachev and the new Soviet policies of perestroika and opening to the West.

In part due to his collegial relationships with President Reagan and other members of the Administration, Shultz was able to exert considerable influence over U.S. foreign policy in regards to these issues. Although he was unable to forge a lasting resolution to the Middle East conflict, he negotiated an agreement between Israel and Lebanon and convinced Israel to begin withdrawing its troops in January 1985, in spite of Lebanon's contravention of the settlement.

He completed the discussions between the United States and China, begun under Secretary of State Alexander Haig, which led to the joint communiqué of August 1982 that has provided stability for U.S.-Chinese relations ever since.

Shultz had not been able to halt the arms-for-hostages deals with Iran that provided funds for the Contras in Nicaragua, which he had opposed, but by 1988 he had helped to broker agreements that eased the disputes of Nicaragua's civil war.

He had other successes in Latin America, but his crowning achievements came in regards to U.S.-Soviet relations. Through positive responses to the overtures of Gorbachev and his Foreign Minister, Eduard Shevardnadze, and through his own initiatives, Shultz helped to draft and sign landmark arms control treaties and other agreements that helped to diminish U.S.-Soviet antagonism.

As a result, under Shultz's leadership, U.S. diplomacy helped to pave the way for the ending of the Cold War during 1989.

James Addison Baker (1989-1992)

James A. Baker was appointed Secretary of State on January 22, 1989, and served until August 23, 1992. Baker brought almost two decades of experience in politics, both behind the scenes and in key administration positions with him to the State Department. As Secretary of State, Baker successfully oversaw United States foreign policy during the end of the Cold War, as well as during the First Persian Gulf War.

As Treasury Secretary during the second Reagan Administration, Baker was instrumental in passing the Plaza Accord of September 1985, a multilateral agreement, which devalued the dollar in order to reduce America's account deficit and help the U.S. economy recover from a recession that had begun in the early 1980s. He also tried to implement the Baker Plan, which proposed using Japan's trade surplus to relieve Third World debt.

Baker served as Secretary of State during a very interesting and important time period in U.S. foreign relations. He was influential in overseeing American foreign policy during the tumultuous and touchy times following communism's downfall in Eastern Europe and the break-up of the former Soviet Union.

As the head of the State Department, Baker was also the driving force behind creating a coalition of nations to repel Saddam Hussein and Iraq from Kuwait during the First Persian Gulf War.

Baker continues to play a role in U.S. diplomacy and international affairs. He served as a Personal Envoy of the United Nations Secretary-General for Western Sahara from 1997 to 2004. In 2006, the former Secretary of State served as the Republican co-chair of the Iraq Study Group, tasked with assessing America's policy toward Iraq.

Lawrence Sidney Eagleburger (1992-1993)

Lawrence Eagleburger was appointed Secretary of State on December 8, 1992 and continued in that position until January 19, 1993. Eagleburger's tenure as Secretary capped off a distinguished 27-year career with the Department of State. He continues to actively engage in foreign policy issues.

When James Baker left his post as Secretary of State in August of 1992 to lead President Bush's reelection campaign, Eagleburger took over the Department of State as Acting Secretary of State until the President gave him a recess appointment as Secretary of State on December 8, 1992. Eagleburger's career service over the years gave him invaluable experience and knowledge in many important areas of U.S. diplomacy.

Most notably, the time he spent in Yugoslavia led him to become President George H.W. Bush's primary advisor during Yugoslavia's disintegration following communism's demise in Eastern Europe. Eagleburger's role as an advisor on Yugoslavian affairs was not without controversy. He gained a reputation as a strong Serbian supporter and denied that there had been atrocities committed in Croatia. As the Department's second-highest ranking official prior to taking over the Secretary's position, Eagleburger also played a key role during the First Persian Gulf War.

Since his retirement, he has remained a strong voice on international and political issues, becoming chairman of the International Commission on Holocaust-Era Insurance Claims in 1998, which worked to resolve unpaid insurance claims for Holocaust survivors. In recent years, Eagleburger has publicly commented on U.S. Middle Eastern policy and served on the Iraq Study Group.

Warren Minor Christopher (1993-1997)

Warren Minor Christopher was nominated Secretary of State by President William Jefferson Clinton in December 1992, confirmed by the U.S. Senate on January 20, 1993, and sworn in the next day. He served in the position for four years and ended his service on January 17, 1997.

Christopher eschewed confrontation in favor of negotiation with friend and foe alike. He encouraged Israel, the Palestinians, and Jordan to sign peace treaties, resulting in the Oslo Accords and the Israel-Jordan peace treaty in 1993 and 1994 respectively. He promoted the Partnership for Peace Program, which advocated the expansion of NATO eastward into the former Soviet bloc nations, in 1994. In 1995 he convinced President Clinton to officially restore diplomatic relations with Vietnam. Later that year, he successfully conducted negotiations between Serbia and Bosnia that resulted in the Dayton Accords and the end of the Bosnian War.

Madeleine Korbel Albright (1997-2001)

Madeleine Korbel Albright was nominated to be the first woman Secretary of State by President William Jefferson Clinton on December 5, 1996, confirmed by the U.S. Senate on January 22, 1997, and sworn in the next day. She served in the position for four years and ended her service on January 20, 2001.

As Secretary of State, Albright promoted the expansion of NATO eastward into the former Soviet bloc nations and the non-proliferation of nuclear weapons from the former Soviet republics to rogue nations, successfully pressed for military intervention under NATO auspices during the humanitarian crisis in Kosovo in 1999, supported the expansion of free-market democratization and the creation of civil societies in the developing world, favored the ratification of the Kyoto Protocol on Global Climate Change, and furthered the normalization of relations with Vietnam.

Colin Luther Powell (2001-2005)

Colin L. Powell was appointed Secretary of State by George W. Bush on January 20, 2001, after being unanimously confirmed by the U.S. Senate. He served for four years, leaving the position on January 26, 2005. He was the first African-American to serve as Secretary of State.

At the beginning of his term, Powell placed an emphasis on reaffirming diplomatic alliances throughout the world, supporting a national missile defense system, working towards peace in the Middle East, and prioritizing sanctions instead of force in potential hot spots such as Iraq. He also focused on reinvigorating U.S. diplomacy through reforms in the Department of State's organizational culture and an infusion of resources for personnel, information technology, security, and facilities.

Powell's term, however, was soon dominated by the challenges the Bush Administration faced after the September 11, 2001, terrorist attacks. Powell was one of the foremost supporters of taking swift military action against al-Qaeda and demanded immediate cooperation from Afghanistan and Pakistan in the U.S. search for those who were complicit in the attacks.

When the Administration's attention shifted to Iraq and the possibility that Saddam Hussein was manufacturing weapons of mass destruction (WMD), Powell pressed to have UN inspectors investigate. In February 2003, Powell presented intelligence to the UN that supported the claim that Iraq had weapons of mass destruction and could produce more. Subsequently, the Administration moved quickly toward preemptive military action against Iraq, despite Powell's advice that war should not begin until a large coalition of allies and a long-term occupation plan were in place. In 2004, some of the intelligence that Powell had brought before the UN in 2003 was found to be erroneous.

Although Afghanistan and Iraq demanded a great deal of Powell's attention during his tenure, he pursued other important U.S. foreign policy initiatives and grappled with various crises that arose between 2001 and 2005. After initially difficult Administration interactions with Russia and China, Powell worked to improve both bilateral relationships. Prominent among these efforts were management of U.S. withdrawal from the U.S.-Russian Anti-Ballistic Missile treaty and the signing of the Moscow Treaty on Strategic Offensive Reductions in May 2002.

In the area of foreign aid, Powell pushed the Administration to increase its commitment to the international fight against AIDS, and oversaw a doubling of development assistance funding. He also pressed for international cooperation to halt the nuclear weapons programs of North Korea and Iran, and the Administration achieved an important nonproliferation success when Libya agreed to give up its weapons programs in 2003.

Powell confronted a variety of international crises as well, including a near war between nuclear powers India and Pakistan in 2001-2002, domestic turmoil in Liberia (2003) and Haiti (2004), and the Indian Ocean tsunami in 2004. His continued belief that Middle East stability required a resolution of the Israeli-Palestinian conflict led him to advocate the 2002 "Road Map" that aimed at creating an independent Palestinian state at peace with Israel. Although President Bush endorsed the plan, Powell was not able to persuade the Administration to make a strong commitment to its implementation.

On November 15, 2004, Powell announced his resignation. After stepping down as Secretary of State, he returned to a busy life in the private sector continuing his work with America's Promise Alliance. He serves on the Boards of

Directors of the Council on Foreign Relations, the Eisenhower Fellowship Program, and the Powell Center at the City College of New York.

Condoleezza Rice (2005-2009)

Condoleezza Rice was nominated for Secretary of State by George W. Bush on November 14, 2004, and assumed office on January 26, 2005. She served for four years, leaving the position on January 20, 2009. She was the first African-American woman to serve as Secretary of State.

As Secretary of State, Rice supported the expansion of democratic governments, and championed the idea of "Transformational Diplomacy," which sought to redistribute U.S. diplomats to areas of severe social and political trouble, address such issues as disease, drug smuggling and human trafficking, and reemphasize aid through the creation of the position of Director of Foreign Assistance.

Rice helped successfully negotiate several agreements in the Middle East, including Israeli withdrawal from and the opening of the Gaza border crossings in 2005 and the August 14, 2006 ceasefire between Israel and Hezbollah forces in Lebanon. Rice organized the Annapolis Conference of November 27, 2007, which focused on finding a two-state solution to the Israeli-Palestinian problem.

Rice also worked actively to improve human rights issues in Iran and supported the passage of a United Nations Security Council Resolution for sanctions against the country unless its uranium enrichment program was curtailed.

Another major concern for Rice was North Korea's nuclear program, and its subsequent testing of a nuclear weapon. Rice was firmly against holding bilateral talks with North Korea, although she welcomed their participation in the Six Party Talks between China, Japan, Russia, North Korea, South Korea, and the United States.

In October 2008, one of Rice's most successful negotiations came to fruition, with the signing of the U.S.-India Agreement for Cooperation Concerning Peaceful Uses of Nuclear Energy (123 Agreement), which would allow civil nuclear trade between the two countries.

Shortly after her term as Secretary of State ended in January 2009, she announced plans to write a book about her diplomatic career. Rice was succeeded as Secretary of State by former First Lady and New York Senator Hillary Rodham Clinton.

Hillary Rodham Clinton (2009-2013)

On January 21, 2009, Hillary Rodham Clinton was sworn in as the 67th Secretary of State of the United States. Secretary Clinton joined the State Department after nearly four decades in public service as an advocate, attorney, First Lady, and Senator. She served until February 1, 2013.

Secretary Clinton was born in Chicago, Illinois on October 26, 1947 to Dorothy Rodham and the late Hugh Rodham.

She attended local public schools before graduating from Wellesley College and Yale Law School, where she met Bill Clinton. In 1974, Secretary Clinton moved to Arkansas, a year later then married Bill Clinton and became a successful attorney while also raising their daughter, Chelsea. She was an assistant professor at the University of Arkansas School of Law, and after working to strengthen the local legal aid office, she was appointed by President Jimmy Carter in 1977 to serve on the board of the Legal Services Corporation, which she later chaired.

During her 12 years as First Lady of the State of Arkansas, she was Chairwoman of the Arkansas Education Standards Committee, co-founded the Arkansas Advocates for Children and Families, and served on the boards of the Arkansas Children's Hospital, and the Children's Defense Fund.

In 1992, Governor Clinton was elected President of the United States, and as First Lady, Hillary Clinton became an advocate of health care reform and worked on many issues relating to children and families. She led successful bipartisan efforts to improve the adoption and foster care systems, reduce teen pregnancy, and provide health care to millions of children through the Children's Health Insurance Program. She also traveled to more than 80 countries as a representative of our country, winning respect as a champion of human rights, democracy and civil society. Her famous speech in Beijing in 1995 -- when she declared that "human rights are women's rights, and women's rights are human rights" – inspired women worldwide and helped galvanize a global movement for women's rights.

With Secretary of State Madeleine K. Albright, Secretary Clinton worked to launch the government's Vital Voices Democracy Initiative. Today, Vital Voices is a non-governmental organization that continues to train and organize women leaders across the globe.

In 2000, Hillary Clinton made history as the first First Lady elected to the United States Senate, and the first woman elected statewide in New York. In the Senate, she served on the Armed Services Committee, the Health, Education, Labor and Pensions Committee, the Environment and Public Works Committee, the Budget Committee and the Select Committee on Aging. She was also a Commissioner on the Commission on Security and Cooperation in Europe.

As a Senator, Clinton worked across party lines to build support for causes important to her constituents and the country, including the expansion of economic opportunity and access to quality, affordable health care. After the terrorist attacks of September 11, 2001, she was a strong advocate for funding the rebuilding of New York and the health concerns of the first responders who risked their lives working at Ground Zero. She also championed the cause of our nation's military and fought for better health care and benefits for wounded service members, veterans and members of the National Guard and Reserves. She was also the only Senate member of the Transformation Advisory Group to the Department of Defense's Joint Forces Command.

In 2006, Senator Clinton won reelection to the Senate, and in 2007 she began her historic campaign for President. In 2008, she campaigned for the election of Barack Obama and Joe Biden, and in November, she was nominated by President-elect Obama to be Secretary of State.

Secretary Clinton is the author of best-selling books, including her memoir, *Living History*, and her groundbreaking book on children, *It Takes A Village*. She and President Clinton reside in New York.

John Forbes Kerry (2013-)

On February 1, 2013, John Forbes Kerry was sworn in as the 68th Secretary of State of the United States, becoming the first sitting Senate Foreign Relations Committee Chairman to become Secretary in over a century.

Secretary Kerry joined the State Department after 28 years in the United States Senate, the last four as Chairman of the Senate Foreign Relations Committee.

Secretary Kerry was born on December 11, 1943, at Fitzsimons Army Hospital in Aurora, Colorado, one of four children of the late Rosemary Forbes Kerry and Richard Kerry, a Foreign Service Officer.

Shortly before he graduated from Yale University, Secretary Kerry enlisted to serve in the United States Navy, and went on to serve two tours of duty. He served in combat as a Swift Boat skipper patrolling the rivers of the Mekong Delta, returning home from Vietnam with a Silver Star, a Bronze Star with Combat V, and three Purple Hearts.

Back in the United States, Secretary Kerry began to forcefully speak out against the Vietnam War. Testifying at the invitation of Chairman J. William Fulbright before the Senate Foreign Relations Committee, he asked the poignant question, "How do you ask a man to be the last man to die for a mistake?" He also began a lifelong fight for his fellow veterans as a co-founder of the Vietnam Veterans of America, and later as a United States Senator who fought to secure veterans' benefits, extension of the G.I. Bill for Higher Education, and improved treatment for PTSD (post-traumatic stress disorder).

In 1976, Secretary Kerry received his law degree from Boston College Law School and went to work as a top prosecutor in Middlesex County, Massachusetts, where he took on organized crime, fought for victims' rights, and created programs for rape counseling. He was elected Lieutenant Governor of Massachusetts in 1982, and 2 years later, he was elected to the United States Senate where he served for 28 years.

In 2009, Secretary Kerry became Chairman of the Senate Foreign Relations Committee, assuming a leadership role on key foreign policy and national security issues facing the United States, including Afghanistan and Pakistan, nuclear nonproliferation, and global climate change. His service as Chairman built on his previous Senate work that included helping to expose the Iran-Contra scandal and leadership on global AIDS.

As Chairman of the Senate Select Committee on POW/MIA Affairs, he worked to learn the truth about American soldiers missing in Vietnam and to normalize relations with that country.

In 2010, as Chairman of the Foreign Relations Committee, Secretary Kerry was instrumental in the ratification of the New START (Strategic Arms Reduction Treaty) Treaty, a vital nuclear arms reduction agreement with Russia that helps steer both countries away from dangerous nuclear confrontations.

In his 28 years on the Senate Foreign Relations Committee, Secretary Kerry chaired the Asia and Middle East subcommittees where he authored and passed major legislation on international drug trafficking, international money laundering, humanitarian aid, and climate change, and he helped negotiate the UN's genocide tribunal to prosecute war crimes in Cambodia.

He also held senior positions on the Finance, Commerce, and Small Business committees, as well as served as a member of the bipartisan Joint Committee on Deficit Reduction, where he worked across party lines to try and reduce the country's debt and strengthen our economy. Prior to his departure from the Senate, Secretary Kerry was the seventh-most senior Senator.

Secretary Kerry was the Democratic Party's nominee for President of the United States in 2004.

Secretary Kerry is the author of best-selling books, including *A Call to Service: My Vision for a Better America* and *This Moment on Earth*, a book on the environment which he co-authored with his wife, Teresa Heinz Kerry. Together they are proud of a blended family that includes two daughters, three sons, and three grandchildren.

Diplomacy Over the Years

1750–1785: Colonial and Revolutionary Period

Colonial era diplomacy focused on two issues: the European balance of power and the colonists' appropriation of land from the Native Americans. Rivalry in Europe, between the French and the British in particular, often influenced the course of events in their North American colonies.

The British and French competed to acquire land and control over the new trading opportunities the colonies often by making alliances with some tribes while alienating others. Sometimes, as in the case of the French and Indian War (which in Europe was referred to as the Seven Years' War), European balance of power politics resulted in conflict in the colonies. As wars in Europe became more heated, fighting broke out between the French and the British in the American colonies. Both sides called upon Native American allies to assist them, exacerbating tensions between the tribes, as well as those between the tribes and colonists. Ultimately, the British Government sent troops and resources to protect its American possessions and taxed the colonists to pay for it. Those taxes became the rallying cry for American independence.

The French and Indian War began in 1754 and ended with the Treaty of Paris in 1763. The war provided Great Britain enormous territorial gains in North America, but disputes over subsequent frontier policy and paying the war's expenses led to colonial discontent, and ultimately to the American revolution.

In 1753, prior to the outbreak of hostilities, Great Britain controlled the 13 colonies up to the Appalachian Mountains, but beyond lay New France, a very large, sparsely settled colony that stretched from Louisiana through the Mississippi Valley and Great Lakes to Canada. In 1757, after several years of stalemate, the war began to turn in favor of Great Britain. British forces defeated French forces in India, and in 1759 British armies invaded and conquered Canada. Spain joined the war on the side of France but Britain's military strength, especially its navy, led to the British seizing the French Caribbean islands, Spanish Cuba, and the Philippines. In the Treaty of Paris (1763), Great Britain secured significant territorial gains, including all French territory east of the Mississippi river, as well as Spanish Florida, although the treaty returned Cuba to Spain.

However, the war had been hugely expensive, and the British government's attempts to impose taxes on colonists to help cover these expenses resulted in increasing colonial resentment of Britain.

The **Albany Plan of Union**, adopted At the Albany Congress on July 10, 1754, was a plan to place the British North American colonies under a more centralized government. Although never carried out, it was the first plan for the colonies to be united under one government. The Pennsylvanian Commissioner to the Congress was Benjamin Franklin. The Albany Plan did not seek to secure independence from Great Britain and many commissioners actually wished to increase imperial authority in the colonies. Its framers saw it instead as a means to reform colonial-imperial relations, while recognizing that the colonies collectively shared certain common interests.

The American Revolution was precipitated, in part, by a series of laws passed between 1763 and 1775 that regulating trade and taxes. This legislation caused tensions between colonists and imperial officials, who made it clear that the British Parliament would not address American complaints that the new laws were onerous. British unwillingness to respond to American demands for change allowed colonists to argue that they were part of an increasingly corrupt and autocratic empire in which their traditional liberties were threatened. This position eventually served as the basis for the colonial Declaration of Independence.

The British Parliament passed the 1764 Currency Act which forbade the colonies from issuing paper currency which made it even more difficult for colonists to pay their debts and taxes. This was followed by the Stamp Tax which required colonists to purchase a government-issued stamp for legal documents and other paper goods. After news of the successful passage of the Stamp Act reached the colonies, the Virginia House of Burgesses passed resolutions denying the British Parliament's authority to tax the colonies. In Boston, colonists rioted and destroyed the house of the stamp distributor. News of these protests inspired similar activities and protests in other colonies, and thus the Stamp Act served as a common cause to unite the 13 colonies in opposition to the British Parliament. In October of 1765, delegates from 9 colonies met to issue petitions to the British Government denying Parliament's authority to tax the colonies. An American boycott of British goods, coupled with recession, also led British merchants to lobby for the act's repeal on pragmatic economic grounds. Under pressure from American colonists and British merchants, the British Government decided it was easier to repeal the Stamp Act than to enforce it.

In 1773 the British Parliament granted the East India Company a monopoly on the tax-free transport of tea which meant that colonial tea traders could not compete. British goods were boycotted and on December 16, 1773, American colonists disguised as Indians boarded East India Company ships in Boston Harbor and threw crates of tea overboard. This famous protest came to be known as the Boston Tea Party.

The British Government ordered the closure of the port of Boston until the East India Company was compensated for the destroyed tea. Parliament also passed several pieces of legislation in 1774 which attempted to place Massachusetts under direct British control. In the American colonies, these laws were referred to as the Intolerable Acts. British control was further solidified by the appointment of General Thomas Gage as military governor of Massachusetts.

Colonial legislatures sent representatives to Philadelphia, and the First Continental Congress convened in September of 1774. The Continental Congress agreed to the Articles of Association on October 20. These Articles listed colonial grievances and called for a locally-enforced boycott in all the colonies to take effect on December 1. The delegates also drafted a petition to King George III laying out their grievances, although by then they doubted that the crisis would be resolved peacefully.

Realizing that further coercive steps would only enrage the colonists and might lead to war, British military governor Gage wrote to London recommending suspension of the Intolerable Acts. Gage hoped to appease many of the colonists and thereby split colonial moderates from radicals. If London was not amenable to his recommendations, Gage stated that he would need significant reinforcements to crush the growing rebellion.

British ministers responded to Gage's suggestions by removing him from his post. They felt that further punitive measures were necessary and pushed Parliament to pass additional trade restrictions on New England. London declared the colonies to be in rebellion, but also offered to stop taxing those colonies that supported the British Government. Conflict was inevitable and the war for American Independence began on April 19, 1775 when British troops and American colonists clashed at Lexington and Concord.

Declaration of Independence

The U.S. Continental Congress endorsed Thomas Jefferson's Declaration of Independence on July 4, 1776, and, with it, the conflict with Britain became a full-fledged War of Independence. Unable to defeat the strong British military on their own, the American colonists required foreign assistance. John Adams approached the French with the "Model Treaty" that protected neutral trade and shipping rights in the event of a war. By issuing the Declaration of Independence the 13 American colonies severed their political connections to Great Britain. The Declaration summarized the colonists' motivations for seeking their independence. By declaring themselves an independent nation, the

American colonists were able to conclude an official alliance with the government of France and obtain French assistance in the war against Great Britain.

The Continental Congress was the formal means by which the American colonial governments coordinated their resistance to British rule during the first two years of the American Revolution. The Congress balanced the interests of the different colonies and also established itself as the official colonial liaison with Great Britain. As the war progressed, the Congress became the effective national government of the country, and, as such, conducted diplomacy on behalf of the new United States.

As British authority crumbled in the colonies, the Continental Congress effectively took over as the de facto national government, thereby exceeding the initial authority granted to it by the individual colonial governments. The Second Congress continued to meet until the Articles of Confederation that established a new national government for the United States took effect on March 1, 1781.

As the de facto national government, the Continental Congress assumed the role of negotiating diplomatic agreements with foreign nations. As the war progressed, the British Parliament banned trade with the colonies and authorized the seizure of colonial vessels on December 23, which served to further erode anti-independence moderates' positions in Congress and bolster pro-independence leaders. Congress responded by opening American ports to all foreign ships except British ones on April 6, 1776.

Congress and the British government made further attempts to reconcile, but negotiations failed when Congress refused to revoke the Declaration of Independence, both in a meeting on September 11, 1776 with British Admiral Richard Howe, and when a peace delegation from Parliament arrived in Philadelphia in 1778. Instead, Congress spelled out terms for peace on August 14, 1779, which demanded British withdrawal, American independence, and navigation rights on the Mississippi River. The next month John Adams was appointed to negotiate such terms with England, however, formal peace negotiations had to wait until after the Confederation Congress took over the reins of government on March 1, 1781, following American victories at Yorktown that resulted in British willingness to end the war.

In 1775 the Continental Congress established the Committee of Secret Correspondence to communicate with sympathetic Britons and other Europeans early in the American Revolution. The committee eventually came to coordinate diplomatic functions for Continental Congress and served as the clearinghouse for transatlantic communication and public relations. In essence, it was the forerunner of the State Department.

Congress initially established the Committee of Correspondence to communicate with colonial agents in Britain and "friends in ... other parts of the world." On the committee were Benjamin Franklin, Benjamin Harrison, Thomas Johnson, John Dickinson, and John Jay. They were soon joined by Robert Morris. Congress had granted the committee sweeping authority to conduct international diplomacy, including the negotiation of clandestine shipments of arms and other similar activities. Owing to the nature of the correspondence, the members began to add the word "secret" to the committee's title, and soon it was known as the Committee of Secret Correspondence. As its diplomatic duties grew, Congress eventually renamed it the Committee for Foreign Affairs on April 17, 1777.

During the American Revolution, the American colonies faced the significant challenge of conducting international diplomacy and seeking the international support it needed to fight against the British. The single most important diplomatic success of the colonists during the War for Independence was the critical link they forged with France. Representatives of the French and American governments signed the Treaty of Alliance and a Treaty of Amity and Commerce on February 6, 1778.

Between 1778 and 1782 the French provided supplies, arms and ammunition, uniforms, and, most importantly, troops and naval support to the beleaguered Continental Army. The French navy transported reinforcements under the Marquis de Lafayette, fought off a British fleet, and protected Washington's forces in Virginia. French assistance was crucial in securing the British surrender at Yorktown in 1781.

With the consent of Vergennes, U.S. commissioners entered negotiations with Britain to end the war, and reached a preliminary agreement in 1782. Vergennes and Franklin successfully presented a united front despite British attempts to drive a wedge between the allies during their separate peace negotiations. The United States, Spain, and France formally ended the war with Britain with the Treaty of Paris in 1783.

Benjamin Franklin: First American Diplomat, 1776–1785

Benjamin Franklin, the most distinguished scientific and literary American of his age, was the first American diplomat. He served from 1776 to 1778 on a three-man commission to France charged with the critical task of gaining French support for American independence. French aristocrats and intellectuals embraced Franklin as the personification of the New World Enlightenment. His likeness appeared on medallions, rings, watches, and snuffboxes, while fashionable ladies adopted the coiffure a la Franklin in imitation of the fur cap he wore instead of a wig. His popularity and diplomatic skill—along with the first American battlefield success at Saratoga—convinced France to recognize American independence and conclude an alliance with the thirteen states in 1778. Franklin presented his credentials to the French court in 1779, becoming the first American Minister (the 18th American century equivalent of ambassador) to be received by a foreign government. Franklin's home in Passy, just outside Paris, became the center of American diplomacy in Europe. When Thomas Jefferson succeeded Franklin in 1785, the French Foreign Minister, Vergennes asked: "It is you who replace Dr. Franklin?" Jefferson replied, "No one can replace him, Sir; I am only his successor."

Articles of Confederation, 1777–1781

Following the Declaration of Independence, the members of the Continental Congress realized that it would be necessary to set up a national government. Delegates finally formulated the Articles of Confederation, in which they agreed to state-by-state voting and proportional state tax burdens based on land values. It served as the written document that established the functions of the national government of the United States. It established a weak central government that mostly, but not entirely, prevented the individual states from conducting their own foreign diplomacy.

Virginia was the first state to ratify on December 16, 1777, other states ratified in 1778 and Maryland was the last to sign on March 1, 1781.

The Continental Congress voted on Jan 10, 1781, to establish a Department of Foreign Affairs; on Aug 10 of that year, it elected Robert R. Livingston as Secretary of Foreign Affairs. The Secretary's duties involved corresponding with U.S. representatives abroad and with ministers of foreign powers. The Secretary was also charged with transmitting Congress' instructions to U.S. agents abroad and was authorized to attend sessions of Congress. A further Act of Feb 22, 1782, allowed the Secretary to ask and respond to questions during sessions of the Continental Congress.

The Articles created a sovereign, national government, and as such limited the rights of the states to conduct their own diplomacy and foreign policy. However, in practice this proved difficult to enforce, and the state of Georgia pursued its own independent policy regarding Spanish Florida, attempting to occupy disputed territories and threatening war if Spanish officials did not work to curb Indian attacks or refrain from harboring escaped slaves. Nor could the Confederation government prevent the landing of convicts that the British Government continued to export to its former colonies. The Articles also did not allow Congress sufficient authority to compel the states to enforce provisions of the 1783 Treaty of Paris that allowed British creditors to sue debtors for pre-Revolutionary debts, an unpopular clause that many state governments chose to ignore. These problems convinced colonial leaders that a more powerful central government was necessary. This led to the Constitutional Convention that formulated the current Constitution of the United States.

Treaty of Paris, 1783

Benjamin Franklin rejected informal peace overtures from Great Britain for a settlement that would provide the thirteen states with some measure of autonomy within the British Empire. Franklin insisted on British recognition of American independence and refused to consider a peace separate from France, America's staunch ally. Franklin did agree to negotiations with the British for an end to the war. Joined by peace commissioners John Adams and John Jay, Franklin engaged the British in formal negotiations beginning on September 27, 1782.

Although Franklin demanded the cessation of Canada to an independent America, he knew that the British Government of Lord Shelburne, opposed to American independence, was unprepared to accept that offer. Two months of hard bargaining resulted in a preliminary articles of peace in which the British accepted American independence and boundaries—a bitter pill to George III—resolved the difficult issues of fishing rights on the Newfoundland banks and prewar debts owed British creditors, promised restitution of property lost during the war by Americans loyal to the British cause, and provided for the evacuation of British forces from the thirteen states. The preliminary articles signed in Paris on November 30, 1782, were only effective when a similar treaty was signed by Britain and France, which French Foreign Minister Vergennes quickly negotiated. France signed preliminary articles of peace with Great Britain on January 20, 1783, which were followed by a formal peace of Paris signed on September 3, 1783.

1784–1800: The Diplomacy of the Early Republic

Following the end of the American Revolution, the United States struggled to define its foreign policy, to determine how to implement it, and to maintain necessary commercial ties with Europe without becoming embroiled in European conflicts and politics. Differences over foreign policy became a basis for the founding of political parties in the new nation as the debate pitted the Federalists, led by the Secretary of the Treasury Alexander Hamilton, against the Jeffersonians, represented by Secretary of State Thomas Jefferson.

The Federalists supported the development of a strong international commerce and, with it, the creation of a navy capable of protecting U.S. merchant vessels. The Jeffersonians favored expansion across the vast continent that the new republic occupied.

The Federalists and Jeffersonians also disagreed over U.S. policy toward political events in Europe. After the outbreak of the French Revolution in 1789, the Federalists distrusted France and encouraged closer commercial ties to England, while the Jeffersonians preferred to support the new French Republic.

Conflict in Europe between France, Britain, and Spain in the late 1790s, resulted in President George Washington declaring American neutrality. The Jay Treaty with Britain (1794) and the Pinckney Treaty with Spain (1795) aimed at preserving this neutrality. In his Farewell Address, Washington promoted a vision of American diplomacy that involved no "entangling alliances" with European powers.

U.S. Debt and Foreign Loans, 1775–1795

During the American Revolution, a cash-strapped Continental Congress accepted loans from France. Paying off these and other debts incurred during the Revolution proved one of the major challenges of the post-independence period. The new U.S. Government attempted to pay off these debts in a timely manner, but the debts were at times a source of diplomatic tension. In order to pay for its significant expenditures during the Revolution, Congress had two options: print more money or obtain loans to meet the budget deficit. In practice it did both, but relied more on the printing of money, which led to hyperinflation. At that time, Congress lacked the authority to levy taxes, and to do so would have risked alienating an American public that had gone to war with the British over the issue of unjust taxation.

The French Government began to secretly ship war materiel to the American revolutionaries in late 1775. This was accomplished by establishing dummy corporations to receive French funds and military supplies. It was unclear whether this aid was a loan or a gift, and disputes over the status of this early assistance caused strong disagreement between American diplomats in Europe. Arthur Lee, one of the American commissioners in France, accused another, Silas Deane, of financial misdealings, while the third member of the commission, Benjamin Franklin, remained aloof. Lee eventually succeeded in convincing Congress to recall Deane. The early French aid would later resurface as one of the disputes behind the 1797 XYZ Affair that led to the Quasi-War with France.

In 1795, the United States was finally able to settle its debts with the French Government with the help of James Swan, an American banker who privately assumed French debts at a slightly higher interest rate. Swan then resold these debts at a profit on domestic U.S. markets. The United States no longer owed money to foreign governments, although it continued to owe money to private investors both in the United States and in Europe.

Constitutional Convention and Ratification, 1787–1789

The Constitutional Convention in Philadelphia met between May and September of 1787 to address the problems of the weak central government that existed under the Articles of Confederation. The United States Constitution that emerged from the convention established a federal government with more specific powers, including those related to conducting relations with foreign governments. Under the reformed federal system, many of the responsibilities for foreign affairs fell under the authority of an executive branch, although important powers, such as treaty ratification, remained the responsibility of the legislative branch. After the necessary number of state ratifications, the Constitution came into effect in 1789 and has served as the basis of the United States Government ever since.

The Constitution does not stipulate existence of departments within the executive branch, but the need for such departments was recognized immediately. Congress passed legislation creating the Department of Foreign Affairs in its first session in 1789, and in the same year changed the name to the Department of State after it added several additional domestic duties to the Department.

The United States and the French Revolution, 1789–1799

The French Revolution lasted from 1789 until 1799. The Revolution precipitated a series of European wars, forcing the United States to articulate a clear policy of neutrality in order to avoid being embroiled in these European conflicts. The French Revolution also influenced U.S. politics, as pro- and anti-Revolutionary factions sought to influence American domestic and foreign policy.

From 1790 to 1794 the French Revolution became increasingly radical. After French King Louis XVI was tried and executed on January 21, 1793, war with Great Britain and Spain was inevitable, and the two powers joined Austria and other European powers in the war against Revolutionary France that had already started in 1791. The United States remained neutral, as both Federalists and Democratic-Republicans saw that war would lead to economic disaster and the possibility of invasion. This policy was made difficult by heavy-handed British and French actions. The British harassed neutral American merchant ships, while the French government had dispatched a controversial minister to the United States, Edmond-Charles Genêt, whose violations of the American neutrality policy embroiled the two countries in the Citizen Genêt Affair until his recall in 1794.

In 1794, the French Revolution entered its most violent phase, the Terror. Under foreign invasion, the French Government had declared a state of emergency, and many foreigners residing in France were arrested, including American revolutionary pamphleteer Thomas Paine, owing to his British birth. Although American minister to France Gouverneur Morris did not obtain Paine's release, Morris was able to intercede successfully on behalf many Americans imprisoned during the Terror, including the American consuls at Dunkirk, Rouen, and Le Havre. Once the Terror ended in late July of 1794, the arrests ended, and Paine, who had been scheduled to be executed, was released.

The United States and the Haitian Revolution, 1791–1804

The Haitian Revolution created the second independent country in the Americas after the United States became independent in 1783. U.S. political leaders, many of them slave-owners, reacted to the emergence of Haiti as a state borne out of a slave revolt with ambivalence, at times providing aid to put down the revolt, and, later in the revolution, providing support to Toussaint L'Ouverture's forces. Due to these shifts in policy and domestic concerns, the United States would not officially recognize Haitian independence until 1862.

The Haitian revolution came to North American shores in the form of a refugee crisis. In 1793, competing factions battled for control of the then-capital of St. Domingue, Cap-Français (now Cap-Haïtien.) The fighting and ensuing fire destroyed much of the capital, and refugees piled into ships anchored in the harbor. The French navy deposited the refugees in Norfolk, Virginia. Many refugees also settled in Baltimore, Philadelphia, and New York. These refugees were predominantly white, though many had brought their slaves with them. The refugees became involved in émigré politics, hoping to influence U.S. foreign policy. Anxieties about their actions, along with those of European radicals also residing in the United States, led to the passage of the Alien and Sedition Acts. The growing xenophobia, along with temporarily improved political stability in France and St. Domingue, convinced many of the refugees to return home.

The beginning of the Federalist administration of President John Adams signaled a change in policy. Adams was resolutely anti-slavery and felt no need to aid white forces in St. Domingue. He was also concerned that L'Ouverture would choose to pursue a policy of state-supported piracy like that of the Barbary States. Lastly, St. Domingue's trade had partially rebounded, and Adams wished to preserve trade links with the colony. Under President Thomas Jefferson's presidency, the United States cut off aid to L'Ouverture and instead pursued a policy to isolate Haiti, fearing that the Haitian revolution would spread to the United States.

The Citizen Genêt Affair, 1793–1794

Edmond Charles Genêt served as French minister to the United States from 1793 to 1794. His activities in that capacity embroiled the United States and France in a diplomatic crisis, as the United States Government attempted to remain neutral in the conflict between Great Britain and Revolutionary France. The controversy was ultimately resolved by Genêt's recall from his position. As a result of the Citizen Genêt affair, the United States established a set of procedures governing neutrality.

Following the overthrow of the monarchy in 1792, the revolutionary French Government sent Edmond Charles Genêt, an experienced diplomat, as minister to the United States. Genêt immediately began to issue privateering commissions upon his arrival in Charleston, with the consent of South Carolina governor William Moultrie. These commissions authorized the bearers, regardless of their country of origin, to seize British merchant ships and their cargo for personal profit, with the approval and protection of the French Government. When Genêt arrived in the U.S. capital of Philadelphia in May to present his credentials, Secretary of State Thomas Jefferson informed him that the United States Cabinet considered the outfitting of French privateers in American ports to be a violation of the U.S. policy of neutrality. Genêt's mission ran into further difficulties when the U.S. Government expressed no interest in a new commercial treaty, as it already enjoyed favorable trading privileges in French ports. The U.S. Cabinet also refused to make advance payments on U.S. debts to the French government.

Genêt ignored American warnings and allowed the outfitting of another French privateer, the Little Democrat. Washington's Cabinet met to consider a response to Genêt's defiant actions. All members agreed to request Genêt's recall. However, Secretary of State Jefferson stopped short of expelling Genet from the United States, as Hamilton had wished. The French government recalled Genêt, and demanded that the U.S. hand him over to the commissioners sent to replace him. President Washington and Attorney General Edmund Randolph, aware that Genêt's return to France would almost certainly result in his execution, allowed Genêt to remain in the United States.

The Genêt affair forced the United States to formulate a consistent policy on the issue of neutrality. Washington's Cabinet signed a set of rules regarding policies of neutrality on August 3, 1793, and these rules were formalized when Congress passed a neutrality bill on June 4, 1794. This legislation formed the basis for neutrality policy throughout the nineteenth century.

John Jay's Treaty, 1794–95

On November 19, 1794 representatives of the United States and Great Britain signed Jay's Treaty, which sought to settle outstanding issues between the two countries that had been left unresolved since American independence. The treaty proved unpopular with the American public but did accomplish the goal of maintaining peace between the two nations and preserving U.S. neutrality.

Tensions between the United States and Britain remained high after the Revolutionary War as a result of three key issues. British exports flooded U.S. markets, while American exports were blocked by British trade restrictions and tariffs. Finally, Britain's impressments of American sailors and seizure of naval and military supplies bound to enemy ports on neutral ships brought the two nations to the brink of war in the late 1700s.

The French Revolution led to war between Britain and France in 1793. Divisions emerged in the United States between those who supported the French, including Secretary of State Thomas Jefferson, and those who supported the British, including Secretary of the Treasury Alexander Hamilton. Fearing the repercussions of a war with Britain, President George Washington sided with Hamilton and sent pro-British Chief Justice John Jay to negotiate with the British Government. The resulting treaty addressed few U.S. interests, and ultimately granted Britain additional rights. President Washington implemented the treaty in the face of popular disapproval, realizing that it was the price of peace with Great Britain and that it gave the United States valuable time to consolidate and rearm in the event of future conflict.

Treaty of San Lorenzo/ Pinckney's Treaty, 1795

Spanish and U.S. negotiators concluded the Treaty of San Lorenzo, also known as Pinckney's Treaty, on October 27, 1795. The treaty was an important diplomatic success for the United States. It resolved territorial disputes between the two countries and granted American ships the right to free navigation of the Mississippi River as well as duty-free transport through the port of New Orleans, then under Spanish control. Prior to the treaty, the western and southern borders of the United States had been a source of tension between Spain and the United States. The U.S. border extended to the Mississippi River, but its southern stretch remained in Spanish territory, and Spanish officials, reluctant to encourage U.S. trade and settlement in a strategic frontier area, kept the Mississippi River closed to American shipping.

The Treaty of San Lorenzo enabled and encouraged American settlers to continue westward expansion, and made frontier areas more attractive and lucrative. Consequently, it was popular with the American public, especially in the West and South. Since Thomas Pinckney was associated with the Federalist Party, the treaty served to bolster the Federalists outside of their New England stronghold and give the party a stronger base in areas where it had traditionally been weak. Diplomatically, the treaty marked a reverse in Spanish policies that attempted to maintain a strong buffer region in North America, while placing the United States in a stronger position in relation to European powers compared to the U.S. concessions made in Jay's Treaty.

Washington's Farewell Address, 1796

To announce his decision not to seek a third term as President, George Washington presented his Farewell Address in a newspaper article September 17, 1796.

Frustrated by French meddling in U.S. politics, Washington warned the nation to avoid permanent alliances with foreign nations and to rely instead on temporary alliances for emergencies. Washington's efforts to protect the fragile young republic by steering a neutral course between England and

France during the French Revolutionary Wars was made extremely difficult by the intense rhetoric flowing from the pro-English Federalists, led by Alexander Hamilton, and the pro-French, personified by Thomas Jefferson. In his farewell address, Washington exhorted Americans to set aside their violent likes and dislikes of foreign nations, lest they be controlled by their passions: "The nation which indulges toward another an habitual hatred or an habitual fondness is in some degree a slave." Washington's remarks have served as an inspiration for American isolationism, and his advice against joining a permanent alliance was heeded for more than a century and a half.

The XYZ Affair and the Quasi-War with France, 1798–1800

The XYZ Affair was a diplomatic incident between French and United States diplomats that resulted in a limited, undeclared war known as the Quasi-War. U.S. and French negotiators restored peace with the Convention of 1800, also known as the Treaty of Mortefontaine. In the late 1700s, the final French Revolutionary government, the Directory, was experiencing problems financing its European wars. Many leaders were also angry that the United States had concluded the Jay Treaty with Great Britain in 1794. Consequently, in 1796 French leaders decided to issue an order allowing for the seizure of American merchant ships, carefully timed to catch as many as possible by surprise. President John Adams dispatched three U.S. envoys to restore harmony between the United States and France—Elbridge Gerry, Charles Cotesworth Pinckney, and John Marshall. In Franxce, the U.S. envoys were approached by several intermediaries, Nicholas Hubbard (later W,) Jean Hottinguer (X), Pierre Bellamy (Y), and Lucien Hauteval (Z.)The French demanded that the United States provide France with a low-interest loan, assume and pay American merchant claims against the French, and lastly pay a substantial bribe to the Foreign Minister. The U.S. envoys were shocked, and also skeptical that any concessions would bring about substantial changes in French policy. President Adams prepared for war, and pro-war Federalists pushed Congress to support him. Leaders of the Democratic-Republican party were suspicious of Adams' motives and demanded that he publicly release the diplomatic correspondence describing the negotiations in France. Adams, knowing its contents, obliged them and released the correspondence, but replaced the names of the French intermediaries with the letters W, X, Y, and Z. Thereafter Adams continued preparations for war, but did not venture to openly declare war. The French attempted to restore relations, and Congress approved a commission to negotiate an agreement with the French government.

1801–1829: Securing the Republic

Opportunities to expand westward strengthened the notion that the United States should continue its quest to occupy more territory of the vast North American continent. The European powers did little to stop the young nation from extending its borders as they were embroiled in the ongoing Napoleonic Wars in Europe. Indeed, the economic pressure of these European conflicts forced the French and the Spanish to sell their Louisiana and Florida territories to the U.S. Government, more than doubling the size of the United States. During this period, the U.S. also built an economy based on trade and commerce, and premised on the same neutrality as outlined by the founders in the Early Republic. The United States even went to war with Britain in 1812, when British actions threatened American neutrality and trading rights. Finally, the United States used the newfound independence of the Latin American states from their former colonial ruler of Spain to establish the idea of an American sphere of influence in the Western Hemisphere and to announce to the European powers the end of the era of colonization in the Americas.

Barbary Wars, 1801–1805 and 1815–1816

The Barbary States were a collection of North African states, many of which practiced state-supported piracy in order to exact tribute from weaker Atlantic powers. Morocco was an independent kingdom, Algiers, Tunis, and Tripoli owed a loose allegiance to the Ottoman Empire. The United States fought two separate wars with Tripoli (1801–1805) and Algiers (1815–1816), although at other times it preferred to pay tribute to obtain the release of captives held in the Barbary States.

The two major European powers, Great Britain and France, found it expedient to encourage the Barbary States' policy and pay tribute to them, as it allowed their merchant shipping an increased share of the Mediterranean trade, and Barbary leaders chose not to challenge the superior British or French navies.

Prior to independence, American colonists had enjoyed the protection of the British Navy. However, once the United States declared independence, British diplomats were quick to inform the Barbary States that U.S. ships were open to attack. In 1785, Dey Muhammad of Algiers declared war on the United States and captured several American ships. The financially troubled Confederation Government of the United States was unable to raise a navy or the tribute that would protect U.S. ships.

In 1795, The U.S. Government dispatched diplomats Joel Barlow, Joseph Donaldson, and Richard O'Brien to North Africa and successfully concluded treaties with the states of Algiers, Tunis, and Tripoli. Under the terms of these treaties, the United States agreed to pay tribute to these states. The treaty with Algiers freed 83 American sailors.

The adoption of the Constitution in 1789 gave the U.S. Government the power to levy taxes and to raise and maintain armed forces, powers which had been lacking under the Articles of Confederation. In 1794, in response to Algerian seizures of American ships, Congress authorized construction of the first 6 ships of the U.S. Navy. In 1801, the Pasha of Tripoli, Yusuf Qaramanli, citing late payments of tribute, demanded additional tribute and declared war on the United States. The United States successfully defeated Qaramanli's forces with a combined naval and land assault by the United States Marine Corps. The U.S. treaty with Tripoli concluded in 1805 included a ransom for American prisoners in Tripoli, but no provisions for tribute.

In 1812, the new Dey of Algiers, Hajji Ali, rejected the American tribute negotiated in the 1795 treaty as insufficient and declared war on the United States.

Algerian corsairs captured an American ship several weeks later. In accordance with an agreement between the Dey and British diplomats, the Algerian declaration was timed to coincide with the start of the War of 1812 between Britain and the United States. The war with Britain prevented the U.S. Government from either confronting Algerian forces or ransoming U.S. captives in Algiers. Once the Treaty of Ghent ended war with Britain, President James Madison was able to request that Congress declare an authorization of force on Algiers, which it did on March 3, 1815. The U.S. Navy, greatly increased in size after the War of 1812, was able send an entire squadron, led by Commodore Stephen Decatur, to the Mediterranean. The Algerians reluctantly accepted the treaty proposed by Decatur that called for an exchange of U.S. and Algerian prisoners and an end to the practices of tribute and ransom. Having defeated the most powerful of the Barbary States, Decatur sailed to Tunis and Tripoli and obtained similar treaties.

Napoleonic Wars and the War of 1812, 1803–1815

Great Britain and France fought for European supremacy, and treated weaker powers heavy-handedly. The United States attempted to remain neutral during the Napoleonic period, but eventually became involved leading to the War of 1812 against Great Britain.

Napoleon Bonaparte seized power in 1799 and in 1803 Britain declared war on France. The United States managed to stay neutral until 1806 when Napoleon issued the Berlin Decree, which forbade trade with Britain. In 1807 the British Government responded with Orders in Council which instituted a blockade of French-controlled Europe, and authorized the British navy to seize ships violating the blockade. Napoleon responded with further trade restrictions in the Milan Decree of 1807.

On June 22, 1807, the H.M.S. *Leopard* bombarded and forcibly boarded the U.S.S. Chesapeake off Norfolk, Virginia in search of British navy deserters. President Jefferson responded with an embargo on all foreign trade in an effort to weaken the British economy. His successor, President James Madison, offered Britain and France the option of ceasing their seizure of U.S. merchant ships in return for U.S. participation in their trade bloc. Napoleon was the first to offer concessions, which Madison accepted pushing the United States closer to war with Britain.

During this period, Madison also had to address a problem created by Secretary of State, Robert Smith, who had personally stated to the British minister his pro-British sympathies. When Madison confronted Smith and offered him a graceful departure as U.S. Minister to Russia, Smith appeared to accept his offer, and then leaked cabinet papers as part of a smear campaign against President Madison. U.S. diplomat Joel Barlow published a reply and swung public opinion against Smith, who resigned on April 1, 1811. Congress passed a declaration of war on June 17, which Madison signed the next day. The war continued into 1815, although diplomats signed the Treaty of Ghent on December 23, 1814. The Treaty restored the political boundaries on the North American continent to the status quo before the war.

Louisiana Purchase, 1803

The Louisiana Purchase refers to the 530,000,000 acres of territory in North America that the United States purchased from France in 1803. Napoleon offered the entire territory of Louisiana for $15 million but there was no provision empowering the President to purchase territory. Jefferson decided to ignore the legalistic interpretation of the Constitution and forgo the passage of a Constitutional amendment to validate the purchase. This decision contributed to the principle of implied powers of the federal government.

Rush-Bagot Pact, 1817 and Convention of 1818

The Rush-Bagot Pact was an agreement between the United States and Great Britain to eliminate their fleets from the Great Lakes, excepting small patrol vessels. The Convention of 1818 set the boundary between the Missouri Territory in the United States and British North America (later Canada) at the forty-ninth parallel. Both agreements reflected the easing of diplomatic tensions that had led to the War of 1812 and marked the beginning of Anglo-American cooperation.

Acquisition of Florida: Treaty of Adams-Onis (1819) and Transcontinental Treaty (1821)

The colonies of East Florida and West Florida remained loyal to the British during the war for American independence, but by the Treaty of Paris in 1783 they returned to Spanish control. After 1783, Americans immigrants moved into West Florida. In 1810, these American settlers in West Florida rebelled, declaring independence from Spain. President James Madison and Congress used the incident to claim the region, knowing full well that the Spanish government was seriously weakened by Napoleon's invasion of Spain. The United States asserted that the portion of West Florida from the Mississippi to the Perdido Rivers was part of the Louisiana Purchase of 1803. Negotiations over Florida began in earnest with the mission of Don Luis de Onís to Washington in 1815 to meet Secretary of State James Monroe. The issue was not resolved until Monroe was president and John Quincy Adams his Secretary of State. Spain ceded East Florida to the United States and renounced all claim to West Florida. Spain received no compensation, but the United States agreed to assume liability for $5 million in damage done by American citizens who rebelled against Spain. Under the Onís-Adams Treaty of 1819 (also called the Transcontinental Treaty and ratified in 1821) the United States and Spain defined the western limits of the Louisiana Purchase and Spain surrendered its claims to the Pacific Northwest. In return, the United States recognized Spanish sovereignty over Texas.

Monroe Doctrine, 1823

In his December 2, 1823, address to Congress, President James Monroe articulated United States' policy on the new political order developing in the rest of the Americas and the role of Europe in the Western Hemisphere.

The statement, known as the Monroe Doctrine became a longstanding tenet of U.S. foreign policy. The three main concepts of the doctrine—separate spheres of influence for the Americas and Europe, non-colonization, and non-intervention—were designed to signify a clear break between the New World and the autocratic realm of Europe. Monroe's administration forewarned the imperial European powers against interfering in the affairs of the newly independent Latin American states or potential United States territories. While Americans generally objected to European colonies in the New World, they also desired to increase United States influence and trading ties throughout the region to their south.

As Monroe stated: "The American continents ... are henceforth not to be considered as subjects for future colonization by any European powers."

1830–1860: Diplomacy and Westward Expansion

During this crucial period, the United States pursued a policy of expansion based on "manifest destiny," the ideology that Americans were in fact destined to extend their nation across the continent. While it negotiated an agreement with Great Britain to secure the Oregon territory, acquiring the valuable territory south of it—including California and its important Pacific harbors—required the use of force, and, in 1845, the United States embarked on its first offensive war by invading Mexico.

The Opening to China: the First Opium War, the United States, and the Treaty of Wangxia, 1839–1844

The Treaty of Wangxia (Wang-hsia) was the first formal treaty signed between the United States and China in 1844. It served as an American counterpart to the Anglo-Chinese Treaty of Nanjing that ended the First Opium War in 1842. The Opium War and these treaties were emblematic of an era in which Western powers tried to gain unfettered access to Chinese products and markets for European and U.S. trade. American trade with China began as early as

1784, relying on North American exports such as furs, sandalwood, and ginseng, but American interest in Chinese products soon outstripped the Chinese appetite for these American exports. The British had already discovered a great market in southern China for smuggled opium, and American traders soon also turned to opium to supplement their exports to China. China imported more goods than it exported. Settling this financial problem eventually led to the First Opium War between Great Britain and China, from 1839 to 1842. After defeating the Chinese the British were in a position to make demands from the Government of China. U.S. negotiators concluded a similar treaty guaranteeing many of the favorable terms awarded the British. In the 1850s, the United States and the European powers grew increasingly dissatisfied with both the terms of their treaties with China, and the Qing Government's failure to adhere to them. The British forced the issue by attacking the Chinese port cities of Guangzhou and Tianjin in the Second Opium War (1857–1858). Under the most-favored-nation clause, all of the foreign powers operating in China were permitted to seek the same concessions of China that Great Britain achieved by force. As a result, France, Russia, and the United States all signed treaties with China at Tianjin in quick succession in 1858.

The agreements reached between the Western powers and China following the Opium Wars came to be known as the "unequal treaties" because in practice they gave foreigners privileged status and extracted concessions from the Chinese.

Webster-Ashburton Treaty, 1842

During Daniel Webster's first term as Secretary of State (1841–1843), the primary foreign policy issues involved Great Britain - the northeast borders of the United States, the involvement of American citizens in the Canadian rebellion of 1837, and the suppression of the international slave trade. The Webster-Ashburton Treaty, signed August 9, 1842, resolved these frictions in Anglo-American relations.

The Oregon Territory, 1846

The Oregon Territory stretched from the Pacific coast to the Rocky Mountains, encompassing the area including present-day Oregon, Washington, and most of British Columbia. Originally Spain, Great Britain, Russia, and the United States claimed the territory. In 1819, under terms of the Transcontinental Treaty, Spain ceded its claims to the territory to the United States. Shortly thereafter the United States contested a unilateral Russian move to grant its citizens a fishing, whaling, and commercial monopoly from the Bering Straits to the 51st parallel. In 1823 President Monroe promulgated his doctrine, which put Russia on notice that the United States did not accept Russian attempts at monopoly. By 1843, increased American immigration on the Oregon Trail to the Territory made the border issue a burning one in Congress. President James Polk proposed a settlement on the 49 degree line to Great Britain. With some minor modifications, which reserved the whole of Vancouver Island to Canada, Great Britain agreed to Polk's suggestion.

The Annexation of Texas, the Mexican-American War, and the Treaty of Guadalupe-Hidalgo, 1845–1848

President James K. Polk oversaw the greatest territorial expansion of the United States - the annexation of Texas in 1845, the negotiation of the Oregon Treaty, and the conclusion of the Mexican-American War in 1848, which ended with the signing and ratification of the Treaty of Guadalupe-Hidalgo in 1848. These events brought within the control of the United States the future states of Texas, California, Nevada, New Mexico, Arizona, Utah, Washington, and Oregon, as well as portions of what would later become Oklahoma, Colorado, Kansas, Wyoming, and Montana.

Founding of Liberia, 1847

The founding of Liberia in the early 1800s was motivated by the domestic politics of slavery and race in the United States as well as by U.S. foreign policy interests. In 1816, a group of white Americans founded the American Colonization Society (ACS) to deal with the "problem" of the growing number of free blacks in the United States by resettling them in Africa. The resulting state of Liberia would become the second (after Haiti) black republic in the world at that time. In 1818 the Society sent two representatives to West Africa to find a suitable location for the colony. In 1820, 88 free black settlers and 3 society members sailed for Sierra Leone. In 1821, a U.S. Navy vessel resumed the search for a place of permanent settlement in what is now Liberia. The local tribes continually attacked the new colony and in 1824, the settlers built fortifications for protection. In that same year, the settlement was named Liberia and its capital Monrovia, in honor of President James Monroe who had procured more U.S. Government money for the project. In 1847, Liberia declared independence from the American Colonization Society in order to establish a sovereign state and create its own laws governing commerce.

United States Maritime Expansion Across the Pacific during the 19th Century

China was the source of some of the most sought after commodities—tea, porcelain, and silk—and Western merchants had sought access to this highly lucrative trade since at least the 17th century. Following U.S. independence, U.S.-based merchants continued to seek opportunity in China. In February 1784 the Empress of China became the first ship to sail from the United States to China. As this trade grew, U.S. traders built a small outpost in China and their interactions with Chinese subjects became more complex and occasionally contentious. The U.S. Government realized that it had to establish formal diplomatic ties in order to protect the interests of its citizens. In the wake of war between Britain and China, and the subsequent opening of diplomatic relations between those two countries, the United States moved to negotiate its own treaty with the Chinese Government. The resulting agreement, the Treaty of Wangxia, was ratified in 1844, and soon thereafter U.S. ministers and consuls took up residence in China's capital and port cities. Making the journey to China and maintaining the U.S. presence there required a network of ports extending across the Pacific Ocean, and as such, the China trade soon drove the United States to expand its presence throughout the Pacific region. When

Commodore Matthew Perry sailed to Japan in 1853, his primary motivation was to establish a foothold that would strengthen the U.S. position for trade and diplomacy in the region. On a smaller scale, as U.S. merchants began to stop at many of the Pacific Islands to replenish supplies and acquire goods to trade with Chinese merchants, the U.S. Government appointed consuls to several of these places. For example, consulates were established in Fiji in 1844, Samoa in 1856, and the Marshall Islands in 1881. The U.S. presence in Hawaii grew out of the need for a substantial base of operations in the Pacific to support U.S. interests in China. Ultimately this need became so great, and the U.S. presence so large, that the United States annexed the islands in 1898.

By 1900, the United States was a recognized world power with substantial commercial, political, and military interests and territorial holdings throughout the Pacific region.

Gadsden Purchase, 1853–1854

The Gadsden Purchase, or Treaty, was an agreement between the United States and Mexico, finalized in 1854, in which the United States agreed to pay Mexico $10 million for a 29,670 square mile portion of Mexico that later became part of Arizona and New Mexico. Gadsden's Purchase provided the land necessary for a southern transcontinental railroad and attempted to resolve conflicts that lingered after the Mexican-American War. The treaty did create the southern border of the present-day United States.

1861–1865: The Civil War and International Diplomacy

In 1861, eleven states seceded from the United States to form the Confederate States of America and, over the course of the next four years, the U.S. fought to bring the Confederate States back under control. During the Civil War the Confederacy repeatedly sought international support for its cause, often calling upon foreign reliance on its cotton exports to obtain it. The Union, on the other hand, strove to prevent other nations from recognizing the Confederacy as a legitimate nation and from getting involved in the Civil War.

One of the most important victories won by the United States during the Civil War was a series of diplomatic victories that ensured that the Confederacy would fail to achieve diplomatic recognition by even a single foreign government. Although this success can be attributed to the skill of Northern diplomats, the anti-slavery sentiments of the European populace, and European diversion to crises in Poland and Denmark, the most important factor stills rises from the battlefields on American soil. The Confederate states were incapable of winning enough consecutive victories to convince European governments that they could sustain independence. Following the U.S. announcement of its intention to establish an official blockade of Confederate ports, foreign governments began to recognize the Confederacy as a belligerent in the Civil War. Great Britain granted belligerent status on May 13, 1861, Spain on June 17, and Brazil on August 1. Other foreign governments issued statements of neutrality.

The blockade had a negative impact on the economies of other countries. Textile manufacturing areas in Britain and France that depended on Southern cotton entered periods of high unemployment, while French producers of wine, brandy and silk also suffered when their markets in the Confederacy were cut off. Although Confederate leaders were confident that Southern economic power would compel European powers to intervene in the Civil War on behalf of the Confederacy, Britain and France remained neutral despite their economic problems, and later in the war developed new sources of cotton in Egypt and India.

In 1862, French Emperor Napoleon III maneuvered to establish a French client state in Mexico, and eventually installed Maximilian of Habsburg, Archduke of Austria, as Emperor of Mexico. Stiff Mexican resistance caused Napoleon to order French withdrawal in 1867, a decision strongly encouraged by a United States recovered from its Civil War weakness in foreign affairs. Throughout the period of French intervention, the overall U.S. policy was to avoid direct conflict with France, and voice displeasure at French interference in Mexican affairs, but ultimately to remain neutral in the conflict.

The Alabama Claims, 1862–1872

The Alabama claims were a diplomatic dispute between the United States and Great Britain that arose from the Civil War. The peaceful resolution of these claims seven years after the war ended set an important precedent for solving serious international disputes through arbitration, and laid the foundation for greatly improved relations between Britain and the United States.

The controversy began when Confederate agents contracted for warships from British boatyards. Disguised as merchant vessels during their construction in order to circumvent British neutrality laws, the craft were actually intended as commerce raiders. The most successful of these cruisers was the Alabama, which was launched on July 29, 1862. It captured 58 Northern merchant ships before it was sunk in June 1864 by a U.S. warship off the coast of France. Together, they sank more than 150 Northern ships and impelled much of the U.S. merchant marine to adopt foreign registry. On September 3, 1863, the British Government impounded two ironclad, steam-driven "Laird rams" that Confederate agent James D. Bulloch had surreptitiously arranged to be built at a shipyard in Liverpool. The United States demanded compensation from Britain for the damage wrought by the British-built, Southern-operated commerce raiders, based upon the argument that the British Government, by aiding the creation of a After years of unsuccessful U.S. diplomatic initiatives, a Joint High Commission meeting in Washington, D.C. during the early part of 1871 arrived at the basis for a settlement. The British Government expressed regret for its contribution to the success of Confederate commerce raiders. This agreement, dated May 8, 1871, and known as the Treaty of Washington, also established an arbitration commission to evaluate the merit of U.S. financial claims on Britain. In addition, the treaty addressed Anglo-American disputes over boundaries and fishing rights. The arbitration commission, which issued its decision in September 1872, rejected American claims for indirect damages, but did order Britain to pay the United States $15.5 million as compensation for the Alabama claims.

1866–1898: Continued Expansion of United States Interests

In the wake of the Civil War, the United States continued to expand into new territory and new markets. In 1867, the U.S. nearly doubled its holdings with the purchase of the territory of Alaska from the Russians. At the same time, U.S. economic power grew, driven by new inventions in communication and transportation that closed the distance from coast to coast, and by a massive influx of immigration that sparked an explosion of industrialization and urbanization throughout the country. This renewed emphasis on exploring international business opportunities resulted in a buildup of U.S. naval forces to protect commercial shipping and overseas interests.

U.S. Diplomacy and the Telegraph, 1866

The development of the electric telegraph greatly changed the way diplomacy was conducted in the 19th century. European foreign ministries first used telegraphy during the early 1850s, but it did not become an important tool in the diplomacy of the United States until the completion of a successful transatlantic cable in 1866. The most significant characteristic of the telegraph was its speed. Even with the additional time required for coding and handling, telegrams were typically available within a few hours of being sent. This speed brought many advantages to policymakers who found that they could respond rapidly to far off crises of whose very existence they would previously have remained ignorant for weeks. But the telegraph also brought disadvantages. The ability to act quickly placed new time pressures upon political leaders, especially since telegraphy could inform newspapers and an expectant public just as swiftly. The acceleration of international disputes posed challenges to foreign ministries, which frequently used delay as a tool in resolving international crises. The long pauses caused by relatively slow communication had previously allowed tempers to cool, provided time for careful, methodical diplomacy, and offered harried political leaders an opportunity to conceive creative solutions to complex problems.

The U.S. Department of State established a telegraph office in 1866, a few months after the permanent establishment of transatlantic telegraphy. Diplomats learned to write more concisely in order to reduce telegraph expenses, which typically increased with the length of messages. Foreign ministries made more frequent use of codes in an (often fruitless) effort to keep the contents of their telegrams secret from spies. In the late 20th and early 21st centuries, new technologies of communication—especially networked computers and fiber optic cables (which carried light rather than electricity)—marked the end of diplomacy by telegraph. Yet, the telegraph deserves to be remembered as the technology that brought diplomacy into the high-speed age of electricity.

The Burlingame-Seward Treaty, 1868

China and the United States concluded the Burlingame-Seward Treaty in 1868 to expand upon the Treaty of Tianjin of 1858. The new treaty established some basic principles that aimed to ease immigration restrictions, and represented a Chinese effort to limit American interference in internal Chinese affairs. Anson Burlingame, a lawyer and former Republican representative to Congress from Massachusetts, became the U.S. Minister to China in 1861 and, under the orders of Secretary of State William Seward, worked to establish the United States as a power in the East. The United States wanted to gain access to profitable trading opportunities and foster the spread of Christianity in Asia, alongside the leading European nations, who also sought to gain inroads in China and Japan.

Despite the reciprocal protections that the Treaty afforded Chinese in the United States and Americans in China, the Treaty ultimately reinforced U.S. trade interests with China under the principle of the most-favored-nation concept, and it ensured a steady flow of low-cost Chinese immigrant labor for U.S. firms.

In the 1850s, Chinese workers migrated to the United States, first to work in the gold mines, but also to take agricultural jobs, and factory work, especially in the garment industry. Chinese immigrants were particularly instrumental in building railroads in the American west, and as Chinese laborers grew successful in the United States, a number of them became entrepreneurs in their own right. As the numbers of Chinese laborers increased, so did the strength of anti-Chinese sentiment among other workers in the American economy. This finally resulted in legislation that aimed to limit future immigration of Chinese workers to the United States, and threatened to sour diplomatic relations between the United States and China.

Sea Power in the 1890s

In 1890, Captain Alfred Thayer Mahan, a lecturer in naval history and the president of the United States Naval War College, published *The Influence of Sea Power upon History, 1660–1783.*He argued that British control of the seas, combined with a corresponding decline in the naval strength of its major European rivals, paved the way for Great Britain's emergence as the world's dominant military, political, and economic power. These lessons, he argued, could be applied to U.S. foreign policy, particularly in the quest to expand U.S. markets overseas.

Accessing these new international markets required three things: a merchant navy, which could carry American products to new markets across the "great highway" of the high seas; an American battleship navy to deter or destroy rival fleets; and a network of naval bases capable of providing fuel and supplies for the enlarged navy, and maintaining open lines of communications between the United States and its new markets. Following the successful conclusion of the Spanish-American War in 1898, the United States gained control of territories that could serve as the coaling stations and naval bases that Mahan had discussed, such as Puerto Rico, Guam, and the Philippines. Five years later, the United States obtained a perpetual lease for a naval base at Guantanamo Bay, Cuba.

Venezuela Boundary Dispute, 1895–1899

The Venezuelan Boundary Dispute officially began in 1841, when the Venezuelan Government protested alleged British encroachment on Venezuelan territory. The dispute dragged on for decades but in 1876 Venezuela broke diplomatic relations with Great Britain, and appealed to the United States for assistance, citing the Monroe Doctrine as justification for U.S. involvement. Finally in 1895 the United States demanded that Britain settle the dispute by arbitration. In 1899 the arbitration commission found in favor of Britain. The Anglo-Venezuelan boundary dispute incident asserted for the first time a more outward-looking American foreign policy, particularly in the Western Hemisphere. Internationally the incident marked the United States as a world power and gave notice that under the Monroe Doctrine it would exercise its claimed prerogatives in the Western Hemisphere.

U.S. Diplomacy and Yellow Journalism, 1895–1898

Yellow journalism was a style of newspaper reporting that emphasized sensationalism over facts. During its heyday in the late 19th century it was one of many factors that helped push the United States and Spain into war in Cuba and the Philippines, leading to the acquisition of overseas territory by the United States. The peak of yellow journalism, in terms of both intensity and influence, came in early 1898, when a U.S. battleship, the Maine, sunk in Havana harbor. U.S. newspaper magnates Hearst and Pulitzer published stories of plots to sink the ship and when a U.S. naval investigation later stated that the explosion had come from a mine in the harbor, the proponents of yellow journalism seized upon it and called for war. By early May, the Spanish-American War had begun. Yellow journalism of this period is significant to the history of U.S. foreign relations in that its centrality to the history of the Spanish American War shows that the press had the power to capture the attention of a large readership and to influence public reaction to international events.

U.S. victory in the Spanish-American War produced a peace treaty that compelled the Spanish to relinquish claims on Cuba, and to cede sovereignty over Guam, Puerto Rico, and the Philippines to the United States. The United States also annexed the independent state of Hawaii during the conflict. Thus, the war enabled the United States to establish its predominance in the Caribbean region and to pursue its strategic and economic interests in Asia.

1899–1913: Defending U.S. International Interests

Following the defeat of Spain, the United States acquired overseas colonies in the Caribbean and the Pacific and pursued a series of policies designed to protect American territories and aggressively expand its international commercial interests. These policies included the promotion of the "Open Door" policy in China and the attachment of the Roosevelt Corollary to the Monroe Doctrine that formally announced the intention to use military force to defend the Western Hemisphere against European incursions. At the same time, President Theodore Roosevelt oversaw the construction of the Panama Canal, which would have profound economic implications for American trade, and engaged in great power diplomacy in the wake of the Russo-Japanese War. In just over a decade, the United States had redefined its national and international interests to include a large overseas military presence, overseas possessions, and direct engagement in setting priorities in international affairs.

The Philippine-American War, 1899–1902

Spain ceded its longstanding colony of the Philippines to the United States in the Treaty of Paris. On February 4, 1899, just two days before the U.S. Senate ratified the treaty, fighting broke out between American forces and Filipino nationalists who sought independence rather than a change in colonial rulers. The ensuing Philippine-American War lasted three years and resulted in the death of over 4,200 American and over 20,000 Filipino combatants. As many as 200,000 Filipino civilians died from violence, famine, and disease. President Theodore Roosevelt proclaimed a general amnesty and declared the conflict over on July 4, 1902. In 1907, the Philippines convened its first elected assembly, and in 1916, the Jones Act promised the nation eventual independence. The archipelago became an autonomous commonwealth in 1935, and the U.S. granted independence in 1946.

Open Door in China, 1899–1900

Secretary of State John Hay created the concept of "Open Door" in China 1900 aimed at promoting equal opportunity for international trade and commerce in China, and respect for China's administrative and territorial integrity. Hay proposed a free, open market and equal trading opportunity for merchants of all nationalities operating in China, based in part on the most favored nation clauses already established in the Treaties of Wangxia and Tianjin. In 1900, however, internal events in China threatened the idea of the Open Door. An anti-foreign movement known as the Boxer Rebellion gathered strength, and began attacking foreign missionaries and Chinese converts to Christianity. It claimed the lives of hundreds of foreign missionaries and thousands of Chinese nationals.

On July 3, 1900, Hay circulated another message to the foreign powers involved in China, this time noting the importance of respecting the "territorial and administrative integrity" of China. Together, the Open Door Notes served the purpose of outlining U.S. policy toward China and expressing U.S. hopes for cooperation with the other foreign powers with a stake in the region. Ironically, Hay articulated the Open Door policy at a time when the U.S. Government was doing everything in its power to close the door on Chinese immigration to the United States.

Japanese-American Relations at the Turn of the Century, 1900–1922

In the first two decades of the twentieth century, the relationship between the United States and Japan was marked by increasing tension and corresponding attempts to use diplomacy to reduce the threat of conflict. Each side had territory and interests in Asia and were concerned the other might threaten these. In 1905, the Japanese started to establish more formal control over South Manchuria by forcing China to give Japan ownership rights to the South Manchurian Railway. In 1908, U.S Secretary of State Elihu Root and Japanese Ambassador Takahira Kogoro formed an agreement in which Japan promised to respect U.S. territorial possessions in the Pacific, its Open Door policy in China, and the limitation of immigration to the United States. The Government of Japan redirected its labor emigrants to its holdings in Manchuria, maintaining that these were not a part of China. For its part, the United States recognized Japanese control of Taiwan and the Pescadores, and the Japanese special interest in Manchuria.

In 1915, the Japanese issued its "Twenty-One Demands" of China, in which it asked that China recognize its territorial claims, prevent other powers from obtaining new concessions along its coast, and take a series of actions designed to benefit the Japanese economically. China turned to the United States for assistance, and U.S. officials responded with a declaration that they would not recognize any agreement that threatened the Open Door. The potential for conflict between the United States and Japan, especially over China, led the two governments to negotiate again. In the Ishii-Lansing Agreement of 1917, Secretary of State Robert Lansing acknowledged that Manchuria was under Japanese control, while Japanese Foreign Minister Ishii Kikujiro agreed not to place limitations on U.S. commercial opportunities elsewhere in China. The two powers also agreed not to take advantage of the war in Europe to seek additional rights and privileges.

Japan and the United States clashed again during the League of Nations negotiations in 1919. The United States refused to accept the Japanese request for a racial equality clause or an admission of the equality of the nations.

The United States, Cuba, and the Platt Amendment, 1901

The Platt Amendment, an amendment to a U.S. army appropriations bill, established the terms under which the United States would end its military occupation of Cuba (which had begun in 1898 during the Spanish-American War) and "leave the government and control of the island of Cuba to its people." It prohibited the Cuban Government from entering into any international treaty that would compromise Cuban independence or allow foreign powers to use the island for military purposes. The United States also reserved the right to intervene in Cuban affairs in order to defend Cuban independence and to maintain "a government adequate for the protection of life, property, and individual liberty." Another condition required Cuba to sell or lease territory for coaling and naval stations to the United States. This clause ultimately led to the perpetual lease by the United States of Guantánamo Bay.

Roosevelt Corollary to the Monroe Doctrine, 1904

President Theodore Roosevelt's assertive approach to Latin America and the Caribbean has often been characterized as the "Big Stick," and his policy came to be known as the Roosevelt Corollary to the Monroe Doctrine. By the 20th century a more confident United States was willing to take on the role of regional policeman. The Roosevelt Corollary stated that the United States would intervene as a last resort to ensure that other nations in the Western Hemisphere fulfilled their obligations to international creditors, and did not violate the rights of the United States or invite "foreign aggression to the detriment of the entire body of American nations." Over the long term the corollary had little to do with relations between the Western Hemisphere and Europe, but it did serve as justification for U.S. intervention in Cuba, Nicaragua, Haiti, and the Dominican Republic.

The Treaty of Portsmouth and the Russo-Japanese War, 1904–1905

The Treaty of Portsmouth formally ended the Russo-Japanese War of 1904–05. The Japanese asked Roosevelt to negotiate a peace agreement, and representatives of the two nations met in Portsmouth, New Hampshire in 1905. The Treaty ultimately gave Japan control of Korea and much of South Manchuria, including Port Arthur and the railway that connected it with the rest of the region, along with the southern half of Sakhalin Island; Russian power was curtailed in the region, but it was not required to pay Japan's war costs. Roosevelt won the Nobel Peace Prize for his efforts in moderating the talks and pushing toward peace.

Dollar Diplomacy, 1909–1913

From 1909 to 1913, President William Howard Taft and Secretary of State Philander C. Knox followed a foreign policy characterized as "dollar diplomacy." Taft believed that the goal of diplomacy was to create stability and order abroad that would best promote American commercial interests. Knox felt that not only was the goal of diplomacy to improve financial opportunities, but also to use private capital to further U.S. interests overseas. "Dollar diplomacy" was evident in extensive U.S. interventions in China, in the Caribbean and Central America, especially in measures undertaken to safeguard American financial interests in the region.

The Chinese Revolution of 1911

In October of 1911, a group of revolutionaries in southern China led a successful revolt against the Qing Dynasty, establishing in its place the Republic of China and ending the imperial system. However the new government failed to unify the country under its control. Foreign nations with investments in China remained neutral throughout the upheaval while the United States was among the first countries to establish full diplomatic relations with the new Republic. Britain, Japan, and Russia soon followed.

The Panama Canal, 1903–1914

The renegotiated Hay-Bunau-Varilla Treaty of 1903 provided the United States with a 10-mile wide strip of land for the canal, a one-time $10 million payment to Panama, and an annual annuity of $250,000. The United States also agreed to guarantee the independence of Panama. Completed in 1914, the Panama Canal symbolized U.S. technological prowess and economic power. Although U.S. control of the canal eventually became an irritant to

U.S.-Panamanian relations, at the time it was heralded as a major foreign policy achievement.

1914–1920: World War One

During his tenure as president, Woodrow Wilson encouraged Americans to look beyond their economic interests and to define and set foreign policy in terms of ideals, morality, and the spread of democracy abroad. The United States continued its efforts to become an active player on the international scene and engaged in action both in its traditional "sphere of influence" in the Western Hemisphere and in Europe during the First World War. Germany's resumption of submarine attacks on passenger and merchant ships in 1917 was the primary motivation behind Wilson's decision to lead the United States into World War I. President Wilson's war aims went beyond the defense of U.S. maritime interests. In his War Message to Congress he declared our object "is to vindicate the principles of peace and justice in the life of the world." The Wilsonian vision for collective security through American leadership in international organizations, like the newly established League of Nations, appealed to the American public, but the United States ultimately declined membership in the League due to Article X of its charter that committed the United States to defending any League member in the event of an attack.

U.S. Invasion and Occupation of Haiti, 1915–34

Increased instability in Haiti in the years before 1915 led to heightened action by the United States to deter foreign influence. Under interventionist policies of the early 20th century, President Woodrow Wilson sent the United States Marines into Haiti to restore order and maintain political and economic stability in the Caribbean after the assassination of the Haitian President in July of 1915. In reality the Wilson administration was protecting U.S. assets in the area and preventing a possible German invasion. This occupation continued until 1934.

The Bullitt Mission to Soviet Russia, 1919

In March of 1919, William Christian Bullitt, an attaché to the U.S. delegation to the Paris Peace Conference, visited Soviet Russia on a clandestine mission. Although Secretary of State Robert Lansing only authorized him to report on political and economic conditions, Bullitt's actual objective was far more ambitious: to broker an agreement between the Allies and Russia's Bolshevik government that would end the Russian Civil War, lift the Allied blockade of that country, and allow the Allies to withdraw the troops they had dispatched to Russia in 1918. Bullitt eventually received a proposal from the Bolshevik government that would have realized these goals, but the Allied leaders at the Paris Peace Conference were unwilling to accept the offer. The failure of the Allies to agree to the proposal secured by the Bullitt mission delayed official U.S. recognition of Soviet Russia for many years.

The Paris Peace Conference and the Treaty of Versailles

The Paris Peace Conference, convened in January 1919 at Versailles just outside Paris, was to establish the terms of the peace after World War. Though nearly thirty nations participated, the representatives of Great Britain, France, the United States, and Italy - known as the "Big Four" - dominated the proceedings. The Treaty of Versailles imposed strict punitive measures on Germany and included a plan to form a League of Nations that would serve as an international forum and an international collective security arrangement. U.S. President Woodrow Wilson was a strong advocate of the League as he believed it would prevent future wars.

The League of Nations, 1920

The League of Nations was an international organization, headquartered in Geneva, Switzerland, to provide a forum for resolving international disputes. It was first proposed by President Woodrow Wilson as part of his Fourteen Points plan for an equitable peace in Europe, but the United States was never a member. The League's main organs were an Assembly of all members and a

Council, made up of five permanent members and four rotating members, along with an International Court of Justice. Most importantly, for Wilson, the League would guarantee the territorial integrity and political independence of member states, authorize the League to take "any action...to safeguard the peace," establish procedures for arbitration and create the mechanisms for economic and military sanctions.

The Washington Naval Conference, 1921–1922

Between 1921 and 1922, the world's largest naval powers gathered in Washington for a conference to discuss naval disarmament and ways to relieve growing tensions in East Asia. Three major treaties emerged out of the Washington Conference: the Five-Power Treaty, the Four-Power Treaty, and the Nine-Power Treaty. The Five-Power treaty was the cornerstone of the naval disarmament program. It called for each of the countries involved to maintain a set ratio of warship tonnage and to stop building capital ships. In the Four-Power Treaty, the United States, France, Britain, and Japan agreed to consult with each other in the event of a future crisis in East Asia before taking action. This treaty replaced the Anglo-Japanese Treaty of 1902, which had been a source of some concern for the United States. In the years following World War I, U.S. policymakers saw Japan as the greatest rising military threat. Heavily militarized and looking to expand its influence and territory, Japan had the potential to threaten U.S. colonial possessions in Asia and the profitable China trade. The final multilateral agreement was the Nine-Power Treaty, which marked the internationalization of the U.S. Open Door Policy in China. The treaty promised that each of the signatories—the United States, Britain, Japan, France, Italy, Belgium, the Netherlands, Portugal and China—would respect the territorial integrity of China. The treaty recognized Japanese dominance in Manchuria but otherwise affirmed the importance of equal opportunity for all nations doing business in the country; for its part, China promised not to discriminate against any country seeking to do business there.

The Dawes Plan, the Young Plan, German Reparations, and Inter-allied War Debts

After the First World War, the victorious European powers demanded that Germany compensate them for the devastation wrought by the four-year conflict. Germany defaulted in January 1923 because of hyperinflation and a currency collapse.

While the United States had little interest in collecting reparations from Germany, it was determined to secure repayment of the more than $10 billion it had loaned to the Allies. Washington repeatedly rejected calls to cancel these debts; it also resisted efforts to link reparations to inter-allied war debts.

In late 1923, the Reparation Commission headed by Charles Dawes met to review the situation. Under the Dawes Plan, Germany's annual reparation payments would be reduced, increasing over time as its economy improved; the full amount to be paid, however, was left undetermined. Over the next four years, U.S. banks lent Germany enough money to enable it to meet its reparation payments to countries such as France and the United Kingdom. These countries, in turn, used their reparation payments from Germany to service their war debts to the United States.

In the autumn of 1928, another committee of experts chaired by Own Young was formed to devise a final settlement of German reparations. In 1929, it proposed a plan that reduced the total amount of reparations demanded of Germany to 121 billion gold marks, almost $29 billion, payable over 58 years. Foreign supervision of German finances would cease and the last of the occupying troops would leave German soil. The advent of the Great Depression doomed the Young Plan from the start. At the Lausanne Conference in 1932, European nations agreed to cancel their reparation claims against Germany, save for a final payment.

The Kellogg-Briand Pact, 1928

The Kellogg-Briand Pact was an agreement to outlaw war. On August 27, 1928, fifteen nations signed the pact at Paris. Signatories included France, the United States, the United Kingdom, Ireland, Canada, Australia, New Zealand,

South Africa, India, Belgium, Poland, Czechoslovakia, Germany, Italy and Japan. Later, an additional forty-seven nations followed suit, so the pact was eventually signed by most of the established nations in the world. The U.S. Senate ratified the agreement by a vote of 85–1, though it did so only after making reservations to note that U.S. participation did not limit its right to self-defense or require it to act against signatories breaking the agreement.

The Great Depression and U.S. Foreign Policy

The Great Depression of the 1930s was a global event that derived in part from events in the United States and U.S. financial policies. As it lingered through the decade, it influenced U.S. foreign policies in such a way that the United States Government became even more isolationist. The key factor in turning national economic difficulties into worldwide Depression seems to have been a lack of international coordination as most governments and financial institutions turned inwards. At the London Economic Conference in 1933, leaders of the world's main economies met to resolve the economic crisis, but failed to reach any major collective agreements. As a result, the Depression dragged on through the rest of the 1930s.

The Depression caused the United States to retreat further into its post-World War I isolationism. A series of international incidents occurred during the 1930s—the Japanese seizure of northeast China in 1931, the Italian invasion of Ethiopia in 1935, and German expansionism in Central and Eastern Europe and the rise of Fascism —but the United States did not take any major action in response or opposition. When these and other incidents occurred, the United States Government issued statements of disapproval but took limited action beyond that.

The London Naval Conference, 1930

The London Naval Conference was an attempt to end an all-out naval arms race. The final treaty limited tonnage of auxiliary ships and tonnage and number of cruisers, as well as the size and gun power of submarines and destroy-ers. In 1935, the powers met for a second London Naval Conference to renego-tiate the Washington and London treaties before their expiration the following year. The Japanese walked out of that conference, but Great Britain, France, and the United States signed an agreement declaring a six-year holiday on building large light cruisers in the 8,000 to 10,000 ton range.

The Mukden Incident of 1931 and the Stimson Doctrine

In 1931, a dispute near the Chinese city of Mukden (Shenyang) precipitated events that led to the Japanese conquest of Manchuria. In response, U.S. Secre-tary of State Henry Stimson issued what would become known as the Stimson Doctrine, stating that the United States would not recognize any agreements between the Japanese and Chinese that limited free commercial intercourse in the region. It proved ineffectual in stopping Japanese aggression. The subse-quent Lytton Commission divided blame for the conflict in Manchuria equally between Chinese nationalism and Japanese militarism. The Manchurian Cri-sis of 1931–33 demonstrated the futility of the 1920s-era agreements on peace, nonaggression and disarmament in the face of a power determined to march forward. Responses like the Stimson Doctrine of non-recognition similarly had little effect.

Good Neighbor Policy, 1933

President Franklin Delano Roosevelt took office determined to improve relations with the nations of Central and South America. Under his leadership the United States emphasized cooperation and trade rather than military force to maintain stability in the hemisphere. In his inaugural address on March 4, 1933, Roosevelt stated: "In the field of world policy I would dedicate this nation to the policy of the good neighbor—the neighbor who resolutely respects himself and, because he does so, respects the rights of others."

Recognition of the Soviet Union, 1933

On November 16, 1933, President Franklin Roosevelt ended almost 16 years of American non-recognition of the Soviet Union following a series of negotiations in Washington, D.C. with the Soviet Commissar for Foreign Affairs, Maxim Litvinov. The U.S. broke off diplomatic relations with Russia, shortly after the Bolshevik Party seized power. Roosevelt hoped that recognition of the Soviet Union would serve U.S. strategic interests by limiting Japanese expansionism in Asia, and he believed that full diplomatic recognition would serve American commercial interests in the Soviet Union, a matter of some concern to an Administration grappling with the effects of the Great Depression. Finally, the United States was the only major power that continued to withhold official diplomatic recognition from the Soviet Union.

New Deal

In 1934, the Roosevelt Administration undertook two initiatives that signaled a desire to reengage economically with the rest of the world. The first was the creation of the Export-Import Bank as an institution designed to finance U.S. trade with the newly-recognized Soviet Union. He created a second Export-Import Bank the following month, this one intended to finance trade with Cuba; in July 1934, the second bank's field of operations was expanded to include all countries save the Soviet Union. In 1935, the two banks were combined and Congress passed legislation granting the newly unified bank more powers and more capital. In the years before the start of the Second World War, while it did extend credits to countries outside the Western Hemisphere such as Italy and China, the Export-Import Bank concentrated its efforts in Latin America, where it proved an important component of the Good Neighbor policy.

The second major foreign economic policy initiative of 1934 was the Reciprocal Trade Agreements Act (RTAA). In March 1934, proclaiming "that a full and permanent domestic recovery depends in part upon a revived and strengthened international trade," Roosevelt asked Congress for authority to negotiate trade agreements based upon reciprocal tariff reductions with other countries. Signed into law on June 12, 1934, the RTAA represented a fundamental shift in U.S. trade policy. The Constitution gives Congress the right to regulate foreign commerce and establish tariff rates. Under the RTAA, Congress granted the president the right – on a temporary basis, subject to renewal after three years – to decrease or increase U.S. tariffs.

The Neutrality Acts, 1930s

In the 1930s, the United States Government enacted a series of laws designed to prevent the United States from being embroiled in a foreign war by clearly stating the terms of U.S. neutrality. On August 31, 1935, Congress passed the first Neutrality Act prohibiting the export of "arms, ammunition, and implements of war" from the United States to foreign nations at war and requiring arms manufacturers in the United States to apply for an export license. The outbreak of the Spanish Civil War in 1936 and the rising tide of fascism in Europe increased support for extending and expanding the Neutrality Act of 1937. Under this law, U.S. citizens were forbidden from traveling on belligerent ships, and American merchant ships were prevented from transporting arms to belligerents even if those arms were produced outside of the United States. The Act gave the President the authority to bar all belligerent ships from U.S. waters, and to extend the export embargo to any additional "articles or materials." Finally, civil wars would also fall under the terms of the Act. The Neutrality Act of 1937 did contain one important concession to Roosevelt: belligerent nations were allowed, at the discretion of the President, to acquire any items except arms from the United States, so long as they immediately paid for such items and carried them on non-American ships—the so-called "cash-and-carry" provision. Since vital raw materials such as oil were not considered "implements of war," the "cash-and-carry" clause would be quite valuable to whatever nation could make use of it. Roosevelt had engineered its inclusion as a deliberate way to assist Great Britain and France in any war against the Axis Powers, since he realized that they were the only countries that had both the hard currency and ships to make use of "cash-and-carry."

In November 1939, a final Neutrality Act passed which lifted the arms embargo and put all trade with belligerent nations under the terms of "cash-and-carry." The ban on loans remained in effect, and American ships were barred from transporting goods to belligerent ports. In October of 1941, after the United States had committed itself to aiding the Allies through Lend-Lease, Roosevelt sought to repeal certain portions of the Act.

1937–1945: Diplomacy and the Road to War

By the late 1930s, the United States continued its efforts to stay out of the hostilities in Europe and Asia although the U.S. government believed war to be inevitable. In 1940, U.S. policy slowly began to shift from neutrality to non-belligerency by providing aid to the nations at war with the Axis Powers—Germany, Italy and Japan. In response to the growing emergency, President Franklin D. Roosevelt called upon the American people to prepare for war. On December 7, 1941, the Japanese attacked the U.S. naval installation at Pearl Harbor, and the United States formally entered the Second World War.

Between 1937 and 1941, most U.S. officials believed that it had no vital interests in China worth going to war over with Japan. Tensions with Japan rose when the Japanese Army bombed the U.S.S. Panay as it evacuated American citizens from Nanjing, killing three. The U.S. Government, however, continued to avoid conflict and accepted an apology and indemnity from the Japanese. An uneasy truce held between the two nations into 1940. In 1940 and 1941, President Franklin D. Roosevelt formalized U.S. aid to China. The U.S. Government extended credits to the Chinese Government for the purchase of war supplies, as it slowly began to tighten restrictions on Japan. Japan signed the Tripartite Pact with Germany and Italy on September 27, 1940 and thereby linked the conflicts in Europe and Asia. Then in mid-1941, Japan signed a Neutrality Pact with the Soviet Union, making it clear that Japan's military would be moving into Southeast Asia, where the United States had greater interests. A third agreement with Vichy France enabled Japanese forces to move into Indochina and begin their Southern Advance.

Faced with serious shortages as a result of the embargo, unable to retreat, and convinced that the U.S. officials opposed further negotiations, Japan's leaders came to the conclusion that they had to act swiftly. Japanese planes bombed the U.S. fleet at Pearl Harbor on December 7, 1941. The following day, the United States declared war on Japan, and it soon entered into a military alliance with China. When Germany stood by its ally and declared war on the United States, the Roosevelt Administration faced war in both Europe and Asia.

Lend-Lease and Military Aid to the Allies in the Early Years of World War II

During World War II, the United States began to provide significant military supplies and other assistance to the Allies in September 1940, even though the United States did not enter the war until December 1941. Much of this aid flowed to the United Kingdom and other nations already at war with Germany and Japan through an innovative program known as Lend-Lease. The United States "lent" the supplies to the British, deferring payment. Over the course of the war, the United States contracted Lend-Lease agreements with more than 30 countries, dispensing some $50 billion in assistance. Although British Prime Minister Winston Churchill later referred to the initiative as "the most unsordid act" one nation had ever done for another, Roosevelt's primary motivation was not altruism or disinterested generosity. Rather, Lend-Lease was designed to serve America's interest in defeating Nazi Germany without entering the war until the American military and public was prepared to fight. At a time when the majority of Americans opposed direct participation in the war, Lend-Lease represented a vital U.S. contribution to the fight against Nazi Germany.

U.S.-Soviet Alliance, 1941–1945

Although relations between the Soviet Union and the United States had been strained in the years before World War II, the U.S.-Soviet alliance of 1941–1945 was marked by a great degree of cooperation and was essential to securing the defeat of Nazi Germany. Without the remarkable efforts of the Soviet Union on the Eastern Front, the United States and Great Britain would have been hard pressed to score a decisive military victory over Nazi Germany. Roosevelt never lost sight of the fact that Nazi Germany, not the Soviet Union, posed the greatest threat to world peace. In order to defeat that threat, Roosevelt confided that he "would hold hands with the devil" if necessary.

Repeal of the Chinese Exclusion Act, 1943

In 1943, Congress passed a measure to repeal the discriminatory exclusion laws against Chinese immigrants and to establish an immigration quota for China of around 105 visas per year. As such, the Chinese were both the first to be excluded in the beginning of the era of immigration restriction and the first Asians to gain entry to the United States in the era of liberalization. The repeal of this act was a decision almost wholly grounded in the exigencies of World War II, as Japanese propaganda made repeated reference to Chinese exclusion from the United States in order to weaken the ties between the United States and its ally, the Republic of China.

Wartime Conferences, 1941–1945

In August 1941, President Franklin Roosevelt and British Prime Minister Winston Churchill met secretly and devised an eight-point statement of war aims known as the **Atlantic Charter**, which included a pledge that the Allies would not accept territorial changes resulting from the war in Europe. Following the Japanese attack on Pearl Harbor, the wartime conferences focused on establishing a second front.

At Casablanca in January 1943, Roosevelt and Churchill agreed to fight until the Axis powers surrendered unconditionally. In a November 1943 meeting in Egypt with Chinese leader Chiang Kai-shek, Roosevelt and Churchill agreed to a pre-eminent role for China in postwar Asia. The next major wartime conference included Roosevelt, Churchill, and the leader of the Soviet Union, Joseph Stalin. Meeting at Tehran following the Cairo Conference, the "Big

Three" secured confirmation on the launching of the cross-channel invasion and a promise from Stalin that the Soviet Union would eventually enter the war against Japan. In 1944, conferences at Bretton Woods and Dumbarton Oaks created the framework for international cooperation in the postwar world. In February 1945, the "Big Three" met at the former Russian czar's summer palace in the Crimea. Yalta was the most important and by far the most controversial of the wartime meetings. Recognizing the strong position that the Soviet Army possessed on the ground, Churchill and an ailing Roosevelt agreed to a number of compromises with Stalin that allowed Soviet hegemony to remain in Poland and other Eastern European countries, granted territorial concessions to the Soviet Union, and outlined punitive measures against Germany, including an occupation and reparations in principle. Stalin did guarantee that the Soviet Union would declare war on Japan within six months. The last meeting of the "Big Three" occurred at Potsdam in July 1945, where the tension that would erupt into the cold war was evident. Despite the end of the war in Europe and the revelation of the existence of the atomic bomb to the Allies, neither President Harry Truman, Roosevelt's successor, nor Clement Atlee, who mid-way through the conference replaced Churchill, could come to agreement with Stalin on any but the most minor issues. The most significant agreement was the issuance of the Potsdam Declaration to Japan demanding an immediate and unconditional surrender and threatening Japan with destruction if they did not comply. With the Axis forces defeated, the wartime alliance soon devolved into suspicion and bitterness on both sides.

The United Nations, 1945

On January 1, 1942, representatives of 26 nations at war with the Axis powers met in Washington to sign the Declaration of the United Nations endorsing the Atlantic Charter, pledging to use their full resources against the Axis and agreeing not to make a separate peace. At the Quebec Conference in August 1943, Secretary of State Cordell Hull and British Foreign Secretary Anthony Eden agreed to draft a declaration that included a call for "a general international organization, based on the principle sovereign equality of all nations." When President Franklin D. Roosevelt met with Soviet Premier Joseph Stalin in Tehran, Iran, in November 1943, he proposed an international organization comprising an assembly of all member states and a 10-member executive committee to discuss social and economic issues. The United States, Great Britain, Soviet Union, and China would enforce peace as "the four policemen." Meanwhile Allied representatives founded a set of task-oriented organizations: the Food and Agricultural Organization (May 1943), the United Nations Relief and Rehabilitation Administration (November 1943), the United Nations Educational, Scientific, and Cultural Organization (April 1944), the International Monetary Fund and the World Bank (July 1944), and the International Civil Aviation Organization (November 1944).

Representatives of 50 nations met in San Francisco April-June 1945 to complete the Charter of the United Nations. In addition to the General Assembly of all member states and a Security Council of 5 permanent and 6 non-permanent members, the Charter provided for an 18-member Economic and Social Council, an International Court of Justice, a Trusteeship Council to oversee certain colonial territories, and a Secretariat under a Secretary General. The United Nations came into existence on October 24, 1945, after 29 nations had ratified the Charter.

1945–1952: The Early Cold War

The United States emerged from World War II as one of the foremost economic, political, and military powers in the world. Wartime production pulled the economy out of depression and propelled it to great profits. In the interest of avoiding another global war, for the first time the United States began to use economic assistance as a strategic element of its foreign policy and offered significant assistance to countries in Europe and Asia struggling to rebuild their shattered economies.

The United States faced increasing resistance from the Soviet Union which had rescinded on a number of wartime promises. As the Soviets demonstrated a keen interest in dominating Eastern Europe, the United States took the lead in forming a Western alliance to counterbalance the communist superpower to contain the spread of communism. At the same time, the United States restructured its military and intelligence forces, both of which would have a significant influence in U.S. Cold War policy.

Atomic Diplomacy

Atomic diplomacy refers to attempts to use the threat of nuclear warfare to achieve diplomatic goals. After the first successful test of the atomic bomb in 1945, U.S. officials immediately considered the potential non-military benefits that could be derived from the American nuclear monopoly. In the years that followed, there were several occasions in which government officials used or considered atomic diplomacy. The Soviet Union successfully exploded its first atomic bomb in 1949, the United Kingdom in 1952, France in 1960 and the People's Republic of China in 1964.

In the first two decades of the Cold War, there were a number of occasions during which a form of atomic diplomacy was employed by either side of the conflict. During the Berlin Blockade of 1948–49, President Truman transferred several B-29 bombers capable of delivering nuclear bombs to the region to signal to the Soviet Union that the United States was both capable of implementing a nuclear attack and willing to execute it if it became necessary. During the Korean War, President Truman once again deployed the B-29s to signal U.S. resolve. In an about face, in 1962, the Soviet deployment of nuclear missiles to Cuba in order to try to force U.S. concessions on Europe became another example of atomic diplomacy.

On June 14, 1946, before a session of the United Nations Atomic Energy Commission (UNAEC), U.S. representative Bernard Baruch, presented a proposal for the creation of an international Atomic Development Authority in the hopes of avoiding unchecked proliferation of nuclear power. The vote was held on December 30, with 10 of the UNAEC's 12 members in favor, while the other two members (the Soviet Union and Poland) abstained. The vote required unanimity to pass. As such, the Polish and Soviet abstentions thwarted the adoption of the Baruch Plan.

Occupation and Reconstruction of Japan, 1945–52

After the defeat of Japan the United States led the Allies in the occupation and rehabilitation of the Japanese state. Between 1945 and 1952, the U.S. occupying forces, led by General Douglas A. MacArthur, enacted widespread military, political, economic, and social reforms. These included The Tokyo War Crimes trials, disbandment of the army and a new constitution as well as large scale land reform to reduce the power of rich landowners, many of whom had supported the war.

The Truman Doctrine, 1947

With the Truman Doctrine, President Harry S. Truman established that the United States would provide political, military and economic assistance to all democratic nations under threat from external or internal authoritarian forces. The Truman Doctrine effectively reoriented U.S. foreign policy, away from its usual stance of withdrawal from regional conflicts not directly involving the United States, to one of possible intervention in faraway conflicts.

The British Government had announced it would no longer provide military and economic assistance to the Greek Government in its civil war against the Greek Communist Party. Truman asked Congress to support the Greek Government against the Communists believing that the Soviet Union supported the Greek Communists. Truman argued that a Communist victory in the Greek Civil War would endanger the political stability of Turkey, which would undermine the political stability of the Middle East. This could not be allowed in light of the region's immense strategic importance to U.S. national security. Truman also argued that the United States was compelled to assist "free peoples" in their struggles against "totalitarian regimes," because the spread of authoritarianism would "undermine the foundations of international peace and hence the security of the United States." In the words of the Truman Doctrine, it became "the policy of the United States to support free peoples who are resisting attempted subjugation by armed minorities or by outside pressures."

George F. Kennan, a career Foreign Service Officer, formulated the policy of "containment," the basic United States strategy for fighting the cold war (1947–1989) with the Soviet Union. "The main element of any United States policy toward the Soviet Union," Kennan wrote, "must be that of a long-term, patient but firm and vigilant containment of Russian expansive tendencies." To that end, he called for countering "Soviet pressure against the free institutions of the Western world" through the "adroit and vigilant application of counter-force at a series of constantly shifting geographical and political points, corresponding to the shifts and maneuvers of Soviet policy." Such a policy, Kennan predicted, would "promote tendencies which must eventually find their outlet in either the break-up or the gradual mellowing of Soviet power."

National Security Act of 1947

The National Security Act of 1947 mandated a major reorganization of the foreign policy and military establishments of the U.S. Government. The act created many of the institutions that Presidents found useful when formulating and implementing foreign policy, including the National Security Council (NSC).

The act also established the Central Intelligence Agency (CIA), which grew out of World War II era Office of Strategic Services. The 1947 law also merged the War Department and Navy Department into a single Department of Defense under the Secretary of Defense, who also directed the newly created Department of the Air Force.

Marshall Plan, 1948

In a June 5, 1947, speech to the graduating class at Harvard University, Secretary of State George C. Marshall called for a comprehensive program to rebuild Europe. Fanned by the fear of Communist expansion and the rapid deterioration of European economies, Congress passed the Economic Cooperation Act in March 1948 and approved funding that would eventually rise to over $12 billion for the rebuilding of Western Europe. The Marshall Plan generated a resurgence of European industrialization and brought extensive investment into the region. It was also a stimulant to the U.S. economy by establishing markets for American goods. Secretary of State Marshall became the only general ever to receive a Nobel Prize for peace. The Marshall Plan also institutionalized and legitimized the concept of U.S. foreign aid programs, which have become an integral part of U.S. foreign policy.

The Berlin Airlift, 1948–1949

At the end of the Second World War, U.S., British, and Soviet military forces divided and occupied Germany. Also divided into occupation zones, Berlin was located far inside Soviet-controlled eastern Germany. The United States, United Kingdom, and France controlled western portions of the city, while Soviet troops controlled the eastern sector. The crisis started on June 24, 1948, when Soviet forces blockaded rail, road, and water access to Allied-controlled areas of Berlin. The United States and United Kingdom responded by airlifting food and fuel to Berlin from Allied airbases in western Germany. In time, the airlift became ever more efficient and the number of aircraft increased. At the height of the campaign, one plane landed every 45 seconds at Tempelhof Airport. By spring 1949, the Berlin Airlift proved successful. The Western Allies showed that they could sustain the operation indefinitely. At the same time, the Allied counter-blockade on eastern Germany was causing severe shortages, which, Moscow feared, might lead to political upheaval. The crisis ended on May 12, 1949, when Soviet forces lifted the blockade on land access to western Berlin.

Creation of Israel, 1948

On November 29, 1947 the United Nations adopted Resolution 181 (also known as the Partition Resolution) that would divide Great Britain's former Palestinian mandate into Jewish and Arab states in May 1948. On May 14, 1948, David Ben-Gurion, the head of the Jewish Agency, proclaimed the establishment of the State of Israel. U.S. President Harry S. Truman recognized the new nation on the same day. The Arab-Israeli War of 1948 broke out when five Arab nations – Lebanon, Syria, Iraq, Egypt and Saudi Arabia - invaded the newly created Israel. The United States maintained an arms embargo against all belligerents. Though the United Nations brokered two cease-fires during the conflict, fighting continued into 1949.

North Atlantic Treaty Organization (NATO), 1949

The North Atlantic Treaty Organization was created in 1949 by the United States, Canada, and several Western European nations to provide collective security against the Soviet Union. NATO was the first peacetime military alliance the United States entered into outside of the Western Hemisphere. The United States viewed an economically strong, rearmed, and integrated Europe as vital to the prevention of communist expansion across the continent.

The Chinese Revolution of 1949

On October 1, 1949, Chinese Communist leader Mao Zedong declared the creation of the People's Republic of China (PRC). The announcement ended the civil war between the Chinese Communist Party (CCP) and the Nationalist Party (KMT), which broke out immediately following World War II. The Nationalists fled to Taiwan. The outbreak of the Korean War, which pitted the PRC and the United States on opposite sides of an international conflict, ended any opportunity for accommodation between the PRC and the United States. Truman's desire to prevent the Korean conflict from spreading south led to the U.S. policy of protecting the Chiang Kai-shek government on Taiwan. Until the 1970s, the United States continued to recognize the Republic of

China, located on Taiwan, as China's true government and supported that government's holding the Chinese seat in the United Nations.

NSC-68, 1950

National Security Council Paper NSC-68 was a Top-Secret report completed by the U.S. Department of State's Policy Planning Staff on April 7, 1950. The 58-page memorandum is among the most influential documents composed by the U.S. Government during the Cold War, and was not declassified until 1975. Its authors argued that one of the most pressing threats confronting the United States was the "hostile design" of the Soviet Union. The authors concluded that the Soviet threat would soon be greatly augmented by the addition of more weapons, including nuclear weapons, to the Soviet arsenal. They argued that the best course of action was to respond in kind with a massive build-up of the U.S. military and its weaponry. NSC 68's recommendations became policy, and the United States Government began a massive military build-up.

Decolonization of Asia and Africa, 1945–1960

Between 1945 and 1960, three dozen new states in Asia and Africa achieved autonomy or outright independence from their European colonial rulers. The creation of so many new countries, some of which occupied strategic locations, others of which possessed significant natural resources, and most of which were desperately poor, altered the composition of the United Nations and political complexity of every region of the globe. The U.S. used aid packages, technical assistance and sometimes military intervention to encourage newly independent nations in the Third World to adopt governments that aligned with the West. The Soviet Union deployed similar tactics in an effort to encourage new nations to join the communist bloc.

The Korean War, 1950–1953

What started as a civil war between North and South Korea became international when the United Nations sided with South Korea and the People's Republic of China (PRC) supported North Korea. The UN sent forces composed of troops from 15 nations to the peninsula to stop the communist advance. By July 1951, the conflict had reached a stalemate and peace talks started. On July 27, 1953, the DPRK, PRC and UN signed an armistice (the ROK abstained) agreeing to a new border near the 38th parallel as the demarcation line between North and South Korea. Both sides would maintain and patrol a demilitarized zone (DMZ) surrounding that boundary line.

The Australia, New Zealand and United States Security Treaty (ANZUS Treaty), 1951

The Australia, New Zealand and United States Security Treaty, or ANZUS Treaty, was an agreement signed in 1951 to protect the security of the Pacific and to stop the spread of communism. Although the agreement has not been formally abrogated, the United States and New Zealand no longer maintain the security relationship between their countries. The 1954 **Southeast Asian Treaty Organization** (SEATO) included all of the ANZUS powers, as well as Britain, France, and several other Asian powers.

Fall of French Indochina, 1954

In the late 1940s, the French struggled to control its colonies in Indochina - Vietnam, Cambodia, and Laos. On May 7, 1954, the French-held garrison at Dien Bien Phu in Vietnam fell after a four month siege led by Vietnamese nationalist Ho Chi Minh. The French pulled out of the region and Vietnam was divided into North and South. The U.S. established its own government in South Vietnam.

The East German Uprising, 1953

On June 16, 1953, workers in East Berlin rose in protest against government demands to increase productivity. Within days, nearly a million East Germans joined the protests and began rioting across hundreds of East German cities and towns. In order to prolong the uprising and win support for the West, the United States established an aid program to feed East Germans. The program, which continued until October 1953, proved popular with East Germans and highlighted the repression and privations of life under communism. In addition to achieving humanitarian objectives through this assistance program, the United States sought to destabilize East Germany and weaken Ulbricht's regime.

The Taiwan Straits Crises: 1954–55 and 1958

Tensions between the People's Republic of China (PRC) and the Republic of China (ROC) in the 1950s resulted in armed conflict over strategic islands in the Taiwan Strait. The United States responded by actively intervening on behalf of the ROC. In January 1955, the U.S. Congress passed the "Formosa Resolution," which gave President Eisenhower total authority to defend Taiwan and the off-shore islands. Eventually, the PRC and ROC came to an arrangement in which they shelled each other's garrisons on alternate days. This continued for twenty years until the PRC and the United States normalized relations.

U.S.-China Ambassadorial Talks, 1955–1970

On August 1, 1955, the United States and the People's Republic of China (PRC) opened a series of ambassadorial-level talks in Geneva to discuss the repatriation of nationals and other issues of mutual concern. Because the two countries did not have formal diplomatic relations, the talks were the principle form of contact between them for sixteen years. They ended when President Richard Nixon visited China and set the stage for eventual U.S. recognition of the People's Republic. Although they accomplished little in terms of formal agreements, the talks did provide China and the United States with an avenue for negotiation, so that misunderstandings did not escalate into outright conflict. In this way, the U.S.-China Ambassadorial Talks served as an important factor in relieving tension in East Asia.

The Warsaw Treaty Organization, 1955

The Warsaw Treaty Organization (also known as the Warsaw Pact) was a political and military alliance established on May 14, 1955 between the Soviet Union and several Eastern European countries. The Soviet Union formed this alliance as a counterbalance to the North Atlantic Treaty Organization (NATO), security alliance concluded between the United States, Canada and Western European nations in 1949. By the 1980s, the Warsaw Treaty Organization was beset by problems related to the economic slowdown in all Eastern European countries. By the late 1980s political changes in most of the member states made the Pact virtually ineffectual. In September 1990, East Germany left the Pact in preparation for reunification with West Germany. By October, Czechoslovakia, Hungary, and Poland had withdrawn from all Warsaw Pact military exercises. The Warsaw Pact officially disbanded in March and July of 1991 following the dissolution of the Soviet Union.

Khrushchev and the Twentieth Congress of the Communist Party, 1956

In February, 1956, Soviet leader Nikita Khrushchev made a keynote address to international communist leaders at the Twentieth Congress of the Communist Party of the Soviet Union. He used his speech to make unexpected and unprecedented condemnations of the policies and excesses of his predecessor, Joseph Stalin, setting off a chain of reaction that led to calls for reform in Eastern Europe and a new policy in the Soviet Union for dealing with the West. Although Khrushchev played a role in shutting down the rebellions in the Soviet satellites in Eastern Europe, he followed up on his address to the Twentieth Party Congress by continuing to advocate reforms and increased cooperation with the West. As a result, there were early signs of détente in the late

1950s, even though progress was delayed first by the U-2 incident and later by the Cuban Missile Crisis.

The Suez Crisis, 1956

On July 26, 1956, Egyptian President Gamal Abdel Nasser nationalized the Suez Canal Company, the joint British-French enterprise which owned and operated Suez Canal. The British and French held secret meetings with Israel, who regarded Nasser as a threat to its security, and on October 29 Israel invaded Egypt advancing to within 10 miles of the Suez Canal. Under the pretext of protecting the Canal, Britain and France landed troops of their own a few days later. The U.S. condemned the invasion and helped broker a UN ceasefire on November 6.

Sputnik, 1957

On October 4, 1957, the Soviet Union launched the earth's first artificial satellite, *Sputnik-1*. The U.S. realized it had fallen behind in developing new technology and this intensified the arms and space races and Cold War tensions.

The Eisenhower Doctrine, 1957

Under the Eisenhower Doctrine, a country could request American economic assistance and/or aid from U.S. military forces if it was being threatened by armed aggression from another state. Eisenhower singled out the Soviet threat in his doctrine by authorizing the commitment of U.S. forces "to secure and protect the territorial integrity and political independence of such nations, requesting such aid against overt armed aggression from any nation controlled by international communism."

The Berlin Crisis, 1958–1961

On November 10, 1958, Soviet Premier Nikita Khrushchev demanded that the United States, Great Britain and France pull their forces out of West Berlin within six months. This ultimatum sparked a three year crisis over the future of the city of Berlin that culminated in 1961 with the building of the Berlin Wall. The divided city highlighted the sharp contrast between the communist and capitalist systems, and the freedom of movement between the sectors had resulted in a mass exodus from the eastern side. The Berlin Wall remained in place until November 9, 1989, when the border between East and West Berlin was reopened and the wall itself was finally dismantled.

U-2 Overflights and the Capture of Francis Gary Powers, 1960

On May 1, 1960, the pilot of an American U-2 spy plane was shot down while flying though Soviet airspace. The fallout over the incident resulted in the cancellation of the Paris Summit scheduled to discuss the ongoing situation in divided Germany, the possibility of an arms control or test ban treaty, and the relaxation of tensions between the USSR and the United States. After extensive questioning by the KGB, Powers was convicted of spying and sentenced to three years in prison and seven more of hard labor. In February, 1962, however, he and a detained American student were traded for a captured Soviet spy, Rudolf Abel. Although Eisenhower refused to end the U-2 program, it was quickly overtaken by new technology, as satellite images replaced aerial photographs. For his part, Khrushchev abandoned his attempts to cooperate with Eisenhower, opting instead to wait for the inauguration of the new U.S. President, John F. Kennedy, elected to office in November, 1960.

1961–1968: The Presidencies of John F. Kennedy and Lyndon B. Johnson

President John F. Kennedy assumed office on January 20, 1961. In his inaugural address, Kennedy proclaimed "Let every nation know, whether it wishes us well or ill, that we shall pay any price, bear any burden, meet any hardship, support any friend, oppose any foe, in order to assure the survival and the success of liberty." Kennedy came into the presidency determined to reenergize the foreign policy establishment. To that end, he assembled a team of young White House and National Security Council advisers—the so-called "best and the brightest"—which included McGeorge Bundy, Walt Rostow, Ted Sorensen and Arthur Schlesinger, Jr. He selected Dean Rusk as his Secretary of State.

The Kennedy administration maintained the belief that Communism was a threat to the United States but implemented the "flexible response" defense strategy, one that relied on multiple options for responding to the Soviet Union, discouraging massive retaliation, and encouraging mutual deterrence.

In April 1961, Kennedy authorized a clandestine invasion of Cuba by a brigade of Cuban exiles, a CIA covert operation approved under President Eisenhower. Relying on faulty intelligence, the operation collapsed in two days with the defeat and capture of anti-Castro forces at the Bay of Pigs. The spectacular failure of this Cold War confrontation was a setback for Kennedy, and one he became determined to overcome.

Tensions with the Soviet Union dominated U.S. foreign policy and reached new heights in late 1962 when the Soviet Union gave the Cuban Government medium-range ballistic missiles to defend against another U.S. invasion. The tense thirteen days of the Cuban Missile Crisis tested the mettle of the Kennedy administration and his team of trusted advisers. Khrushchev agreed to remove the missiles, averting nuclear war, but resolving little between the two nations.

Kennedy authorized sending troops and military advisers to the U.S.-backed nation of South Vietnam and steadily increased their numbers throughout his presidency. The administration was determined not to lose either the nation of South Vietnam or the broader region of Southeast Asia to communism.

Kennedy's assassination in November 1963 brought his Vice President, Lyndon B. Johnson to the presidency. Dean Rusk continued to serve as Secretary of State and stressed to the new President the necessity of continuity in foreign policy. President Johnson vowed to the nation that it would keep its commitments "from South Vietnam to West Berlin." By 1967, nearly 500,000 troops were in Vietnam. Following the surprise defeat of the Tet Offensive in 1968 and facing dwindling public support for the war, Johnson announced that he would not seek a second term as President.

USAID

The administrations of John F. Kennedy and Lyndon B. Johnson marked a revitalization of the U.S. foreign assistance program, signified a growing awareness of the importance of humanitarian aid as a form of diplomacy, and reinforced the belief that American security was linked to the economic progress and stability of other nations. Kennedy insisted that the United States must "narrow the gap between abundance here at home and near starvation abroad." While Johnson believed that the United States should extend food aid for humanitarian reasons, he also favored conditioning food aid agreements on the recipient nation's ability to implement necessary "self help" agricultural reforms.

Alliance for Progress and Peace Corps, 1961–1969

Growing out of the fear of increased Soviet and Cuban influence in Latin America, the 1961–1969 Alliance for Progress was in essence a Marshall Plan for Latin America. The United States pledged $20 billion in assistance (grants and loans) and called upon the Latin American governments to provide $80 billion in investment funds for their economies. It was the biggest U.S. aid program toward the developing world up to that point—and called for substantial reform of Latin American institutions.

Since the Peace Corps' founding, more than 187,000 men and women have joined the Peace Corps and served in 139 countries. There are 7,749 Peace Corps Volunteers currently serving 73 countries around the world.

The Limited Test Ban Treaty, 1963

This treaty did not have much practical effect on the development and proliferation of nuclear weapons, but it established an important precedent for future arms control. Both superpowers entered the 1960s determined to build or maintain nuclear superiority. As the United States, Soviet Union and United Kingdom tested new nuclear technologies in the earth's atmosphere, concerns emerged worldwide about the potential effects of radioactive fallout on the people exposed to it. This led to the formation of activist groups and public discussion of the issue. The Limited Test Ban Treaty 1963 banned all nuclear tests in the atmosphere, in space, or underwater and stopped the spread of radioactive nuclear material through atmospheric testing. It also set the precedent for a new wave of arms control agreements , especially the 1968 Nuclear Non-Proliferation Treaty.

The 1967 Arab-Israeli War

The 1967 Arab-Israeli War marked the failure of the Eisenhower, Kennedy, and Johnson administrations' efforts to prevent renewed Arab-Israeli conflict following the 1956 Suez War. The administration's concept of "land-for-peace" solidified following the war. " UN Security Council Resolution 242, adopted on November 22, called for Israel's withdrawal from "territories occupied in the recent conflict" in exchange for "termination of all claims or states of belliger-ency and respect for and acknowledgment of the sovereignty, territorial integ-rity and political independence of every State in the area and their right to live in peace within secure and recognized boundaries free from threats or acts of force." Interpreted differently by Israelis and Arabs, this resolution has re-mained the bedrock of all subsequent U.S. efforts to resolve the Arab-Israeli dispute.

Soviet Invasion of Czechoslovakia, 1968

On August 20, 1968, the Soviet Union led Warsaw Pact troops in an invasion of Czechoslovakia to crack down on reformist trends in Prague. Although the Soviet Union's action successfully halted the pace of reform in Czechoslovakia, it had unintended consequences for the unity of the communist bloc. The So-viet invasion of Czechoslovakia was significant in that it delayed the splinter-ing of Eastern European Communism and was concluded without provoking any direct intervention from the West. It also temporarily derailed progress toward détente between the Soviet Union and the United States.

1969–1976: The Presidencies of Richard M. Nixon and Gerald R. Ford

Nixon was convinced that power was the core dynamic of the international system; while willing to take advantage of summit meetings for political and diplomatic purposes, he was highly skeptical about personal diplomacy. His central concern through his presidency lay in managing great power relationships in the bipolar international system. As the relationship between Nixon and Kissinger matured, they evolved into a close partnership, generally with Nixon laying out the broad outlines of policy and Kissinger executing the detailed actions necessary to implement broad policy. Nixon ended America's involvement in the Vietnam War, opened the door to China and started the 'dawn of détente' with Moscow. After Nixon's resignation, Ford emphasized continuity in foreign policy, continuing Nixon's policy of détente with the Soviet Union and the Strategic Arms Limitation Talks (SALT). He continued to develop U.S. relations with the People's Republic of China, conducting a summit in Beijing in December 1975. He also worked with Kissinger in securing the Helsinki Accords, which were signed in August 1975, and a second Egyptian-Israeli Disengagement Agreement, which was signed in September 1975. The first months of his presidency saw the invasion and conquest of South Vietnam by North Vietnam in March–April 1975, followed quickly by the *Mayaguez* incident.

The South Asia Crisis and the Founding of Bangladesh, 1971

In 1971, an internal crisis in Pakistan resulted in a third war between India and Pakistan and the secession of East Pakistan, creating the independent state of Bangladesh. These developments resulted in a decline in U.S. influence in South Asia and India's emergence as the most significant power on the subcontinent. U.S. prestige was damaged in both nations, in Pakistan for failing to help prevent the loss of East Pakistan and in India for supporting the brutality of the Pakistani regime's actions in what became Bangladesh. In contrast, the Soviet relationship with India became stronger.

The 1973 Arab-Israeli War

The 1973 Arab-Israeli War was a watershed for U.S. foreign policy toward the Middle East. It forced the Nixon administration to realize that Arab frustration over Israel's unwillingness to withdraw from the territories it had occupied in 1967 could have major strategic consequences for the United States. The war thus paved the way for Secretary of State Henry Kissinger's "shuttle diplomacy" and ultimately, the Israeli-Egyptian peace treaty of 1979.

During the war, Arab members of the Organization of Petroleum Exporting Countries (OPEC) imposed an **oil embargo** against the United States in retaliation for the U.S. decision to re-supply the Israeli military and to gain leverage in the post-war peace negotiations. In April, Nixon announced a new energy strategy to boost domestic production to reduce U.S. vulnerability to oil imports and ease the strain of nationwide fuel shortages.

Helsinki Final Act, 1975

The Helsinki Final Act was an agreement signed by 35 nations that concluded the Conference on Security and Cooperation in Europe, held in Helsinki, Finland. The multifaceted Act addressed a range of prominent global issues and in so doing had a far-reaching effect on the Cold War and U.S.-Soviet relations. These shifts helped bring an end to Soviet dominance in Eastern Europe and the end of the Cold War.

1977–1981: The Presidency of Jimmy Carter

President Jimmy Carter took office in January 1977 pledging to restore a sense a morality to both domestic and foreign policy. Carter envisioned that his for-

eign policy, "derived from a longer view of global change," would move the
United States away from operating within a bipolar or tripolar context to one
taking into account an increasingly complicated and interdependent world.
His approach emphasized the maintenance of peace, the pursuit of human
rights, the achievement of nuclear non-proliferation, the necessity of international cooperation, and a focus on the developing world rather than on East-
West concerns. In defining this policy, Carter admitted that the United States
did not alone possess the answers to the world's problems. It should not impose unilateral solutions, although it could take the lead in advancing policies
designed to create a "just and stable" international order. In doing so, the
United States would maintain its strategic interests.

The Soviet invasion of Afghanistan took place a month after Iranian militants stormed the U.S. Embassy in Tehran and took Americans hostage. In
addition to these crises, Carter faced a mounting series of domestic economic
problems, including increases in gasoline prices, rising inflation, and rising
unemployment. Carter responded to the Soviet invasion by embargoing grain
sales, banning technology exports, and prohibiting U.S. participation in the
upcoming 1980 Moscow Summer Olympics.

The changing political landscape in Western Europe also had a significant
impact on U.S.-Western European relations during this time. In the 1970s,
communist parties in Western Europe, particularly in Italy, became more independent from policy set in Moscow. Communist groups throughout the region worked more closely within their national systems, and in some cases
even entered into ruling coalition governments. This movement, known as
Eurocommunism, altered how Washington and its overseas representatives
worked with European policymakers. Previously U.S. policy limited the United
States to working only with anti- or non-communist groups and politicians. In
response to the trend toward Eurocommunism, the Carter administration decided that U.S. diplomats should engage with a broader cross-section of politicians, opinion makers, and the public.

In September 1978 following talks with Chinese leaders, the United States
acknowledged "the Chinese position that there is but one China and Taiwan is

part of China." The exchange of accredited ambassadors and the operation of Embassies enabled both parties to negotiate diplomatic disputes and pursue mutual interests.

Camp David Accords and the Arab-Israeli Peace Process

The Camp David Accords, signed by President Jimmy Carter, Egyptian President Anwar Sadat, and Israeli Prime Minister Menachem Begin in September 1978, established a framework for a historic peace treaty concluded between Israel and Egypt in March 1979. From the start of his administration, Carter and his Secretary of State, Cyrus Vance, pursued intensive negotiations with Arab and Israeli leaders, hoping to reconvene the Geneva Conference, which had been established in December 1973 to seek an end to the Arab-Israeli dispute.

The Panama Canal and the Torrijos-Carter Treaties

One of President Jimmy Carter's greatest accomplishments was negotiating the Torrijos-Carter Treaties, which were ratified by the U.S. Senate in 1978. These treaties gave the nation of Panama eventual control of the Panama Canal. The Torrijos-Carter Treaties allowed the United States to defend itself from charges of imperialism made by Soviet-aligned states.

The Soviet Invasion of Afghanistan and the U.S. Response, 1978–1980

At the end of December 1979, the Soviet Union sent thousands of troops into Afghanistan and immediately assumed complete military and political control of Kabul and large portions of the country. This event began a decade-long attempt by Moscow to subdue the Afghan civil war and maintain a friendly and socialist government on its border. The United States and its European allies sharply criticized the Soviet move into Afghanistan and devised numerous measures to compel Moscow to withdraw. After ten years of grinding insurgency Moscow finally withdrew, at the cost of millions of lives and billions of dollars. In their wake, the Soviets left a shattered country in which the Taliban, an Islamic fundamentalist group, seized control, later providing Osama bin Laden with a training base from which to launch terrorist operations worldwide.

1981–1988: The Presidency of Ronald W. Reagan

Reagan objected to the implied moral equivalency of détente, insisting instead on the superiority of representative government, free-market capitalism, and freedom of conscience over what he viewed as godless, collectivist, Communism. This more confrontational approach – the "clash of good and evil" - eventually came to be labeled the "Reagan Doctrine," which advocated opposition to Communist-supported regimes wherever they existed, as well as a willingness to directly challenge the Soviet Union.

The Reagan administration advocated a wide array of initiatives that heightened confrontation with the U.S.S.R. and its allies. Reagan engineered a significant increase in U.S. defense spending designed to modernize existing forces and achieve technological advances the Soviet Union could not match. At the same time he offered conciliations such as decreasing nuclear weapon stockpiles, which eventually resulted in the landmark Strategic Arms Reduction Treaty (START). The emergence of Mikhail Gorbachev as the principal Soviet leader provided Reagan with a partner willing to engage in substantive negotiations. A series of summit meetings ensued which reduced tensions and produced concrete results, such as the 1987 Intermediate-Range Nuclear Forces Treaty (INF) that eliminated the deployment of theater-level nuclear missiles in Europe. The accomplishments of this administration are viewed in the light of events that occurred after Ronald Reagan left office in January 1989. Within a year, the Berlin Wall fell, and by the end of 1991 the Soviet Union had collapsed, signaling the end of the Cold War. There is no question that Ronald Reagan and his foreign policy advisers played key roles in this remarkable turn of events.

Central America, 1981–1993

President Reagan amplified concerns expressed by President Carter and Congress about foreign support of Central American leftist guerrilla forces. Secretary of State Alexander Haig accused the Sandinista government of exporting terrorism to El Salvador and in April 1981, Reagan terminated economic assistance to Nicaragua citing its involvement in supporting Salvadoran rebels. After several failed diplomatic attempts to dissuade Managua from supporting FMLN activities, Reagan opted to support a clandestine guerrilla force to quash the Sandinista training and arming of Salvadoran guerillas. These "Contras," as in "counterrevolutionaries," were primarily ex-Nicaraguan National Guard members who had gathered in Honduran territory. The Contras launched their first major attack against the Sandinistas in March 1982. In response, the Sandinistas undertook a dramatic build-up of military manpower assisted by Soviet and Cuban advisers and weaponry, mostly from the Soviet bloc. Reagan redoubled his commitment to the Contras in his second term, however, the Tower Commission set up after the Iran-Contra scandal reported that White House staff members had been using extralegal funds raised from arms sales to Iran and foreign donors to arm the Contras prior to October 1986.

In August 1987, Central American leaders signed a peace accord at Esquipulas, Guatemala. The plan focused on democratization and regional security, backed with a system of verification. The civil war in El Salvador lasted until 1991, when the FMLN reached a peace accord with the Salvadoran Government under United Nations supervision. In Guatemala, fighting between leftist groups and the military continued into the mid-1990s. Washington continued to perceive threats in Central America and on December 20, 1989, President George H.W. Bush dispatched over twenty thousand troops to invade Panama and arrest its head of state, Manuel Noriega who had nullified a presidential election won by opposition candidate Guillermo Endara. Noriega was tried in a United States court and convicted on charges of drug trafficking, money laundering, and racketeering.

1989–1992: The Presidency of George H.W. Bush

The collapse of the Soviet Union in 1991 created a massive shift in the international balance of power and left the United States as the sole remaining superpower.

Bush strove to build what he termed in his September 11, 1991, address before a joint session of congress "new world order," one "freer from the threat of terror, stronger in the pursuit of justice, and more secure in the quest for peace." During his presidency, apartheid in South Africa came to an end leading to increased U.S. foreign aid and reinvestment by American companies. The Asia Pacific Economic Cooperation, or APEC, was formed in 1989 as an informal forum in which member nations could discuss free trade and economic cooperation along the Pacific Rim. From the perspective of the United States, it has been a crucial institution for economic engagement within the region. On November 9, 1989, thousands of jubilant Germans brought down the most visible symbol of division at the heart of Europe—the Berlin Wall. In Poland Solidarity emerged and Hungary opened its borders to the west. A new non-communist government took over in Czechoslovakia and communist dictators in Romania and Bulgaria were deposed. By the summer of 1990, all of the former communist regimes of Eastern Europe were replaced by democratically elected governments and the Soviet Union had collapsed. Some former soviet satellites like Yugoslavia would soon implode.

During his visits to Washington, politics, economic reforms, and security issues dominated the conversations between Yeltsin and Bush. Of paramount concern was securing the nuclear arsenal of the former Soviet Union and making certain nuclear weapons did not fall into the wrong hands. Bush made it clear that funding was available from the United States to secure nuclear, chemical and biological weapons in the former Soviet Union. The Nunn-Lugar Act established the Cooperative Threat Reduction Program in November 1991 to fund the dismantling of weapons in the former Soviet Union, in accordance with the START and INF Treaties and other agreements.

Tiananmen Square, 1989

The establishment of formal diplomatic relations between the United States and the People's Republic of China in 1979, together with Chinese Vice Premier Deng Xiaoping's economic reforms, inaugurated a decade of vibrant cultural exchange and expanding economic ties between the two countries. However, the Chinese Government's violent suppression of demonstrations in Tiananmen Square on June 4, 1989, cooled U.S.-Chinese relations. To the present day, the Department of State marks the anniversary of the suppression by issuing a statement calling on the Chinese Government to end harassment of those who participated in the protests and to fully account for those killed, detained, or missing.

The Gulf War, 1991

Iraq began to threaten Kuwait early in July 1990 and the United States staged maneuvers in the Gulf to warn Iraq against taking military action against the United Arab Emirates and Kuwait. Despite this show of U.S. force, President George H.W. Bush adopted a conciliatory policy toward Saddam Hussein in hopes of moderating the Iraqi regime and policies. But on August 2, 1990, a force of one hundred thousand Iraqi troops invaded Kuwait and overran the country in a matter of hours. The invasion of Kuwait led to a United Nations Security Council embargo and sanctions on Iraq and a U.S.-led coalition air and ground war, which began on January 16, 1991, and ended with an Iraqi defeat and retreat from Kuwait on February 28, 1991. Although the United States was aware of Hussein's threats to Kuwait, it did not anticipate the Iraqi military incursion.

The Madrid Conference, 1991

On March 6, 1991, President George H. W. Bush told Congress, "The time has come to put an end to the Arab-Israeli conflict." Bush's declaration was followed by eight months of intensive shuttle diplomacy by Secretary of State James Baker, culminating in the Madrid Peace Conference in October 1991.

The Conference, co-chaired by Bush and Soviet President Mikhail Gorbachev, was attended by Israeli, Egyptian, Syrian, and Lebanese delegations, as well as a joint Jordanian-Palestinian delegation. For the first time, all of the parties to the Arab-Israeli conflict had gathered to hold direct negotiations—a historically unprecedented event. Following Madrid, Israeli, Syrian, Jordanian, and Palestinian representatives continued to meet for bilateral talks in Washington, and multilateral talks commenced in Moscow in 1992. Yet by 1993, the Washington talks had become deadlocked and were overtaken by secret Israeli-Palestinian and Israeli-Jordanian negotiations, which produced the Israeli-Palestinian Declaration of Principles (the so-called "Oslo Accord") of September 1993 and the Israeli-Jordanian peace treaty of October 1994.

1993–2000: The Presidency of William J. Clinton

Clinton faced many high profile foreign affairs issues from redefining the role of NATO in the post-Soviet era and dealing with Russia to Somalia and the war in Bosnia.

In 1991 the central government of Somalia collapsed, the country descended into chaos, and a humanitarian crisis of staggering proportions began to unfold. The United States sent food aid via Operation Provide Comfort starting in August 1992 but distribution was hampered by warlords.. In December 1992, President Bush sent U.S. troops to Somalia to assist with famine relief as part of the larger United Nations effort. On October 3, 1993 two Black Hawk helicopters were shot down in a battle which lead to the deaths of 18 U.S. soldiers and hundreds of Somalis. The deaths turned the tide of public opinion in the United States. President Bill Clinton pulled U.S. troops out of combat four days later, and all U.S. troops left the country in March 1994. The United Nations withdrew from Somalia in March 1995. Fighting continued in the country.

During this time President Clinton ordered the national security bureaucracy to consider how and when the United States should become involved in peacekeeping operations. Presidential Decision Directive 25, issued on May 3,

1994, outlined a series of factors which must consider before involving the United States in peacekeeping.

In 1991 and 1992, Yugoslavia disintegrated under the pressures of ethnic conflict, economic issues, and the demagoguery of Serbian President Slobodan Milosevic. The secessions of Slovenia and Croatia triggered warfare in both new nations. Serbian forces executed widespread "ethnic cleansing" in occupied areas, creating horrific scenes of refugees and concentration camps. Bosnia's declaration of independence led to a three year long war. In July 1994, Bosnian Serb commanders launched an offensive against the eastern enclaves of Srebrenica and Zepa; they massacred over 7,000 men in Srebrenica. The mass killing served as a tipping point to western resolve to bring a decisive end to the conflict. Convening in London on July 21, NATO agreed on the effective end of the "dual key" policy for controlling air strikes, with authority for strikes delegated to UN and NATO commanders in the field. The alliance further agreed that any future attacks on safe areas would result in a sustained air offensive.

When a mortar shell exploded in the Markala marketplace in Sarajevo on August 25, NATO executed Operation Deliberate Force, an intense two-week series of attacks on Serb military positions. The combination of the ground offensive, NATO's air campaign, and Holbrooke's tireless diplomacy yielded a cease-fire by the end of September. On November 1, negotiations among the three parties opened at Dayton AFB, OH. The parties reached a hard-fought agreement on November 21 and the Dayton Accords, formally the General Framework Agreement for Peace in Bosnia and Herzegovina, were signed in Paris on December 14.

"Bill and Boris" met eighteen times, nearly as often as their predecessors had met throughout the entire Cold War as relations between the United States and Russia improved. Clinton promised Yeltsin strong support in the form of financial assistance to promote various programs, including funds to stabilize the economy, to house decommissioned military officers, and to employ nuclear scientists.

Clinton and Yeltsin also continued the bilateral cooperation, begun by Ronald Reagan and Mikhail Gorbachev, to manage the most tangible, and terrifying, relics of the Cold War. The control of nuclear weapons had always been one of the most difficult issues for the two superpowers to negotiate. The task in the 1990s, however, was complicated by the fact that Russia did not maintain control over the entire Soviet inventory; some strategic (long-range) and theater (intermediate range) nuclear weapons were also still based on the territory of at least Ukraine, Belarus, and Kazakhstan. In November 1994, Russia, Ukraine, Belarus, and Kazakhstan finally agreed to adhere to INF; then, the following month, the four countries formally ratified START I.

The Bush Administration (2001-2009)

Eight months into Bush's first term as president, the September 11, 2001 terrorist attacks occurred. In response, Bush launched the global War on Terror, an international military campaign which included the war in Afghanistan – home base of Osama Bin Laden - launched in 2001.The war led to the collapse of the Taliban regime. In his 2002 State of the Union Address, Bush referred to an axis of evil including Iraq, Iran and North Korea as a "grave and growing danger" that threatened the peace of the world. The war in Iraq was launched in 2003 on the grounds that Saddam Hussein posed a global threat because of his weapons of mass destruction. The Bush Administration argued that it had the right to "wage preemptive war" but the Bush Doctrine as it became known, lost the United States considerable support overseas and damaged the President's standing at home in many quarters. The Taliban re-emerged as a powerful force in Afghanistan in 2006 forcing Bush to commit more ground troops to the fight. Further fighting in Iraq between sectarian groups also forced the President to send 21,500 additional troops – the Surge - in January, 2007.

Bush was an outspoken critic of North Korea and in 2002 declared "We will not permit the world's most dangerous regimes to threaten us with the world's most destructive weapons." In 2007 the President also increased economic sanctions on Syria for supporting terrorism.

Other foreign affairs landmarks include $44 billion contributed by the U.S. Government to fight aids in Africa as part of the President's Emergency Plan for AIDS Relief program.

The Obama Administration (2009-2016)

President Obama nominated his Democratic presidential rival Hilary Rodham Clinton as his Secretary of State and they sought to improve relations with allies and end the war in Iraq. In his inaugural address, the President talked about "working tirelessly with old friends and former foes."

At her confirmation hearings she said, "The best way to advance America's interests in reducing global threats and seizing global opportunities is to design and implement global solutions." We must use "smart power" she said – "the full range of tools at our disposal – diplomatic, economic, military, political, legal and cultural – picking the right tool or combination of tools for each situation. With smart power, diplomacy will be the vanguard of our foreign policy."

Main landmarks were the 2008 Great Recession that had global impact, the Arab Spring protests that saw the overthrow of several Middle East governments, ongoing Israeli-Palestinian conflict, the civil war in Syria, Russia's invasion of the Crimea and the emergence of ISIL as the world's most well-funded and well-organized terror group.